Multi-National City

SNAPSHOTS

1

FROM

NEW YORK

TO

SILICON VALLEY

2

FROM

NEW DELHI

TO

NEW YORK

3

FROM

SILICON VALLEY

TO

NEW DELHI

More often than not, in the Multi-National City the crowd is invisible, except if you look closely at its jammed highways, its empty parking lots, and its silent electronic screens. As a time machine that mixes past, present, and future, the MNC is haunted by old memories and by visionary hallucinations. It is both the apotheosis and the opposite of a romanticized "global village." It is also the modern metropolis writ large but transformed. Its new forms of alienation are met by the old anti-urban dream of recovering a lost home, but now in casual, domesticated corporate campuses rather than in uptight suburban houses. And it reinvents modernity's masses as individualized, mass-customizable persons while in the process, effacing their singularity. But the MNC also reproduces modernity's salutary, catalytic estrangements and its wrenching, liberating disenchantments, though these are often expressed paradoxically in new pathologies: instead of (modern) fatigue, (postmodern) stress; instead of (modern) shock, (postmodern) boredom.

1

FROM **NEW YORK** TO **SILICON VALLEY**

1.01 Silicon Valley, from space, c. 1999.

1.02 Genentech, Inc. "Founding Fathers" Robert A. Swanson and Dr. Herbert W. Boyer, 1976. Sculpture by Larry Anderson, 1992.

1.03 Goldman Sachs, Sand Hill Road, Palo Alto, California, 1998. Architect unknown.

1.01

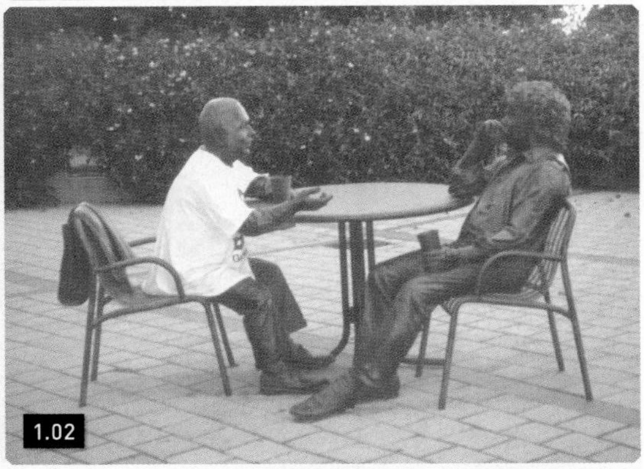
1.02

1.03

The Spectral City

→ p. 20

Intel Corporation, Santa Clara, California, 1998. Architect unknown.

1.04 Interior on screen.

1.05 Entrance.

1.06–1.07 John Portman and Associates, Embarcadero Center, San Francisco, 1982.

1.04

1.05

1.06

1.07

The Ruin, or The Regime of the Potted Plant

→ p. 21

1.08 John Portman and Associates, Embarcadero Center, San Francisco, 1982. Atrium.

1.09 John Portman and Associates, Peachtree Center, Atlanta, 1976. Atrium.

1.08

1.09

The Atrium Principle

→ p. 23

1.10 Hawley and Peterson, Qume Corporation, Santa Clara, 1980. Atrium.

1.11–1.13 Devcon Construction, Cisco Systems, San Jose, 1999.

1.14 Hawley and Peterson, Qume Corporation, Santa Clara, 1980. Exterior.

1.10

1.11

1.12

1.13

1.38

1.39

Benchmark

→ p. 32

1.40 Gensler and Associates, Digital Corporation, Santa Clara, 1976.
1.41 Plan.

1.42 MBT Associates, IBM Santa Theresa, San Jose, 1974.
1.43 Site plan.

1.44 Gensler and Associates, Oracle Corporation, Redwood City, 1990. Detail.

1.40

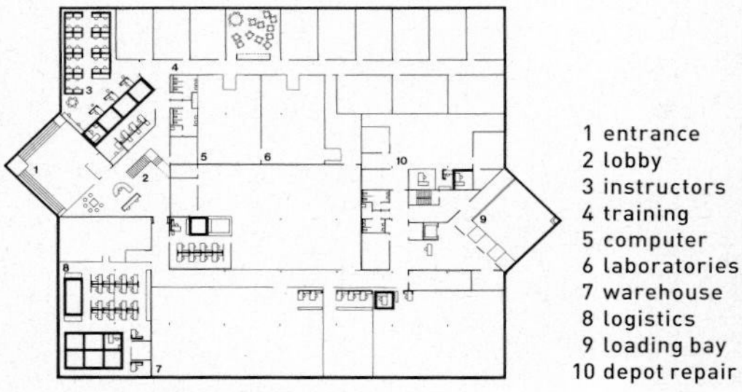

Digital Corporation (plan)

1.41

1.42

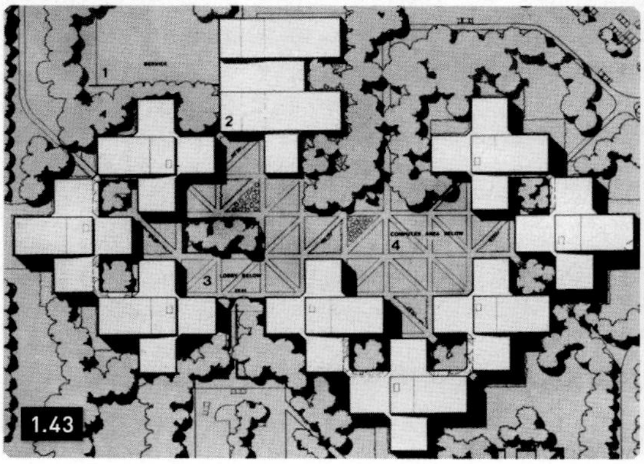

1.43

1.44

The Developer or, Virtual Reality

→ p. 30

Gensler Associates, Oracle Corporation, Redwood City, 1990.

1.36 **Site plan.**
1.37 **Night view.**
1.38 **Video stills.**
1.39 **View from street.**

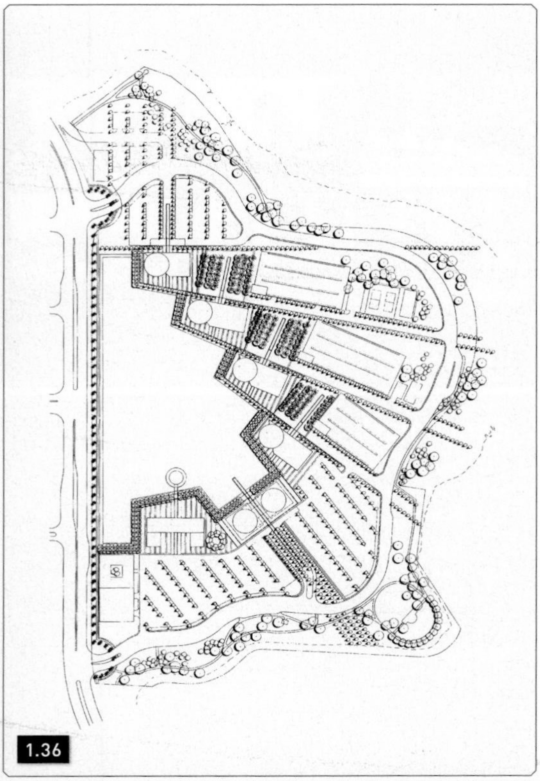

1.36

1.37

1.31–1.35

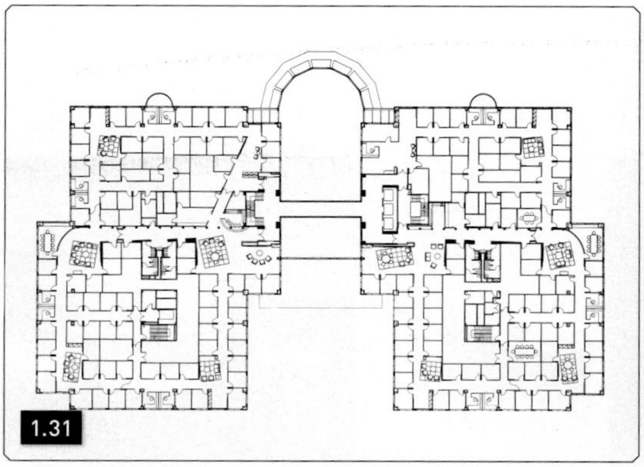

1.31

1.32

1.33

1.34

1.35

Users

→ p. 28

1.28 Gensler Associates, Apple Computer, Cupertino, 1993. User Defined Area.

1.29 Apple iMac advertisement, c. 1998.

1.30 Hellmuth, Obata, and Kassabaum, Nortel Networks, 2001.

1.31– 1.32 Gensler and Associates, Apple Computer, Cupertino, 1993. Plan and User Defined Area.

1.33– 1.34 Hellmuth, Obata, and Kassabaum, Adobe Corporation, San Jose, 2001.

1.35 Market Post Tower, MAE West Internet hub, San Jose, 1985. Architect unknown.

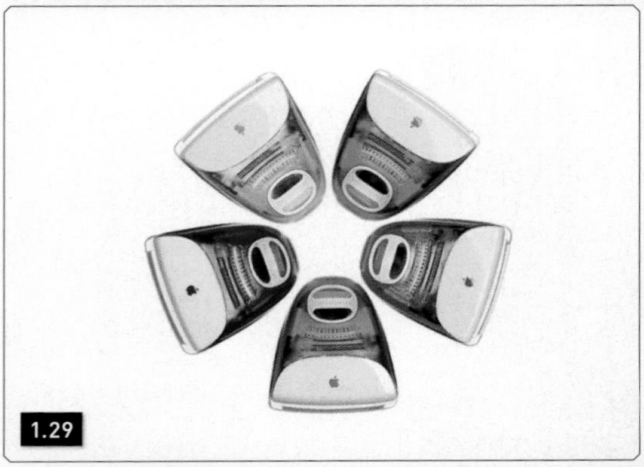

1.29

1.28

1.30

PCPC

→ p. 27

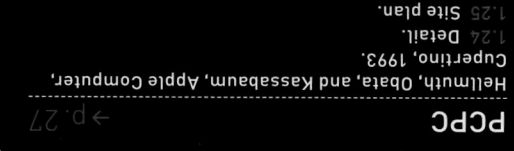

Hellmuth, Obata, and Kassabaum, Apple Computer, Cupertino, 1993.
1.24 Detail.
1.25 Site plan.
1.26 Courtyard.

1.27 The Irvine Company, North Park Apartment Village, San Jose, 2003.

1.24

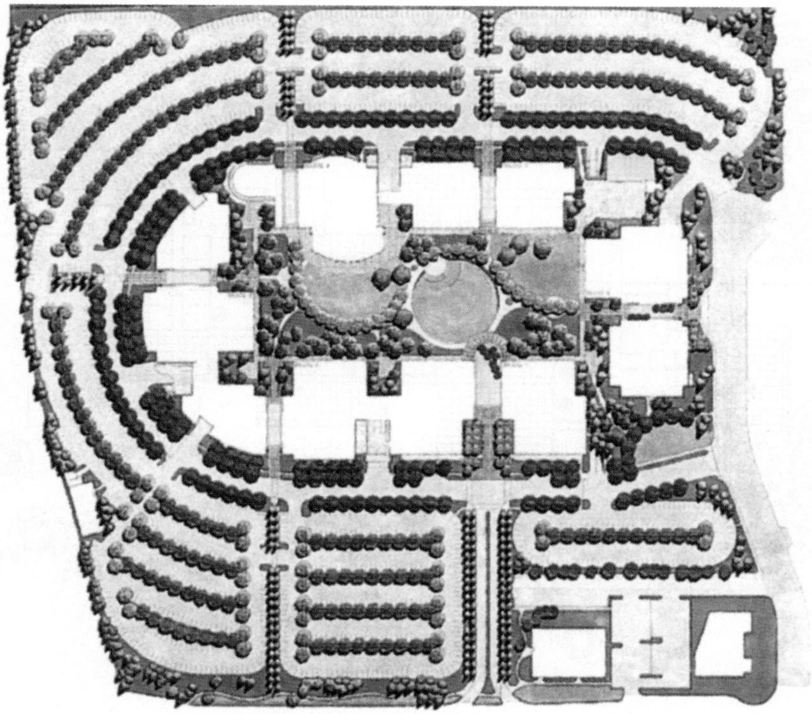
1.25

1.26

1.27

Interior Design

→ p. 26

1.20 Hellmuth, Obata, and Kassabaum, Xerox PARC, Palo Alto, 1975.
1.21 Plan.

1.22–1.23 Hellmuth, Obata, and Kassabaum, Apple Computer, Cupertino, 1993. Atrium.

1.20

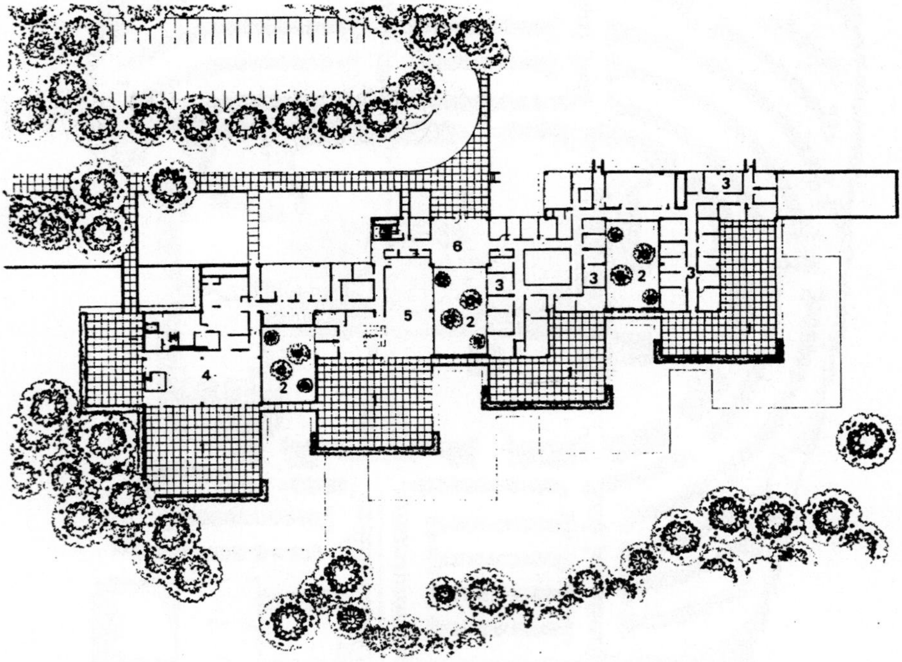

1.21

1.22

1.23

1.19
2500 Sand Hill Road
Matrix Partners
The Nasdaq Stock Market, Inc.
Russell Reynolds Associates, Inc.

1.14

The Continuous Interior, or From Wall Street to Sandhill Road → p. 25

1.15 ARPANET, 1969. Diagram.

1.16 Sand Hill Road, Palo Alto, 2003.

1.17 Stanford Research Institute, Palo Alto, 1946. Architect unknown.

1.18 Kleiner Perkins Caufield and Byers, Sand Hill Road, Palo Alto. Date and architect unknown.

1.19 NASDAQ, Sand Hill Road, Palo Alto. Date and architect unknown.

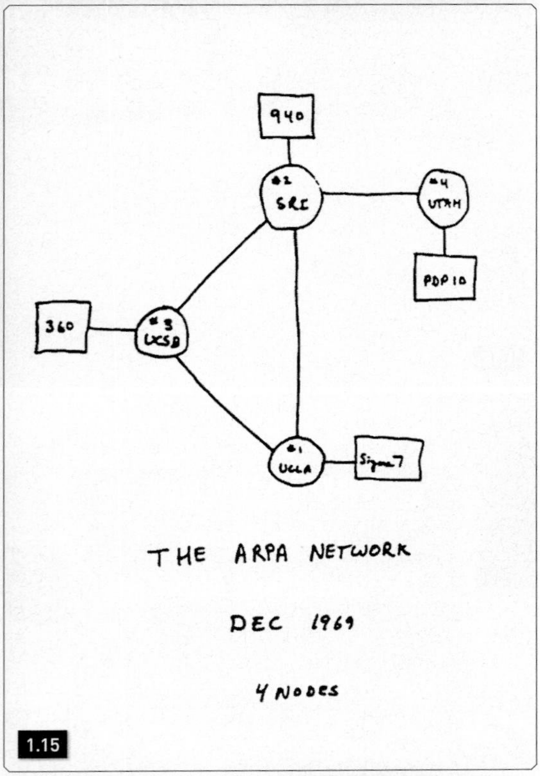

1.15

1.16

1.17

1.18

Shell and Core

→ p. 33

1.45 Sobrato Development Companies, SONICblue, Santa Clara, 2003.

1.46 Office park lawn, Mountain View, 2002.

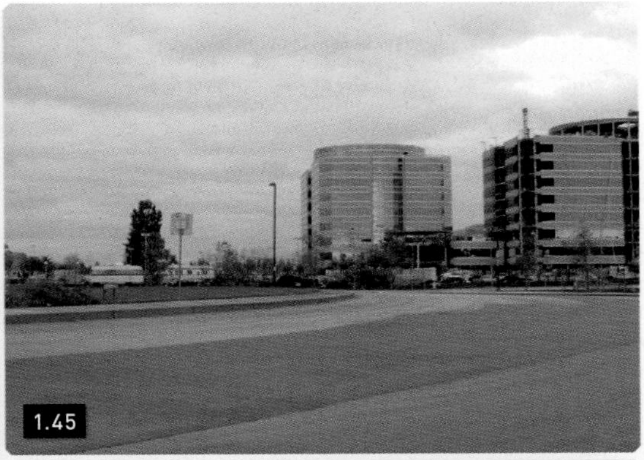

1.45

1.46

The Golf Course Principle

→ p. 34

Studios Architecture, Silicon Graphics, North Charleston Campus (now Googleplex), Mountain View, 1997.

1.47 Plan.
1.48 Aerial View.
1.49-1.50 Landscape.

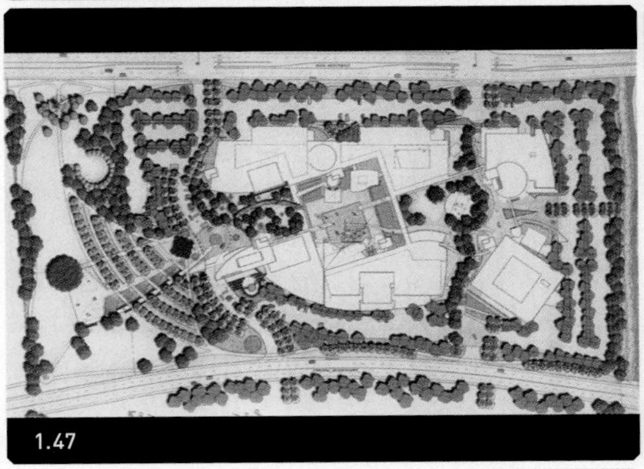

1.47

1.48

1.49

1.50

From Seagram to SGI

→ p. 36

Studios Architecture, E*Trade, Menlo Park, 1999.
1.51 Coffee bar.
1.52 Plan.

1.53–1.54 Studios Architecture, 3Com, Santa Clara, 1999.

1.51

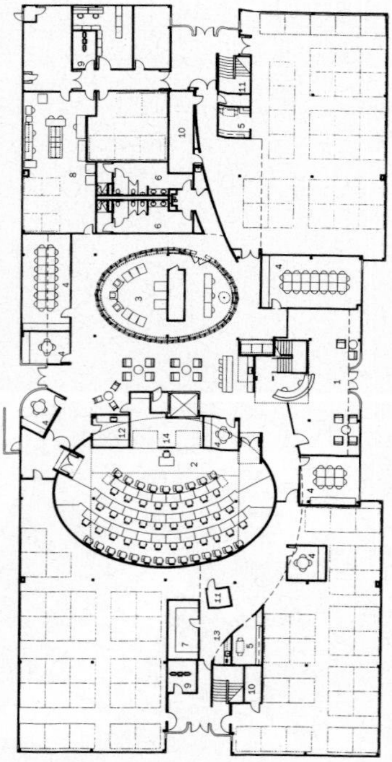

1.52

1.53

1.54

The (Exit) Sign

→ p. 37

Hellmuth, Obata, and Kassabaum, with interiors by Studios Architecture, Excite@Home, Redwood City, 2000.

1.55 Night view.
1.56 Interior after bankruptcy.
1.57 Exterior.
1.58 Landscape with "@" sign after bankruptcy.

1.59 Vacant office park, Mountain View, 2003.

1.60 Vacant offices, Mountain View, 2003.

1.61 Office park signage, erased, Mountain View, 2003.

1.55

1.56

1.57

1.58

1.59

1.60

1.61

From Hardware to Software → p. 38

Studios Architecture, Silicon Graphics, North Charleston Campus (now Googleplex), Mountain View, 1997.
1.62–1.63 Courtyard.
1.64 Coffee bar with white board.

1.62

1.64

1.63

CVRP → p. 39

1.65 Hellmuth, Obata, and Kassabaum, Apple Computer, Cupertino, 1993.

1.66 Sun Microsystems, Santa Clara, 2001. Architect unknown. View from Interstate 101.

Devcon Construction and Cisco Systems, Coyote Valley Research Park, San Jose, 2000.
1.67 Site plan.
1.68–1.69 Renderings.

1.70 Coyote Valley, San Jose, 2003.
1.71 Cayote Valley, San Jose, View from Interstate 101, 2003.

1.65

1.66

1.67

1.68 A light rail system (at right) would serve the Coyote Valley Research Park.

1.69 The "Main Street" portion of Cisco's proposed Coyote Valley Research Park.

1.70

1.71

FROM
NEW DELHI
TO
NEW YORK

2

2.01 Herbert Baker, Council House, New Delhi, 1927.

2.02 Herbert Baker and Edwin Lutyens, Imperial Complex, New Delhi, 1927, Detail.

2.01

2.02

Ground Zero

→ p. 60

2.03–2.04 Wallace Harrison et al, United Nations Headquarters, New York, 1950.

2.03

2.04

Follow the Money

→ p. 60

2.05 Gordon Bunshaft of Skidmore, Owings & Merrill, Lever House, New York, 1952. View from Seagram Building.

2.06 Ludwig Mies van der Rohe and Philip Johnson, Seagram Building, New York, 1958.

2.07 Gordon Bunshaft of Skidmore, Owings & Merrill, Union Carbide Building, New York, 1960.

2.05

2.06

2.07

Whiskey (An Interlude)

→ p. 61

2.08 Kevin Roche John Dinkeloo and Associates, JP Morgan Headquarters, New York, 1987.

2.09 Gordon Bunshaft of Skidmore, Owings & Merrill, Union Carbide Building, 1960. Lobby (JPMorganChase), 2003.

2.08

2.09

Crystals

→ p. 62

Kevin Roche John Dinkeloo and Associates
2.10 Union Carbide Headquarters, Danbury, 1982.
2.11 United Nations Plaza, New York, original master plan, 1969.
2.12 United Nations Plaza, New York, 1983.
2.13 Union Carbide Headquarters, Danbury, 1982. Office.
2.14 United Nations Plaza, New York, 1983.

2.10

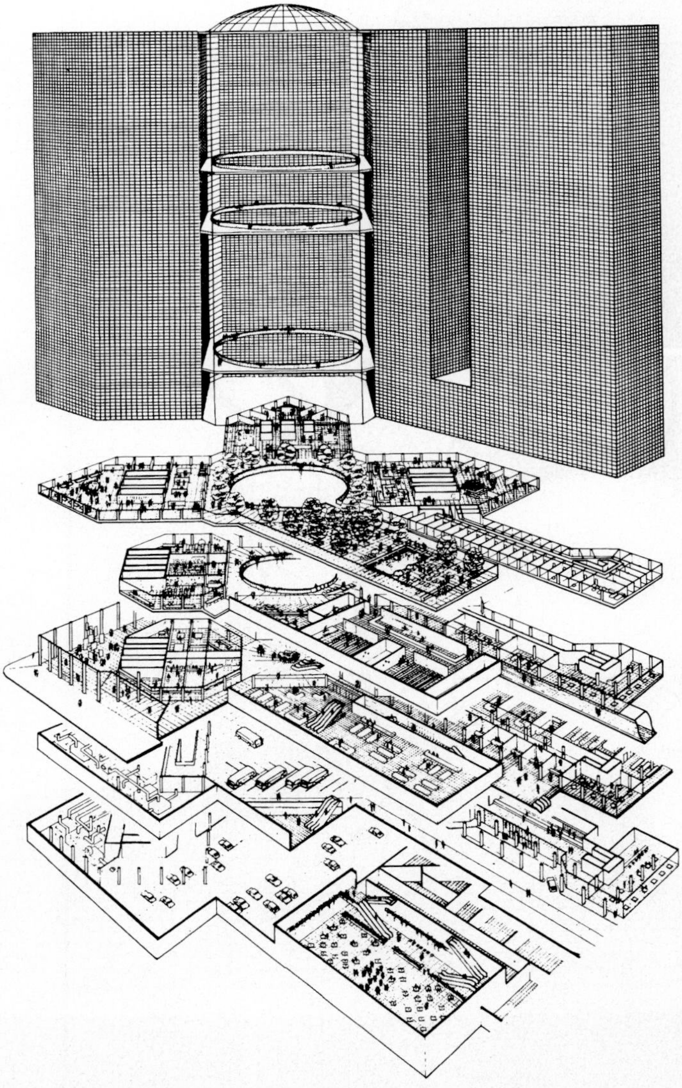

2.11

2.12

2.13

2.14

World Trade

→ p. 62

2.15 Gordon Bunshaft of Skidmore, Owings & Merrill, Chase Manhattan Bank Headquarters, New York, 1961.

2.16 Gordon Bunshaft of Skidmore, Owings & Merrill, Chase Manhattan Bank Headquarters, New York, 1961.

2.17 Skidmore, Owings & Merrill, original scheme for World Trade Center, New York, 1958. Rendering.

2.15

2.16

2.17

Towers, or Public Relations

→ p. 64

2.18 Minoru Yamasaki and Emery Roth & Sons, World Trade Center, New York, 1964, completed 1973. Model photograph by Balthazar Korab.

2.18

Plazas

→ p. 64

2.19 Gordon Bunshaft of Skidmore, Owings & Merrill, Marine Midland Bank Headquarters, New York, 1967.

2.20 Gordon Bunshaft of Skidmore, Owings & Merrill, Marine Midland Bank Headquarters with Chase Manhattan Bank Headquarters (beyond), New York, 1967 and 1961, respectively.

2.21 Gordon Bunshaft of Skidmore, Owings & Merrill, Chase Manhattan Bank Headquarters, New York, 1961.

2.22 Gordon Bunshaft of Skidmore, Owings & Merrill, Marine Midland Bank Headquarters, New York, 1967. Plaza with planters and Chase plaza beyond, 2003.

2.19

2.20

2.21

2.22

The Continuous Interior, Again

→ p. 65

2.23 Minoru Yamasaki and Emery Roth & Sons, World Trade Center, New York, 1973. Elevators.

Planes

→ p. 65

2.24 Port Authority of New York and New Jersey, World Trade Center press kit, inside cover, 1964. Avery Architectural and Fine Arts Library, Columbia University.

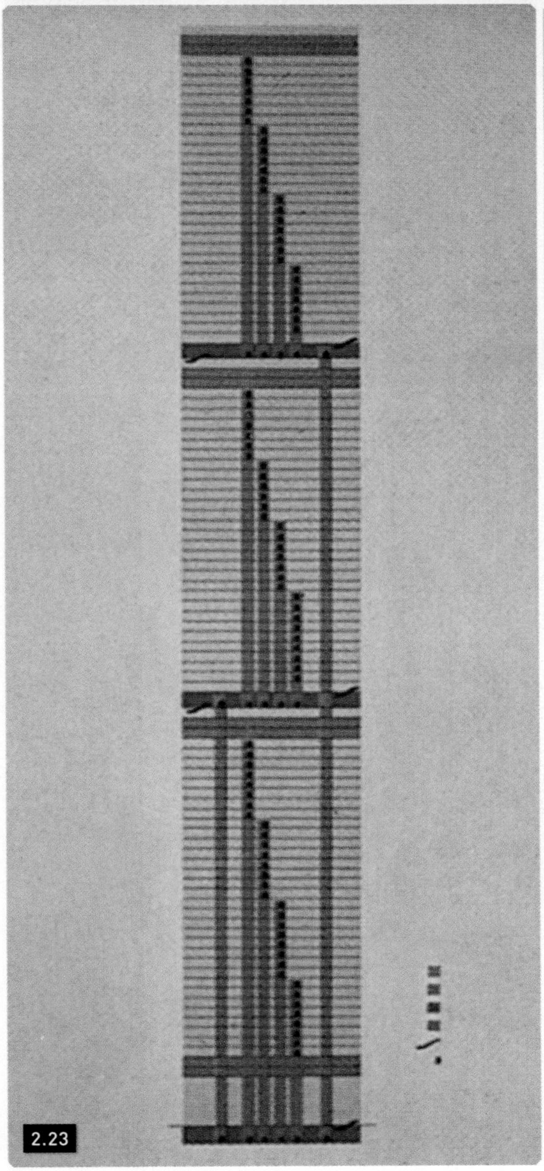

2.23

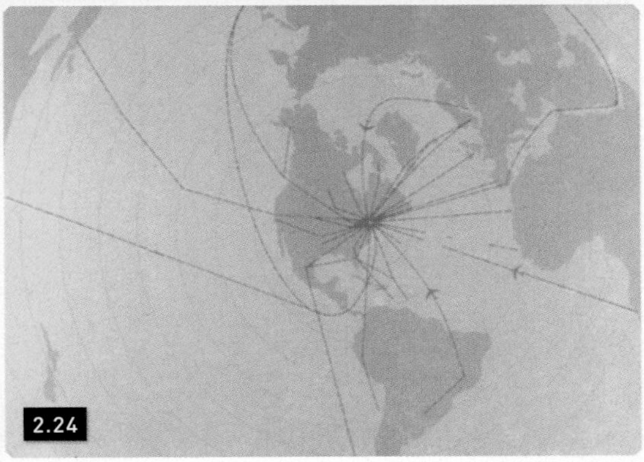

2.24

Trees

→ p. 66

Rai Y. Okamoto et al, *Urban Design Manhattan*, 1969.
2.25 Manhattan CBDs, conceptual diagram.
2.26 New office cluster, section.
2.27 Access Tree.
2.28 Office Projections Diagram.
2.29 Form Response Diagram.
2.30 Long Range Movement Systems.
2.31 Office clusters and typical Access Tree, model.

2.32 Wallace Harrison and Max Abramovitz,
XYZ Buildings, New York, 1972.

2.26

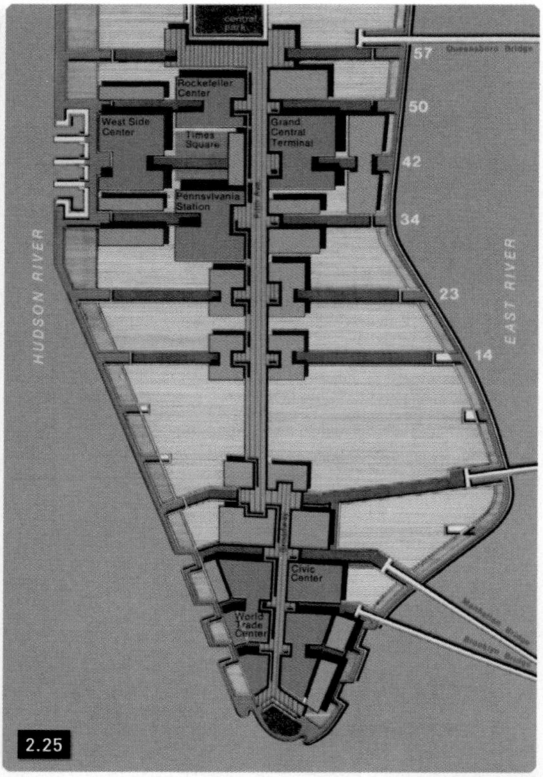

2.25

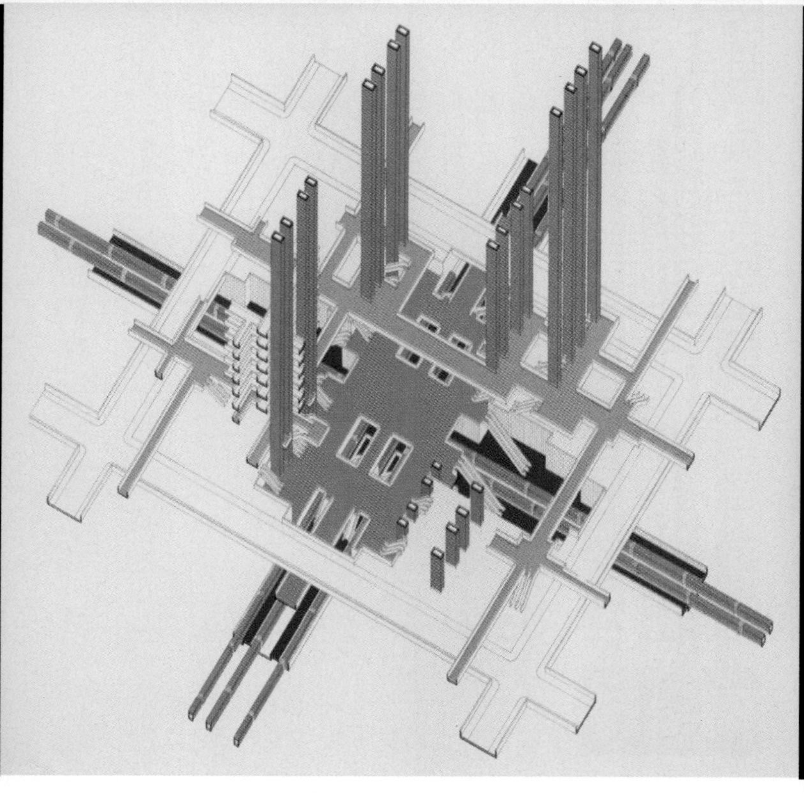

2.27

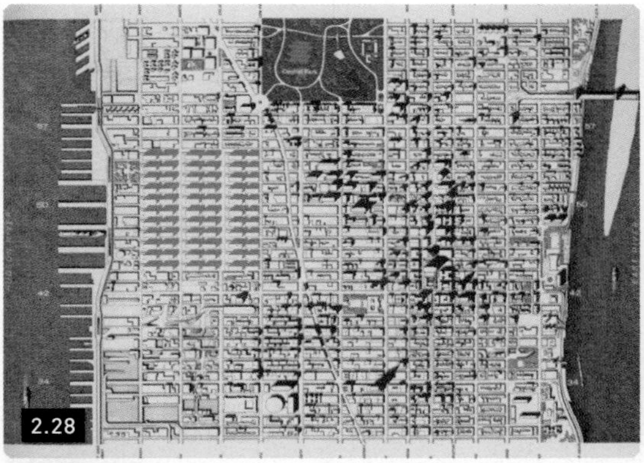
2.28

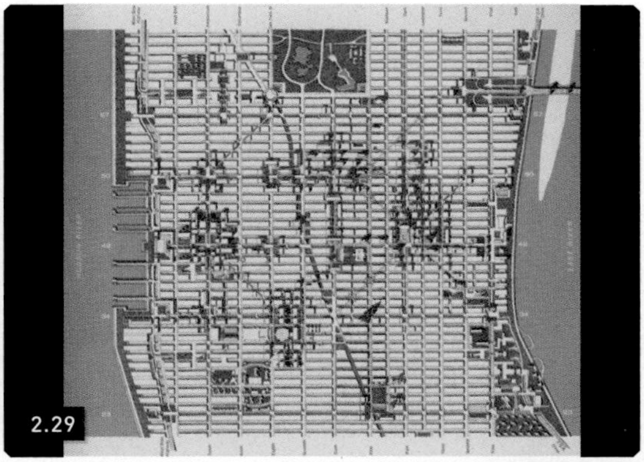
2.29

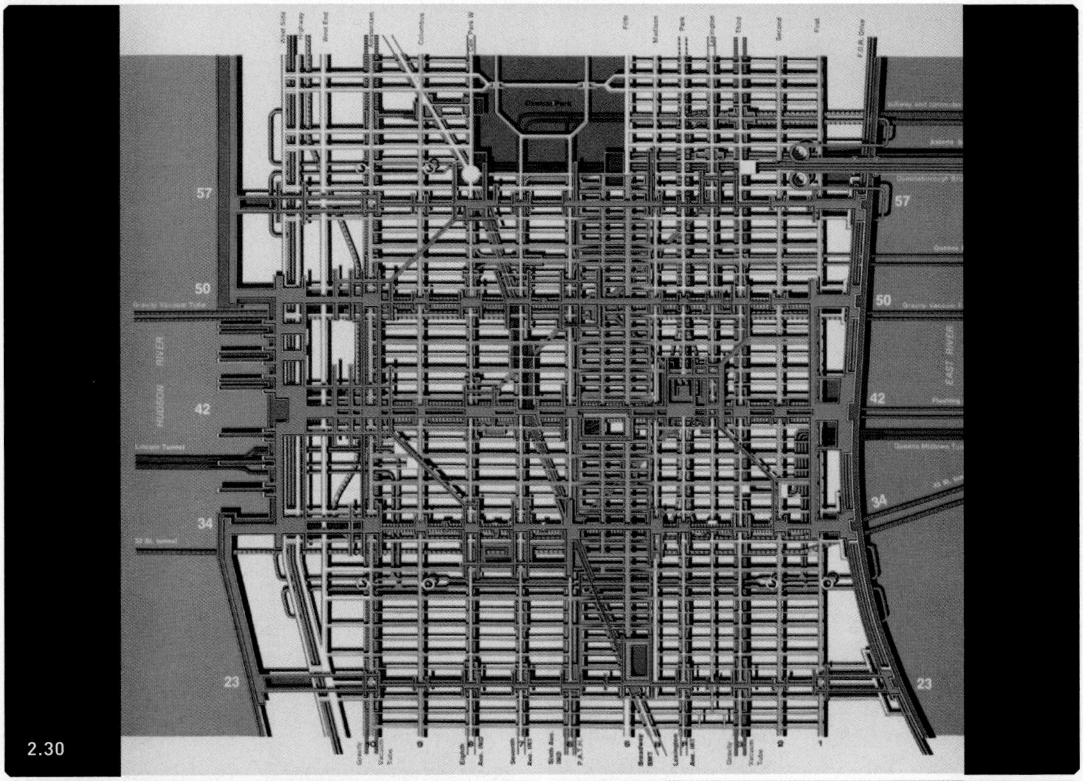

2.30

2.31

2.32

The Citi is (Not) a Tree → p. 68

2.33–2.34 **Hugh Stubbins and Associates, Citicorp Center, New York, 1977.**
2.35 **Atrium.**
2.36 **Sunken plaza.**
2.37 **Façade.**
2.38 **Sketch.**

2.39 **Carson & Lundin, and Kahn & Jacobs, First City National Bank, 399 Park Avenue, New York, 1961.**

2.34

2.33

2.35

2.36

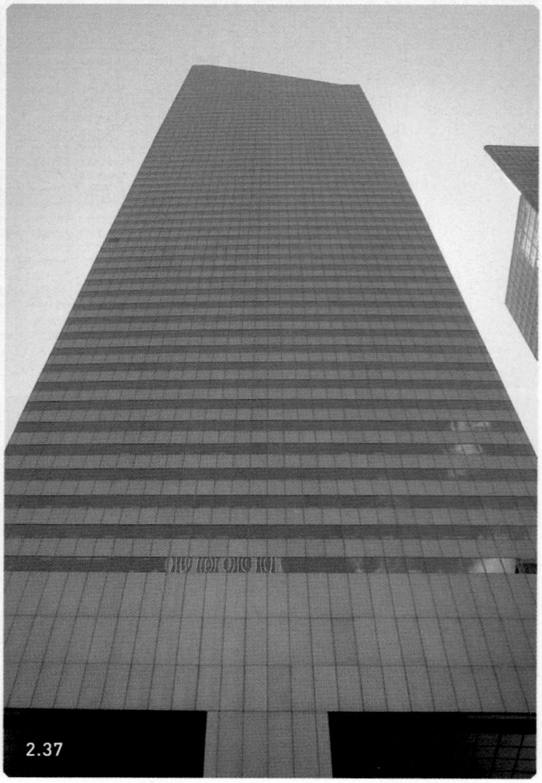

2.37

2.38

2.39

The Atrium, Again → p. 71

2.40 Edward Larrabee Barnes, IBM Building, New York, 1983. Philip Johnson, AT&T Building, New York, 1983.

2.41 Edward Larrabee Barnes, IBM Building, New York, 1983.

2.42 Philip Johnson, AT&T Building, New York, 1983.

2.43 Eero Saarinen and Associates, Bell Laboratories, Holmdel, 1966.

2.44 Kevin Roche John Dinkeloo and Associates, Ford Foundation Headquarters, New York, 1968.
2.45 Atrium.

Edward Larrabee Barnes, IBM Building, New York, 1983.
2.46 Base.
2.47 Atrium.
2.48 Philip Johnson, AT&T Building, New York, 1983. Atrium.
2.49 Exterior, with Trump Tower on left.

2.50 Der Scutt with Swanke Hayden and Connell, Trump Tower, New York, 1983.
2.51 Atrium.

2.40

2.41

2.42

2.43

2.44

2.45

2.46

2.47

2.48

2.49

2.50

2.51

World Finance

→ p. 72

2.52–253 Cesar Pelli and Associates, World Financial Center, New York, 1988.
2.54 Atrium.
2.55 View from Jersey City.

2.52

2.53

2.54

2.55

Off Center

→ p. 73

2.56 Cesar Pelli and Associates, Goldman Sachs Building, Jersey City, 2004.

2.57 Cesar Pelli and Associates, World Financial Center, New York, 1988. Reflected view from Jersey City.

2.58 Cesar Pelli and Associates, Bloomberg Headquarters, New York, 2005.
2.59 Entry court.

2.56

2.57

2.58

2.59

TWC

→ p. 74

2.60 David Childs of Skidmore, Owings & Merrill, Time Warner Center, New York, 2004.
2.61 Axonometric showing programmatic mixture.
2.62 Façade.
2.63 Interior mall.
2.64 Atrium with glass wall by Jaime Carpenter.
2.65–2.66 Interior mall.

2.60

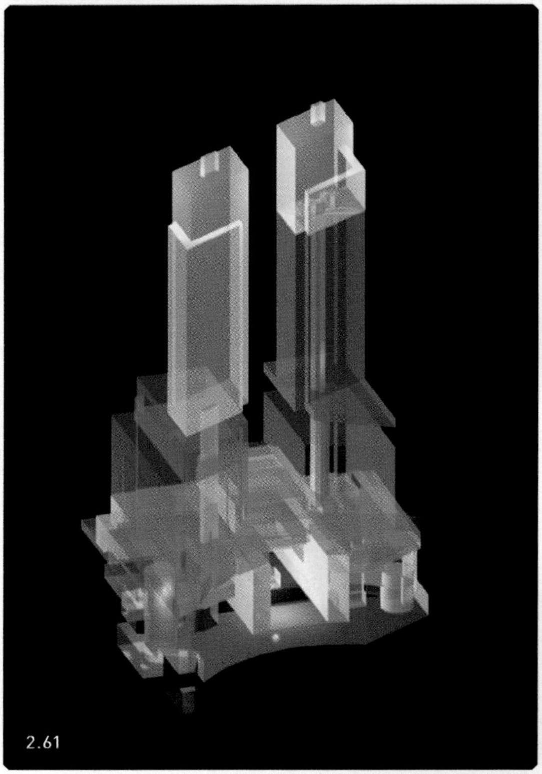

2.61

2.62

2.63

2.64

2.65

2.66

The Centripetal/Centrifugal Spiral

→ p. 77

2.67 The Centripetal/Centrifugal Spiral, with selected office development sites, c. 2002.

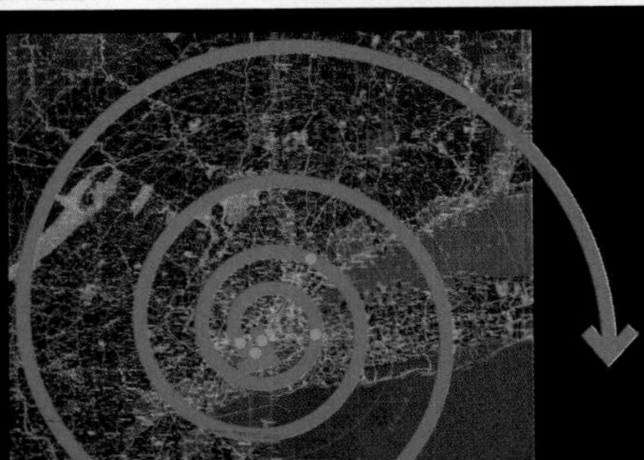

2.67

Number One

→ p. 78

2.68 Martin/Baxi Architects, No. 1 Broadway Penthouse, 2001.

2.68

A Report

→ p. 79

2.69 World Trade Center site, 15 September 2001.

FROM **SILICON VALLEY** TO **NEW DELHI**

3

3.01 RSP Architects and Planners, International Tech Park Ltd. (ITPL), Bangalore, 2002.

World Class

→ p. 97

3.02 RSP Architects and Planners, International Tech Park Ltd. (ITPL), Bangalore, 2002.

3.03 Export Promotion Industrial Park, Bangalore, 2002. Map.

3.02

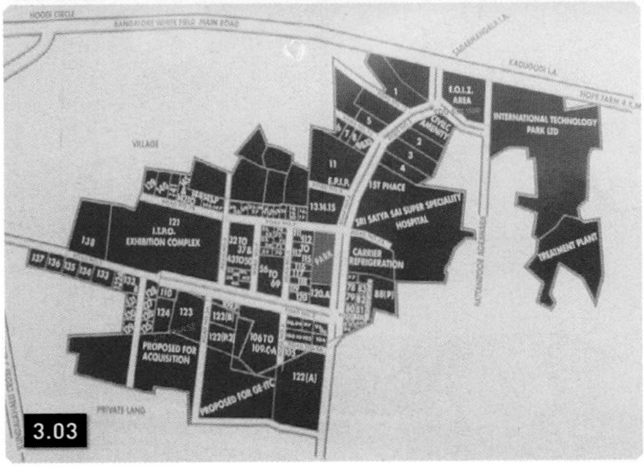

3.03

Digital (Park)

→ p. 98

3.04–3.05 Karan Grover, Digital Park, Bangalore, 2002.

3.04

3.05

Euphoria in the Cafeteria

→ p. 98

3.06 Sundaram Architects, Infosys, Bangalore, 2002. Corporate Care Center.
3.07 Food court.

3.06

3.07

NRI

→ p. 99

3.08 Edward Durell Stone, United States Embassy, New Delhi, 1954.
3.09 Fence, 2002.
3.10 Portico.
3.11 Party, mid-1960s.
3.12 Entry, 2002.

3.13 Herbert Baker and Edwin Lutyens, Imperial complex, New Delhi, 1927.

3.08

3.09

3.10

3.11

3.12

3.13

IIC

→ p. 101

3.14 **Joseph Allen Stein, India International Center, New Delhi, 1962.**

chandigarh.com

→ p. 102

3.15 Balkrishna V. Doshi, Indian Institute of Management, Bangalore, 1985.
3.16 Plan.

Le Corbusier
3.17 High Court, Chandigarh, 1958.
3.18 Secretariat, Chandigarh, 1958.
3.19 Assembly Building, Chandigarh, 1963.
3.20 Open Hand Monument, Chandigarh, 1985.

3.21 Quark City, Chandigarh. Rendering, 2004. Architect unknown.

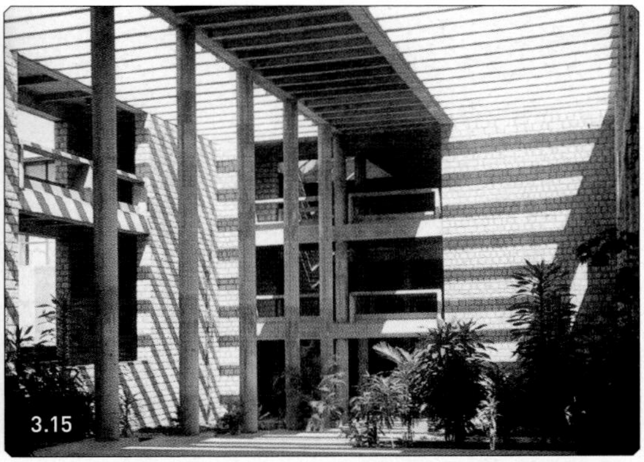
3.15

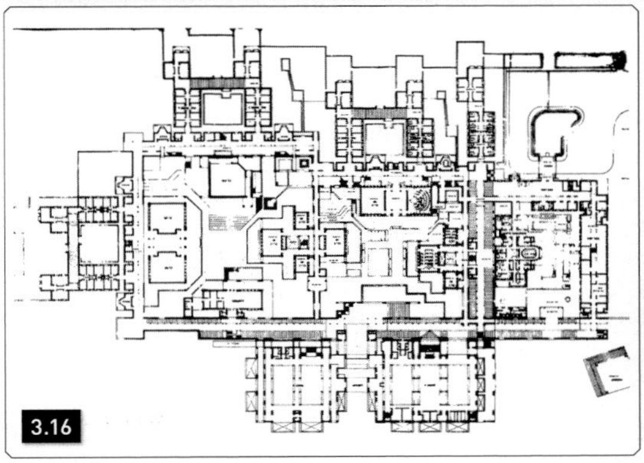
3.16

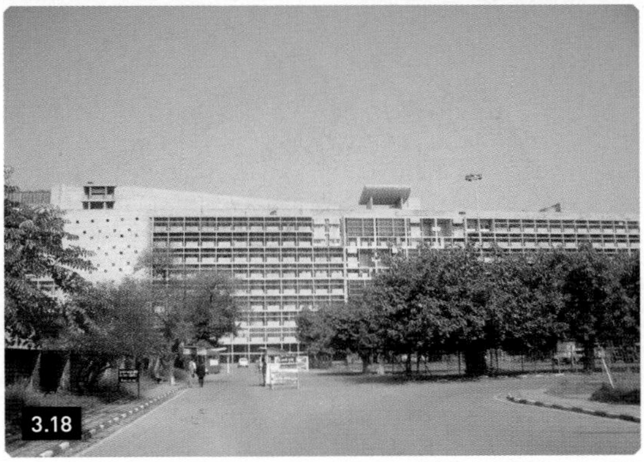
3.18

3.17

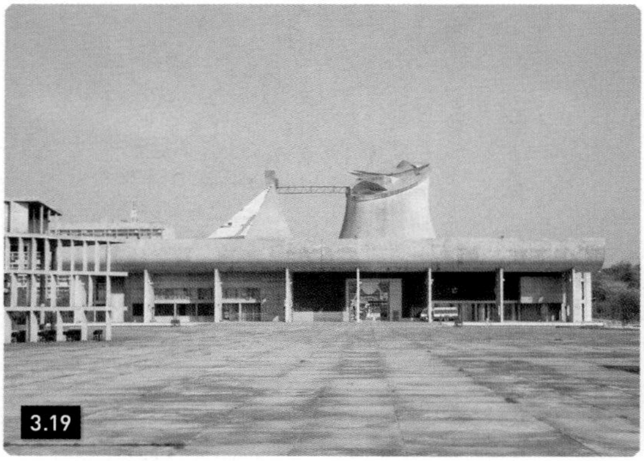

3.19

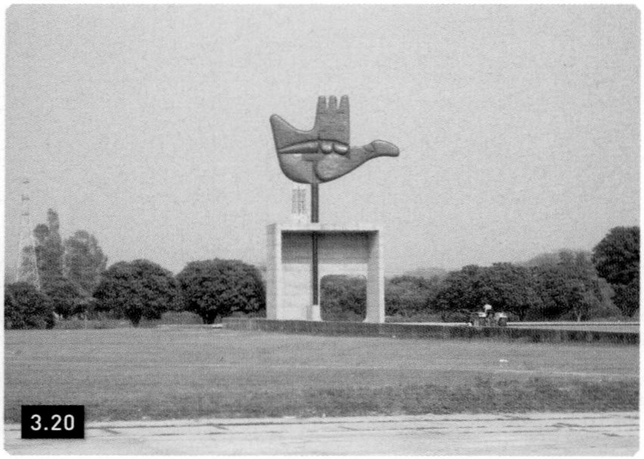

3.20

3.21

An Error

→ p. 104

3.22 Le Corbusier in Chandigarh, c. 1950.

3.23 Le Corbusier, Le Modulor, original version, 1945.

3.24 Le Corbusier, 1/6000 error in Le Modulor, 1955.

3.25 Diagram showing graphic effect of mathematical "error" in Le Modulor. Drawing by Urtzi Grau.

3.26 Le Corbusier, High Court, Chandigarh, 1958. Modulor.

3.27 Le Corbusier, Governor's House, Chandigarh. Unbuilt. Diagrams from *Modulor 2*, 1958.

3.28 Le Corbusier, Le Modulor, 1955.

3.22

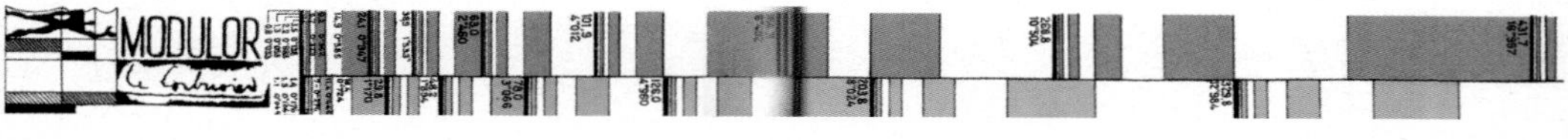

3.23

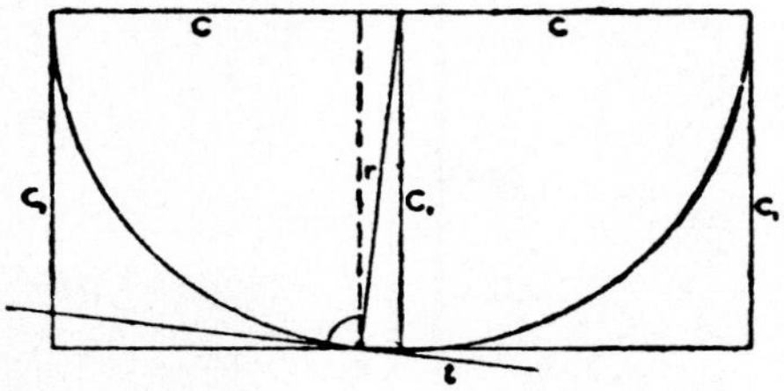

3.24

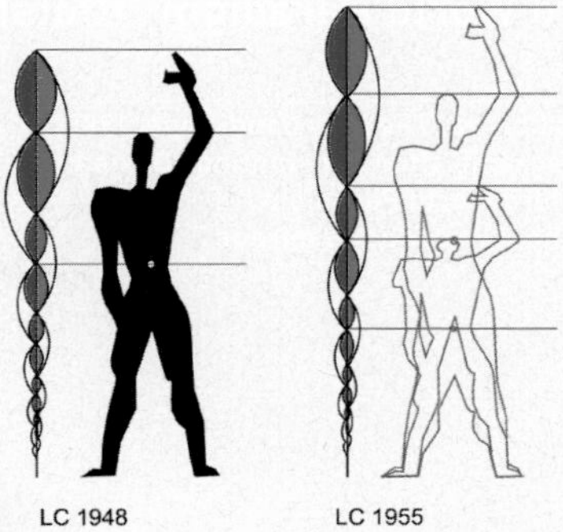

3.25

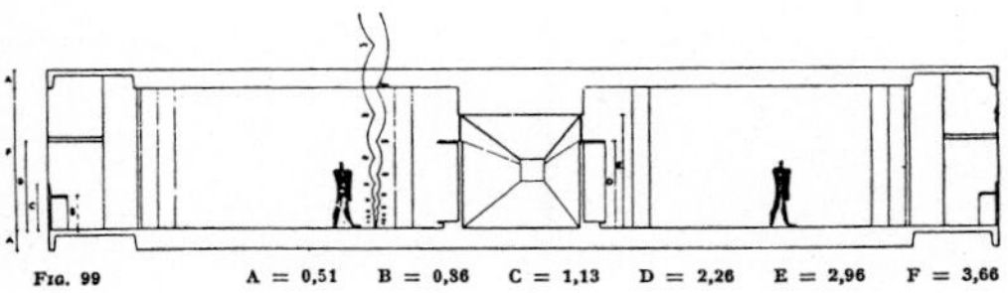

3.26

3.27

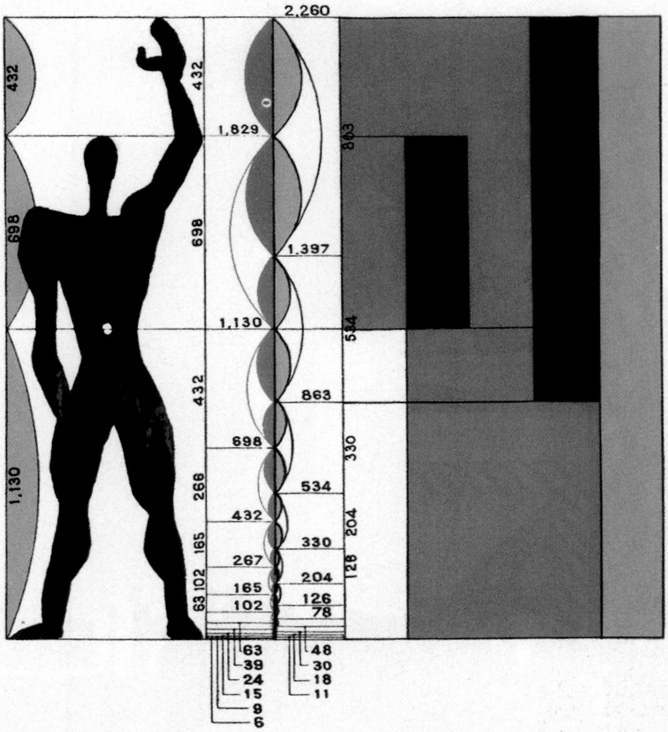

3.28

"Third World Paradigm" (Dots)

→ p. 106

Charles Correa, *The New Landscape*, 1985.
3.29 Diagrams after Constantinos Doxiadis.
3.30 "Third World Paradigm."
3.31 "The Metropolis as mirage."

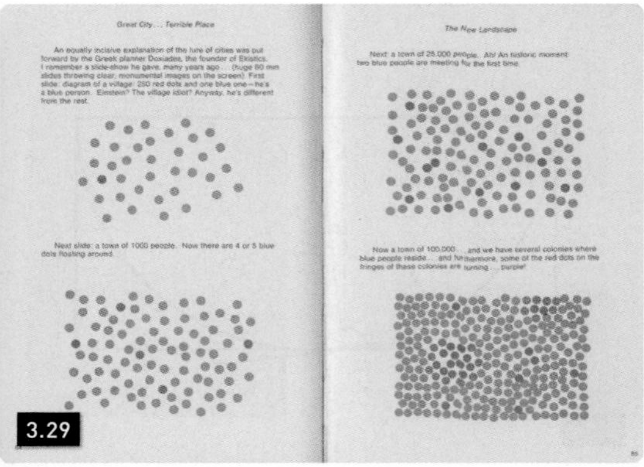

Great City . . . Terrible Place

An equally incisive explanation of the lure of cities was put forward by the Greek planner Doxiades, the founder of Ekistics. I remember a slide-show he gave, many years ago . . . (huge 60 mm slides throwing clear, monumental images on the screen). First slide: diagram of a village: 250 red dots and one blue one—he's a blue person. Einstein? The village idiot? Anyway, he's different from the rest.

Next slide: a town of 1000 people. Now there are 4 or 5 blue dots floating around.

The New Landscape

Next: a town of 25,000 people. Ah! An historic moment: two blue people are meeting for the first time.

Now a town of 100,000 . . . and we have several colonies where blue people reside . . . and furthermore, some of the red dots on the fringes of these colonies are turning . . . purple!

3.29

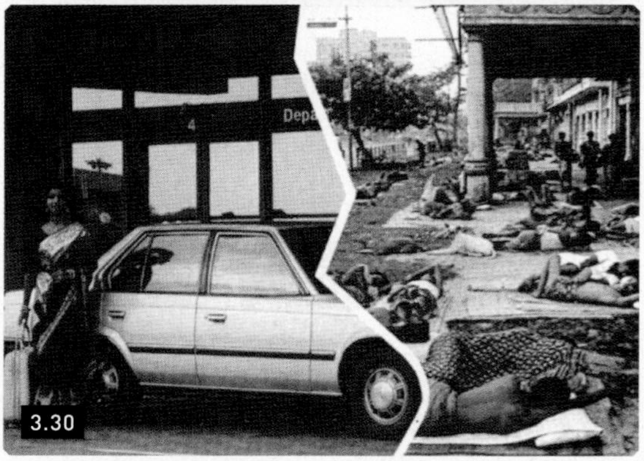

3.30

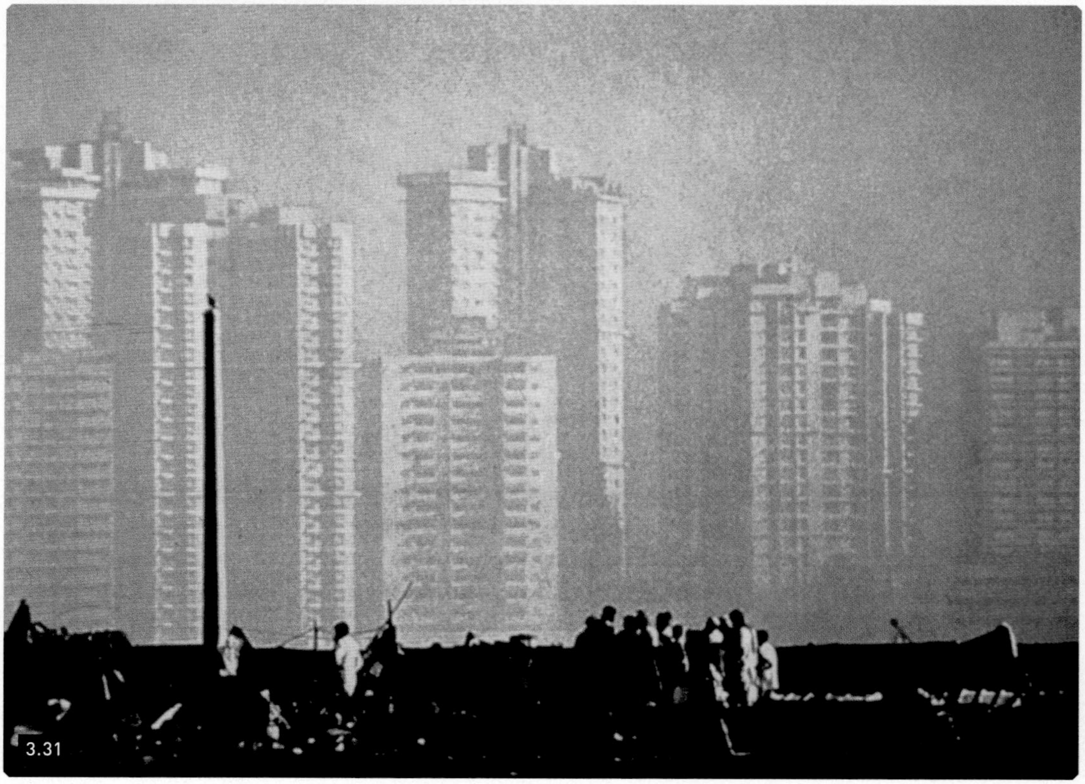

3.31

Sandstone (Red)

→ p. 107

Charles Correa

3.32 Visvesvaraya Center, Bangalore, 1980.
3.33 Hindustan Lever Pavilion, New Delhi, 1961.
3.34–3.35 Life Insurance Corporaton of India (Jeevan Bharati), New Delhi, 1986.
3.36 British Council, New Delhi, 1992.
3.37 India Permanent Mission to the United Nations, New York, 1992.

3.33

3.32

3.34

3.35

3.36

3.37

Mini-Mega

→p. 109

Raj Rewal
3.38, 3.41 State Trading Corporation Headquarters, New Delhi, 1976.
3.39 Standing Conference of Public Enterprise (SCOPE), New Delhi, 1989.
3.40 Standing Conference of Public Enterprise (SCOPE), New Delhi, 1989. Axonometric.

3.42 Ralph Lerner, Indira Gandhi National Centre for the Arts, New Delhi, 1999.

3.38

3.39

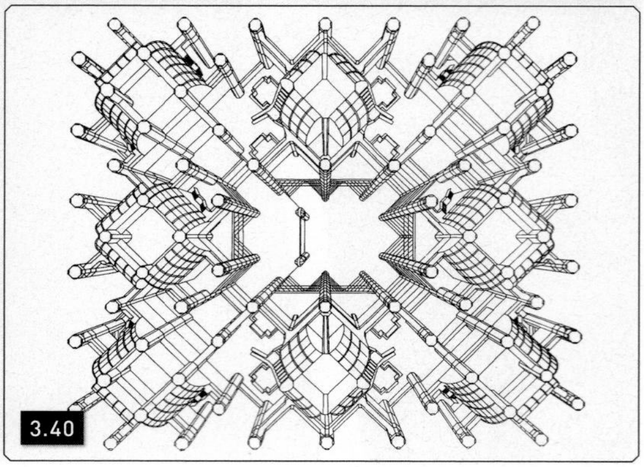
3.40

CENTRAL COTTAGE INDUSTRIES EMPORIUM
Jawahar Vyapar Bhawan

3.41

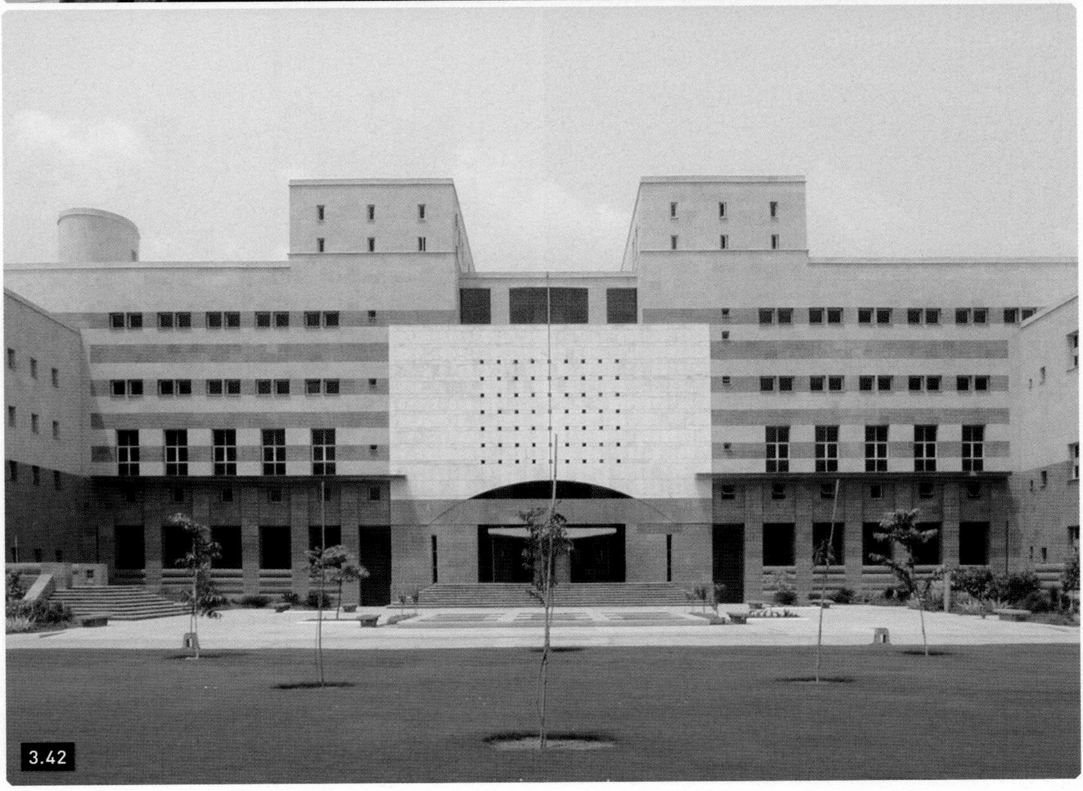

3.42

Import-Export

→ p. 110

3.43 Raj Rewal, International Trade Fair, New Delhi, 1972.

3.43

Global Village

→ p. 111

3.44 Charles Correa, National Crafts Museum, New Delhi, 1990.

3.44

National Science

→ p. 112

3.45 Achyut Kanvinde, National Science Museum, New Delhi, 1990.

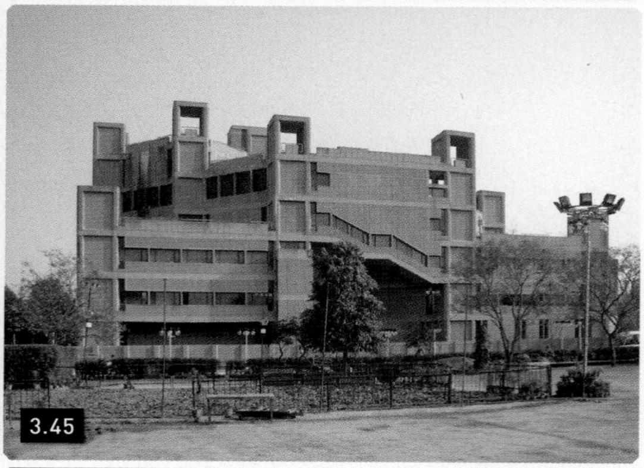

3.45

All that is solid...

→ p. 113

3.46 Kuldip Singh, New Delhi Town Hall, 1980.

3.46

Hafeez

→ p. 113

Hafeez Contractor
3.47 DLF Group Headquarters, New Delhi, 1997.
3.48–3.49 in advertisements from *Architecture + Design*, 2002.

DLF City, Gurgaon

3.50 1999.
3.51 c. 2004, map.
3.52 1999.

3.53 Hafeez Contractor, Lake Castle, Mumbai, 1999.

3.47

3.48

3.49

3.50

3.51

3.52

3.53

Very, Very American!

→ p. 115

3.54 Spazzio Architects, Adobe India, Noida, 2003.

3.54

Princeton, Gurgaon

→ p. 116

Hafeez Contractor, DLF City, Gurgaon, 2004.
3.55–3.56 DLF Princeton Estate.
3.57 DLF Carlton Estate.

3.55

3.56

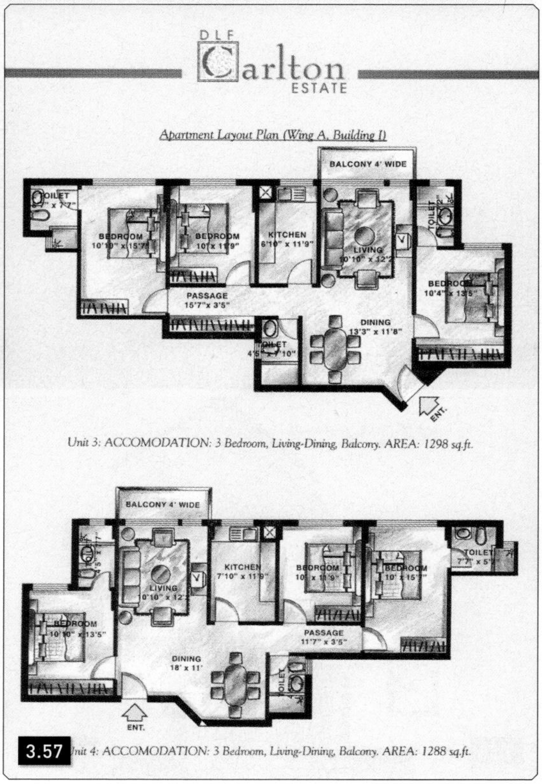

3.57

Inside Outsourcing → p. 116

3.58–3.59 Hafeez Contractor, DLF Plaza Tower, DLF City, Gurgaon, 1999.

3.60 DLF Golf Links, DLF City, Gurgaon, 1999.

3.61 *India Today*, 18 November 2002. Cover.

3.62 Hafeez Contractor, GE Capital Call Center, DLF City, Gurgaon, 2002.
3.63 with DLF Princeton Estate beyond.

Framework Interiors
3.64 GE Capital Call Center, DLF City, Gurgaon, 2002.
3.65 "Multinational Design for the Multinational Mind," *Architecture + Design*, 2002.

3.66 Framework Interiors, "Multinational Design for the Multinational Mind," *Architecture + Design*, 2002.

Hafeez Contractor
3.67–3.68 DLF Gateway Tower, DLF City, Gurgaon, 1999.
3.69–3.71 DLF Square Tower, DLF City, Gurgaon, 1999.

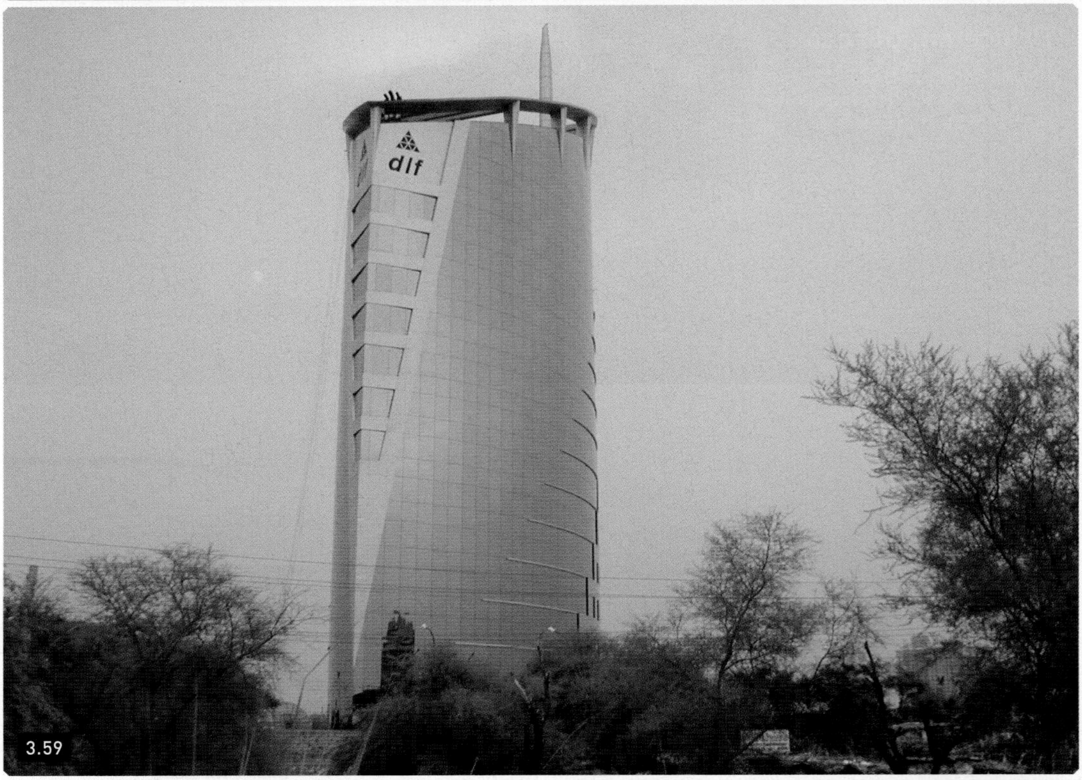

3.59

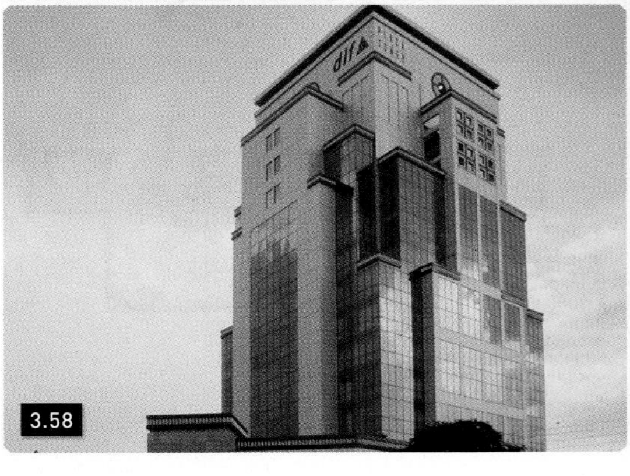
3.58

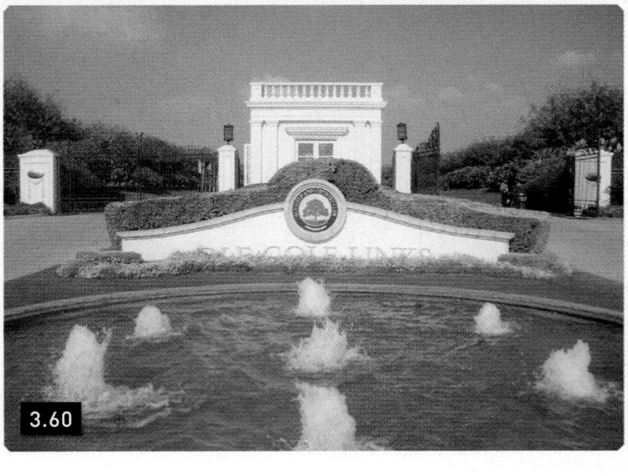
3.60

3.61

3.62

3.63

3.64

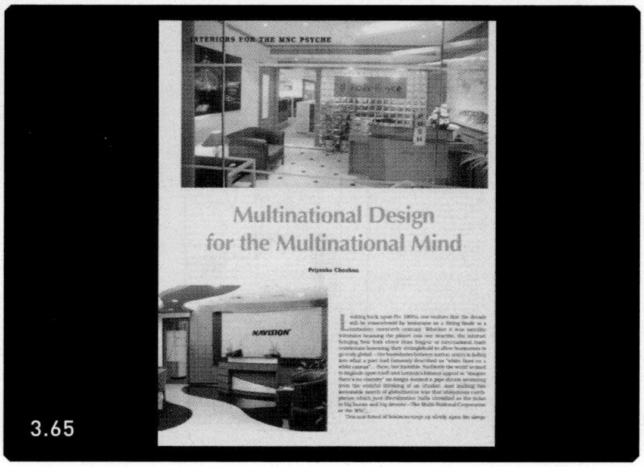

3.65

3.66

3.67

3.68

3.69

3.70

3.71

Generators (Backup)

→ p. 119

3.72 Hafeez Contractor, Ericsson Headquarters, DLF City, Gurgaon, 2004.
3.73 with DLF Gateway Tower beyond.

3.72

3.73

"Nature"

→ p. 120

3.74 Rahul Mehrotra Associates, Hewlett Packard campus, Bangalore, 2002. Site plan.

3.75 Rahul Mehrotra Associates, Hewlett Packard campus, Bangalore, 2002.

3.76 Rahul Mehrotra Associates, Hewlett Packard campus, Bangalore, 2002.

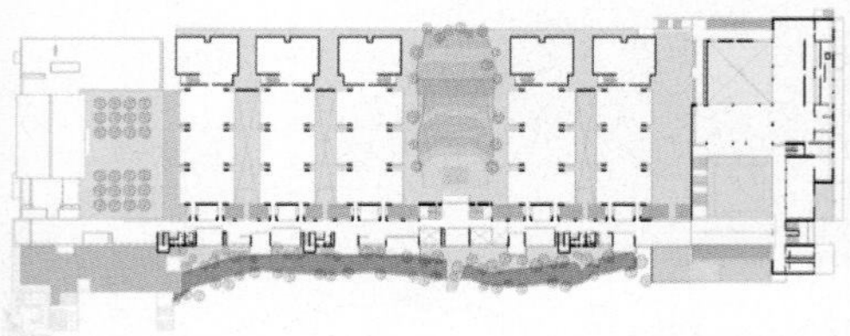

3.74

3.75

3.76

Normal?

→ p. 120

3.77 "A globe building for a 'global' corporation," Bangalore, 2002.

3.78 Sikka Associates, Global Business Park, Gurgaon, 1999.

3.79 Global curtain wall, Gurgaon, 1999.

3.80 City of Logos. Hafeez Contractor, DLF Square Tower, DLF City, Gurgaon, 1999.

3.81–3.82 DLF City, Phase V, Gurgaon, 2004.

3.77

3.78

3.79

Fidelity
citibank
FLUOR
Sona
AVAYA
GLOBALCONNECT
Max New York Life
3.80

3.81

3.82

A set of non-contiguous spatial islands held together by their brand name, DLF City is the Multi-National City (MNC) in microcosm. Located in Gurgaon, outside of New Delhi, its gated enclaves go by such names as DLF Windsor Court, DLF Beverly Park, DLF Carlton Estate, and DLF Princeton Estate. On its islands also float other islands, like the GE Capital call center, DLF Gateway Tower, DLF Square Tower, and Ericsson India.

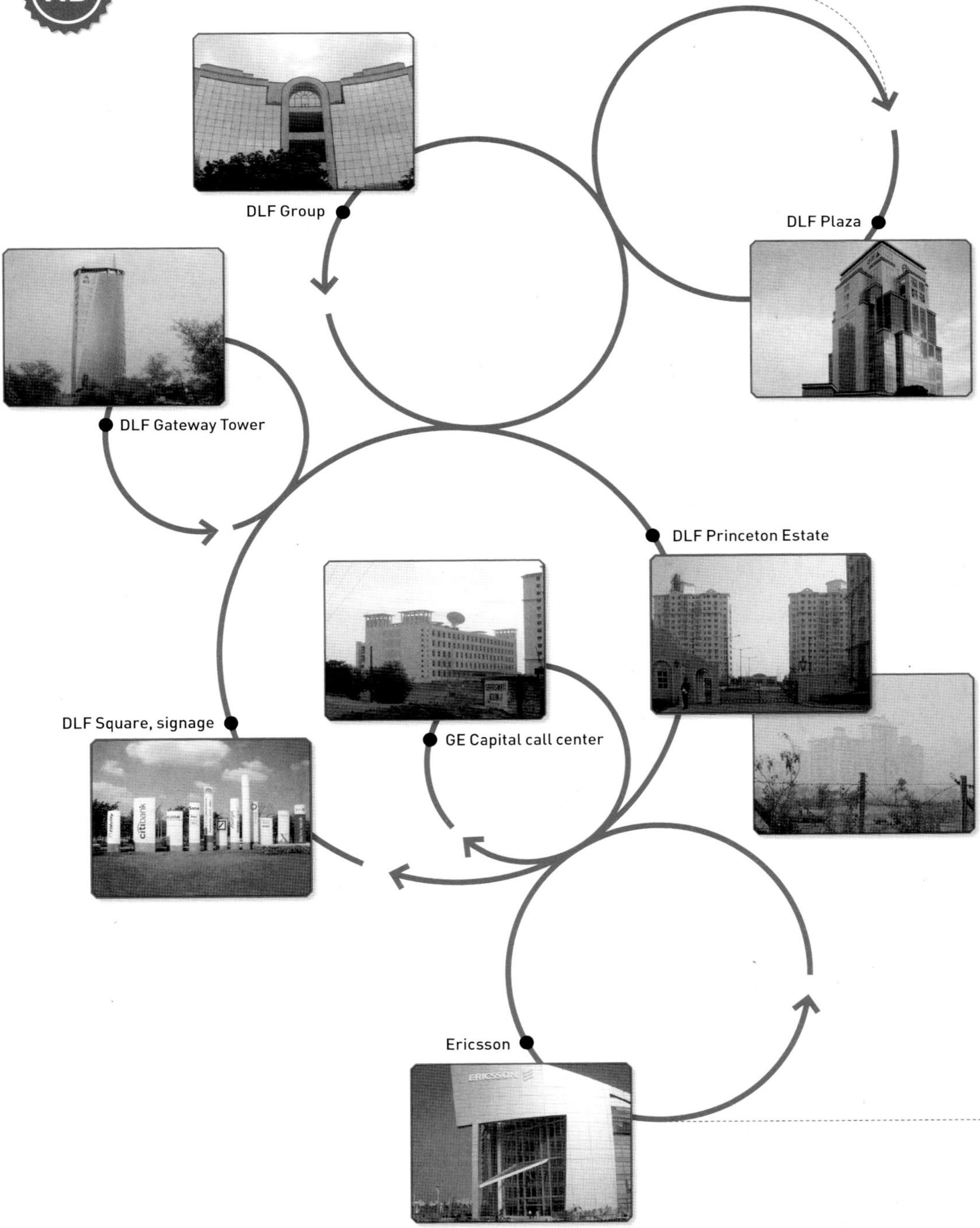

For Neelan

MULTI-NATIONAL CITY
ARCHITECTURAL ITINERARIES

Reinhold Martin and Kadambari Baxi

INTRODUCTION
MULTI-NATIONAL CITY

0

------------------------> This is a guidebook, a tour of the monuments of corporate globalization. Its itineraries lead to a series of possible futures for architecture and urbanism—some desirable, others not. Between their lines runs just one question: can architecture and urbanism help inaugurate a *science of the imaginary*?

By "imaginary" we mean a very real collective imagination, a dreamscape that includes objects like buildings and cities. And by "science" we mean careful, rigorous analysis and speculation. To demonstrate, we follow three itineraries through three contemporary cities and their histories. These cities—like so many others—are caught within the feedback loops of the information age: Silicon Valley in northern California; New York's internal suburbias; and Gurgaon, a burgeoning corporate city outside of New Delhi. This choice of cities is largely circumstantial and by no means exhaustive. In linking them we merely hope to exemplify a set of propositions, as follows:

1. A city is never simply in one place.
2. You cannot always see a city.
3. A city is a figment of the imagination that is also a tangible thing.
4. Every building imagines a city, and a world.
5. Every building can imagine another city, and another world.

We take for granted the often cited statistic that more than half of humanity now lives in cities. This statistic conjures images of both horror and promise: sprawling slums, somnambulent shoppers, and a new, potentially cosmopolitan sociability all at once. We aim only to explore its historical penumbra as well as its architectural afterimages. Past, present, and future co-exist in the cities we examine. Hence we also aim, with the help of architecture, to trace the untimeliness, the double-take that is among the real meanings of the term "globalization."

Once upon a time, anyone trained in the rudiments of modern architecture could stand in front of any building whatsoever and discern its structural system, the font and source of modernist virtue. They possessed, in effect, an x-ray vision. Today, we must retrain ourselves to look at any building whatsoever and see the worlds that it imagines, and the forces—historical, economic, social, aesthetic, and technological—that pass through it. We must acquire a new x-ray vision. But this new vision must also be peripheral. That is, it must be simultaneously *centripetal* and *centrifugal* in order to take in the swirling vortex that we call the Multi-National City.

The Multi-National City is the city of corporate globalization. But that is not all it is. We use the term "multi-national" here rather than the more conventional "global" or the more current "transnational" to emphasize the multiplicities to be found within what is often understood to be a homogeneous monoculture. A figure that seems anachronistic or untimely in one context—like the term "multi-national corporation" might seem in the United States (with its overtones of the 1970s)—is often all too timely in another. Thus in postmodern India, land of the acronym, "multi-national corporation" is commonly shortened to MNC, to describe the treacherously sublime dreamspaces materialized in brand new office buildings, call centers, gated residential enclaves, shopping malls, and other such artifacts of the multi-national imaginary.

And so we borrow the letters MNC while insisting on their ambiguity. To be sure: the Multi-National City, with its promise of new freedoms for some and new oppressions for so many others, remains shadowed by the Multi-National Corporation, much like delirious, metropolitan New York was and remains shadowed by big business. And like the new corporations, the new city is both here and there at once. In addition, as the anthropologist Arjun Appadurai once put it with respect to the "developing" world, "your past is their future" (though perhaps it is also the other way around). Globalization simultaneously links and separates in both space and time. Consider, for example, the case of the Indian software engineer working for an MNC in Gurgaon who obtains a green card to work for that same company in Silicon Valley, traveling on occasion to visit her relatives in New Jersey and partake of themed shopping experiences in New York. Does she traverse many different spaces, many different cities—past, present, and future, here and there, inside and out—or just one?

In re-reading MNC as Multi-National City, we have also attempted to describe architecture's role in the emergent city or cities formed around MNCs (Multi-National Corporations)—including their exclusions, their wars, and the crises of national sovereignty that they precipitate. But the MNC is more than just another new, privatized megalopolis indifferent to national borders. It is also a city that—despite itself, perhaps—is never total, never complete. No nation, corporation, or conglomerate can contain it. It is full of holes. In its enigmas, in its abstractions, in its persistent non-communication, the MNC is the city of strangers rediscovered. Despite its apparent uniformity, it harbors a multitudinous crowd.

FROM THE METROPOLIS TO THE MNC

More often than not, in the Multi-National City the crowd is invisible, except if you look closely at its jammed highways, its empty parking lots, and its silent electronic screens. As a time machine that mixes past, present, and future, the MNC is haunted by old memories and by visionary hallucinations. It is both the apotheosis and the opposite of a romanticized "global village." It is also the modern metropolis writ large but transformed. Its new forms of alienation are met by the old anti-urban dream of recovering a lost home, but now in casual, domesticated corporate campuses rather than in uptight suburban houses. And it reinvents modernity's masses as individualized, mass-customizable persons while in the process, effacing their singularity. But the MNC also reproduces modernity's salutary, catalytic estrangements and its wrenching, liberating disenchantments, though these are often expressed paradoxically in new pathologies: instead of (modern) fatigue, (postmodern) stress; instead of (modern) shock, (postmodern) boredom.

The MNC therefore reflects an urban crisis—not the crisis *in* the cities that erupted in the West in the 1960s, but the worldwide crisis *of* the cities that followed. And if the modernist future was both imagined and realized in the great, grinding metropolis, this crisis is now ultimately a crisis of the future itself. In today's permanent state of emergency, crisis has become a norm and has thereby been stripped of its capacity to prefigure anything new and revolutionary. Similarly, the city of the future has become a permanent, private dystopia. But this dystopia must be confronted with the secret that it still conceals: the utopian promise of another world. Such a world is not going to be found in the city as we know it. Instead, it must be discovered elsewhere, in cities that are no longer cities, and in houses that are no longer homes. But nor is this other world to be found somewhere "out there," somewhere new (where the modernists searched), somewhere supposedly exotic (where their heirs continue to search), or somewhere ordinary (where their hopes are betrayed). Instead, the outside—the new, impossibly utopian, *other* city, the city of the future—must be imagined *on the inside*. Think of the MNC turned inside-out.

Here, we have been the beneficiaries of a tradition in which already-existing cities have served as models for new architectures: *The Architecture of the City* (Rossi), *Learning from Las Vegas* (Venturi, Scott Brown, Izenour), *Delirious New York* (Koolhaas). But where these others have attempted to rescue the modern city at its apocalypse—with appeals to historical memory, to the commercial strip that delimits its borders, or to its repressed delirium—we record its quiet collapse without remorse.

In multiplying and linking our cities, we also depart from the well-developed tradition of architectural and urban analysis that counters the dissolute (post)modern city by probing the depths of specific, rooted *places*: the archaic monuments of a Eurocentric collective memory (Rossi), the semiotic surfaces of Las Vegas (Venturi, Scott Brown, Izenour), or New York's retroactive dreamscapes (Koolhaas). But neither are we content merely to brand the new city "generic" and thereby return architecture and urbanism to a post-International Style universality.

Instead, we travel. Between cities, between cultures, between time zones, and between historical epochs. In transit, we encounter the Multi-National City, where the metropolitan "stranger" has become a "Resident Alien" and the city, a spiraling vortex. Thus, if the modern metropolis—the city of strangers—continues to captivate us, it is because it remains populated by these figures and by invisible others even as it approaches obsolescence. This book is haunted by its memory, but also by its ghostly afterlife.

THE ITINERARIES

The Grand Tour, which was once a staple in the education of an architect, has long been instrumental in reinforcing Euro-American architecture's internal, familial lore. This has generally involved excursions into a mythical past located far, far away. And it has generally entailed a "from-to" structure that doubles back on itself. In the original Grand Tour, you traveled from eighteenth century London to the archaeologically reconstructed Rome of Piranesi and back again, in a closed loop. Following such routes, architects have for centuries ventured outward in both space and time only to return home with their myths intact. Whether these myths are founded on geographical, cultural, or temporal distance (the "East" of Le Corbusier's youthful sojourn, or ancient Rome forever revisited), their primary function has been to confirm the closure of what passes for architecture, even as they appear to open it up.

So too for the MNC, which is both closed and open at once. The difference? Like the new corporations that support it, it is organized as a network of lateral connections rather than as an architectural family tree. Its constant deferrals, "from this to this to this to this to that," do not make it any less foundational, any less metaphysical than Athens, Rome, New York, or Las Vegas have been for others. On the contrary, the ubiquity of the MNC renders it all the more mystified. It is a kind of flattened-out Olympus harboring an ever present pantheon catalogued in an arcane iconography of logos and brands, whose epics tell of mergers and acquisitions, initial public offerings and bankruptcies. Like our predecessors, who for generations have entered monuments to other, older deities—temples, churches, skyscrapers ("cathedrals of commerce"), and casinos—and exclaimed "Architecture!" we can only react in amazement when presented with this spectacle. Except that we are amazed at the degree to which the MNC's mythologies are so blindly accepted as a guidebook for our profession.

Our own, counter-guide thus follows three itineraries that connect to themselves and to others in an indefinite series of feedback loops. Each story is told in words, pictures, and diagrams. Our first itinerary moves from New York to Silicon Valley, in which the paradoxes of the modern metropolis—the oppressive freedoms offered by abstraction and alienation—migrate to the lost highways, cubicle farms, and parking lots of northern California, new homes for the Multi-National Corporation. Our second itinerary moves from New Delhi to New York, in which the architectural representation of empire (formerly exemplified by the British Raj) is displaced onto the global city, headquartered simultaneously in Manhattan, in its suburbs, and in its doubles around the world, new homes for the Multi-National Corporation. And our third itinerary moves from Silicon Valley to New Delhi, in which the protocols of the information economy—including connectivity, dislocation, and privatization—are amplified and transported to a privately developed new New Delhi, DLF City/Gurgaon, a new home for the Multi-National Corporation.

LOOPHOLES, OR FROM TYPOLOGY TO TOPOLOGY

Each building we encounter on these trips can be considered "Architecture!" precisely to the degree that it feigns an architectural character, and our choices are guided mainly by those instances in which this effort is most obvious. The more transparent the sleight-of-hand is, the more evidently it problematizes architecture's self-definition *as architecture*. Here, where architecture strains from its commercial margins to adhere to internal rules systematically enforced in the media, the museums, and the academy, it reveals most clearly the outside interests served by these rules. Since, like it or not, the further inside you go, the further outside you get. We therefore seek out these paradoxical holes in architecture's well-disciplined interior, these loopholes, in limit cases where the symptoms are most evident, rather than in academically canonized objects hopelessly enveloped by the mists of respectability.

Our account aims primarily to conjure this volatile mixture in just one of its aspects: the office building. In the MNC, the office building is not a "type." It is a cross-section of the city itself. Its functional instability incorporates ever-expanding spheres of everyday life into its domain, rendering the neat classifications of both typology and functionalism helpless in its presence. The contemporary office building therefore undoes typology from within, with extraordinary efficiency. And through its topological inversions, it collapses what used to be called "program"—work, living, recreation, etc.—into a black hole of programmed productivity, or "serious fun," 24/7.

ISLANDS

In the MNC, there are islands everywhere: enclaves and slums, gated communities, self-contained shopping malls, manicured corporate campuses, weather-sealed atriums, barricaded office buildings, prisons, refugee camps. Is it possible, then, that the island form can be activated to reawaken utopia, its ultimate progenitor? Or is this form condemned forever to equivocate, promising another world even as it constructs a world apart, fortified and invisible?

DOUBLE AGENCY

This book is driven by a sense of responsibility that plots a perilous course between the Scylla of earnest moralism and the Charybdis of an equally earnest cynicism. In doing so, it aspires to a double agency that never leaves behind the risk of complicity that attends the practice of architecture and urbanism. And as with the structural ambivalence native to the double agent, our position does not come without a price. The double agent is at home nowhere and everywhere, a decidedly untrustworthy figure engaged in the perpetual construction of credibility. This book is a strategic transfer of intelligence attempted by two double agents and their co-conspirators—all of them, both real and imagined.

Q: WHAT IS TO BE DONE?
A: UTOPIAN REALISM.

The stakes of this game are high—so high that the question of utopia must also be put back on the architectural table. But it must not be misread as a call for a perfect world, a world apart, an impossible totality that inevitably fades into totalitarianism. Instead, utopia must be read literally, as the "non-place" written into its etymological origins that is "nowhere" not because it is ideal and inaccessible, but because, in perfect mirrored symmetry, it is also "everywhere." Utopia is both glamorous and boring, exceptional and prosaic. Among its heralds is that denizen of the modern metropolis, Herman Melville's Bartleby the Scrivener, an anonymous, modest clerk working in lower Manhattan who, when asked literally to reproduce what the 1960s would later call "the system," simply and politely refused, declaring "I would prefer not to."

Utopia is a specter, a ghost that infuses everyday reality with other, possible worlds, rather than some otherworldly dream. And like all ghosts, that specter is never quite dead, returning to haunt the present and the future. In architecture, we can call this haunting "utopian realism." Utopian realism is a movement that may or may not exist, all of whose practitioners are double agents. Naming them, or their work, would blow their cover. (They may or may not all be architects.) So you, too, could be a utopian realist. Utopian realism is critical. It is real. It is (other)worldly. It is enchantingly secular. It thinks differently. It is a style with no form. And it is utopian not because it dreams impossible dreams, but because it recognizes "reality" itself as—precisely—an all-too-real dream enforced by those who would prefer to accept things as they are. Utopia's ghost floats within this dream, conjured time and again by those who would prefer not to.

FEEDBACK: A FEW SIMPLE RULES FOR ARCHITECTS

Based on our observations, we have therefore extrapolated a possible future out of each itinerary. This takes the form of an architectural project (*Feedback*) that appears as an unannounced stop at the end of each tour. These counter-projects obey a few simple rules:

1. Remember history, and never forget the future.
2. Take advantage of all available techniques.
3. When it doubt, turn it inside-out; if that does not work, turn it upside-down.
4. There is no such thing as program; there is only what actually happens.
5. Think Different(ly).™

The projects are fictional in that the built realities they visualize will not be found outside these pages. But they are real in that they are written directly into the very real histories they follow, as projects. They apply the lessons of the MNC to itself, to test the system's internal tolerances, its limit cases. In doing so, they glimpse utopia as a twilight of the idols, a hole in the screen that leads out of the closed loops that each "from-to" vector follows, even as it seems to lead back in.

Thus, where the modernist arrow of progress—scientifically sharpened and technologically propelled—runs down a one-way street, in the MNC this arrow traces circles through the cul-de-sacs and parking lots of time. This can be cause for confusion ("Where are we going?"), hope ("Where are we going?"), or dismay ("Where are we going?"). But in all cases, the answer is never as certain as "nowhere," since the encompassing vastness of the MNC spells history's recurrence ever anew. We are going to where we have just been, but in another place and in another time.

Where for the moderns, space was the raw material of both conquest and emancipation, in the MNC it has thus been displaced by the enigmas of time. If our night is your day, work on the future continues literally around the clock. And so for all their brutality, the MNC's topological inversions allow us to bend time's arrow by remixing its histories—turning them back in on themselves, and perhaps back out again. We do so with few delusions. We do not claim to reverse the portentous tendencies that our subject so obviously embodies by supplying an enticing, comprehensive alternative. We only claim to render their inevitability in doubt by extrapolating their circles, in order to make it possible to imagine something else, something new, something other.

Exacerbate or ameliorate? Yes.

MNC Monuments. Corporate headquarters, offices, call centers, apartment buildings, and logos in Silicon Valley, New York, and New Delhi/Gurgaon.

1

2

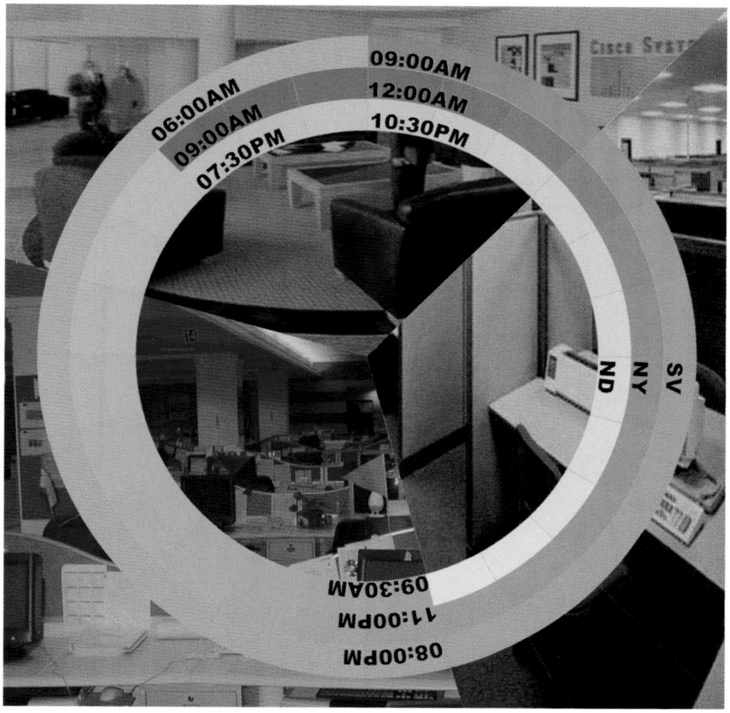

[1] MNC Top to Bottom. Adobe headquarters in San Jose, Citicorp (now Citigroup) Center in New York, and DLF Gateway Tower in Gurgaon.
[2] MNC Internal Timezones. Office/call center interiors in Silicon Valley, New York and New Delhi/Gurgaon linked by a 24-hour work cycle.

1

2

[1] MNC Continuous Interiors. Taxis, airplanes, elevators, lounges, and lobbies in a closed loop, intercut with interiors from Martin/Baxi Architects proposals.
[2] MNC Sky. Reflections in Silicon Valley, New York, and New Delhi/Gurgaon, intercut with Martin/Baxi Architects proposals.

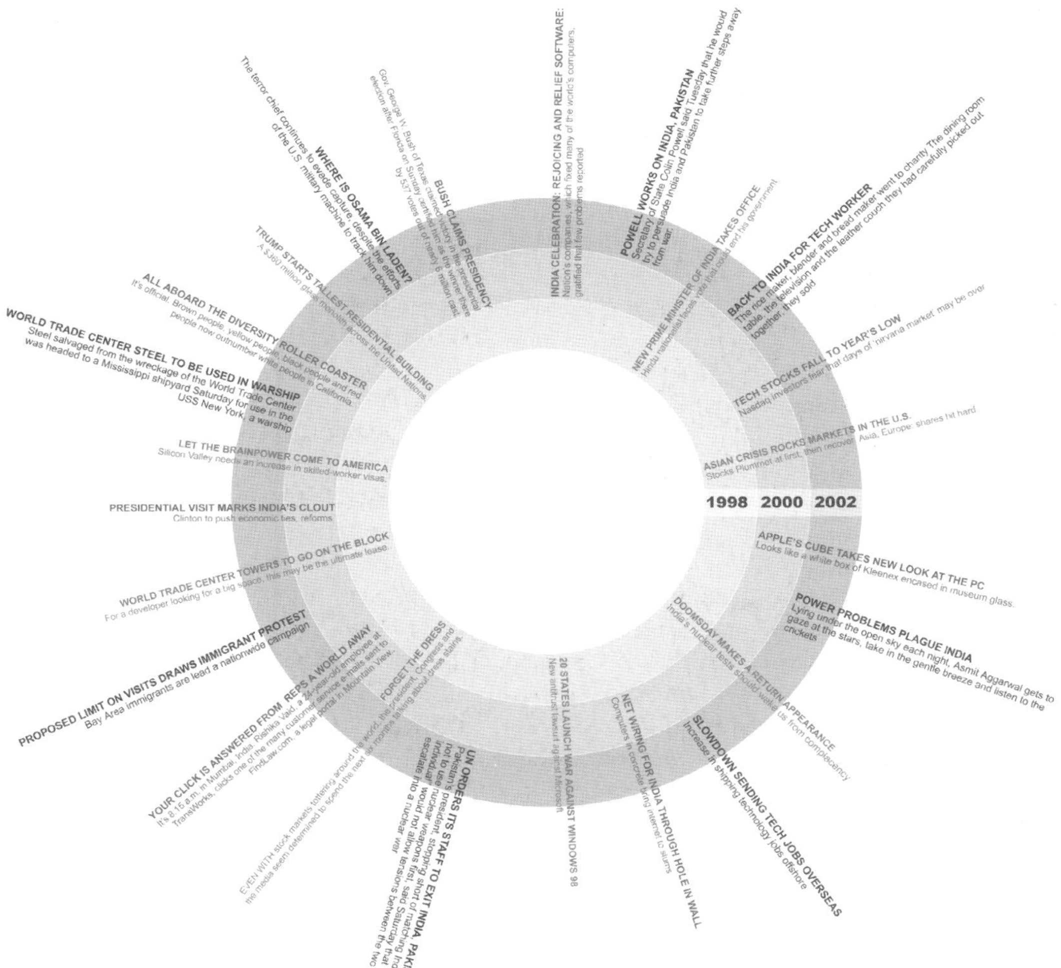

1998 2000 2002
INDIA CELEBRATION: REJOICING AND RELIEF SOFTWARE:
POWELL WORKS ON INDIA, PAKISTAN
BACK TO INDIA FOR TECH WORKER
TECH STOCKS FALL TO YEAR'S LOW
ASIAN CRISIS ROCKS MARKETS IN THE U.S.
APPLE'S CUBE TAKES NEW LOOK AT THE PC
Looks like a white box of Kleenex encased in museum glass.
POWER PROBLEMS PLAGUE INDIA
SLOWDOWN SENDING TECH JOBS OVERSEAS
NET WIRING FOR INDIA THROUGH HOLE IN WALL
20 STATES LAUNCH WAR AGAINST WINDOWS 98
UN ORDERS ITS STAFF TO EXIT INDIA, PAKISTAN
FORGET THE DRESS
YOUR CLICK IS ANSWERED FROM REPS A WORLD AWAY
PROPOSED LIMIT ON VISITS DRAWS IMMIGRANT PROTEST
Bay Area immigrants are lead a nationwide campaign
WORLD TRADE CENTER TOWERS TO GO ON THE BLOCK
PRESIDENTIAL VISIT MARKS INDIA'S CLOUT
Clinton to push economic ties, reforms
LET THE BRAINPOWER COME TO AMERICA
Silicon Valley needs an increase in skilled-worker visas.
WORLD TRADE CENTER STEEL TO BE USED IN WARSHIP
ALL ABOARD THE DIVERSITY ROLLER COASTER
TRUMP STARTS TALLEST RESIDENTIAL BUILDING
WHERE IS OSAMA BIN LADEN?
BUSH CLAIMS PRESIDENCY

MNC Newslinks. How each city imagines the others. The keywords "Silicon Valley," New York," and "New Delhi" as they appear in each other's headlines, selected from the online archives of The Mercury News (San Jose), The New York Times, and The Times of India, and arranged in a circular timeline.

FROM **NEW YORK** TO **SILICON VALLEY**

1

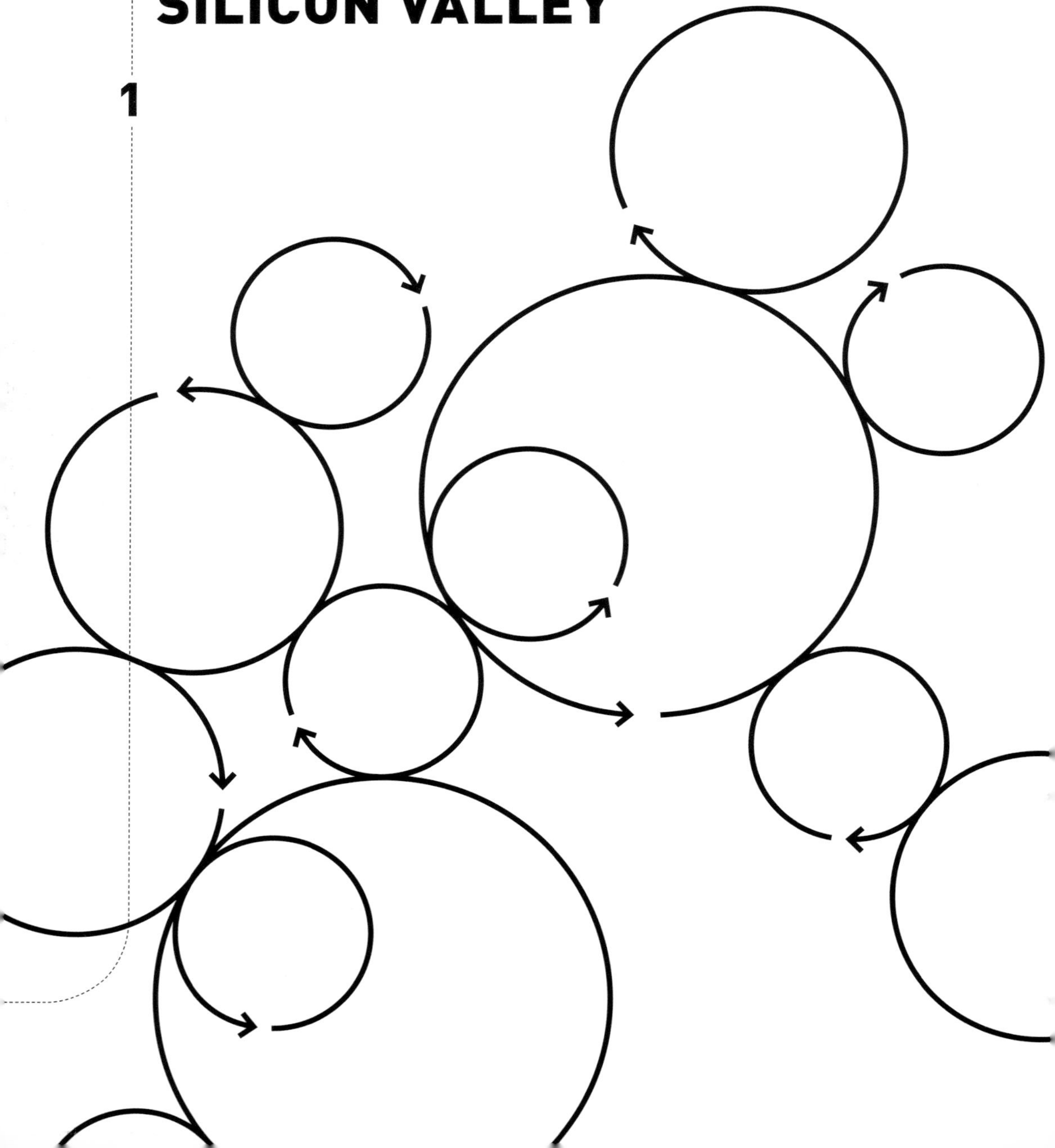

Silicon Valley does not exist. It never did. You will not find it on any map. You will not find any road signs that announce its immanent appearance, nor will you find any monuments that mark its downtown, nor even an intersection that bears its name. There is simply nothing there, far more literally than in nearby Oakland as famously described by Gertrude Stein. Silicon Valley is a phantasm, a construction. It is, therefore, a city.

Yes, geographically speaking, there is something like a valley stretching west of the San Francisco Bay between two ridges in northern California and running southward from San Francisco's hilly streets, through the campuses—academic, military, and industrial—that begin north of Palo Alto and extend down past San Jose. Geologically speaking, this valley is the product of two fault lines, the San Andreas and the Hayward, out of which the ridges have erupted. And its soil, its very foundation, contains the same Adobe™ clay that (indirectly) gave the maker of Photoshop™ and Illustrator™ its name.[1]

But only over time does Silicon Valley become visible, driving south along Interstate 101. Here unfolds the geological time compressed into the hard materiality of the Valley's name—the imported, semi-conducting silica sands out of which its future erupted. And here too is the historical time, the timeline of "progress" named by that name. This line of "progress" leads from north to south along an axis of exuberant development ("sprawl") driven by high-technology industries. But it also runs east to west, originating in New York, the mechanized, modern metropolis and capital of the twentieth century, and passing through the cleft in time marked by this Valley and by its fault lines, into the twenty-first.

1.1

1.2

1.3

Most of the plentiful hagiographies devoted to Silicon Valley's academic and corporate "founders" (often described, with Oedipal conviction, as "founding fathers") emphasize the new balance of power that they ultimately secured in the techno-economic imaginary of the postwar United States.[2] The story goes something like this: technological and managerial innovation

1. Adobe Systems Inc. was actually named after Adobe Creek, which ran behind company co-founder John Warnock's home in Los Gatos, California. See http://www.adobe.com/aboutadobe/pressroom/pdfs/fastfacts.pdf.

2. A partial list of books devoted to Silicon Valley's corporate culture and histories includes David A. Kaplan, *The Silicon Boys and Their Valley of Dreams* (New York: Perennial, 2000); Michael Lewis, *The New New Thing: A Silicon Valley Story* (New York: W.W. Norton, 2000); Po Bronson, *Nudist on the Late Shift and Other True Tales of Silicon Valley* (New York: Random House, 1999); and David A. Vise and Mark Malseed, *The Google Story* (New York: Delacorte Press, 2005). Relevant scholarly works include Martin Kenney, ed. *Understanding Silicon Valley: The Anatomy of an Entrepreneurial Region* (Stanford, CA: Stanford University Press, 2000); Annalee Saxenian, *Regional Advantage: Culture and Competition in Silicon Valley and Route 128* (Cambridge, MA: Harvard University Press, 1994); Manuel Castells and Peter Hall, *Technopoles of the World: The Making of 21st Century Industrial Complexes* (New York: Routledge, 1994); Andrew Ross, *No-Collar: The Humane Workplace and Its Hidden Costs* (New York: Basic Books,

on the west coast, underwritten by speculative finance capital—"venture capital"—originating in the east. But this same story also tells of the clumsiness of Wall Street in getting on board for the ride, and of the Street's timidity when confronted with the Valley's frontier spirit, its manifest destiny written in silicon. And so New York appears in this Valley only as a kind of ghost, the specter of capital coursing through all the old channels flowing from Wall Street—Goldman Sachs, Morgan Stanley, the Rockefellers, and so on. This ghost haunts Silicon Valley's forever young "next generations," its "new new things."

1.4

1.5

1.6

1.7

THE SPECTRAL CITY

In the 1970s and 1980s Venrock, the Rockefeller family's venture capital firm, made successful investments in startups called Intel, Apple, and 3Com. So it may not be surprising to find another Rockefeller investment looming over another monument to Silicon Valley's urban paradox. And it is a paradox, since it entails—simultaneously—a suburbanization of the city and an urbanization of the suburbs that is hardly confined to northern California. The investment in question was made by David Rockefeller in partnership with Trammel Crow, Prudential Insurance, and John C. Portman, FAIA, beginning in 1968, in what was to become the Embarcadero Center in downtown San Francisco, completed in 1982. Essentially Rockefeller Center with an atrium, Embarcadero Center belonged to an even more ambitious venture begun by the San Francisco Redevelopment Agency in 1959. Around the same time, the World Trade Center, having been invented by the private Downtown-Lower Manhattan Association led by Rockefeller, was being passed into the public custody of the Port Authority of New York and New Jersey. But the reverse was happening in San Francisco. There, the public agency was soliciting private investors, thus consolidating another set of forces that allowed Rockefeller, Portman, and company to conjure a vision for the downtown—and for Downtown as such—that secured its fate as a suburban paradise.[3]

Rem Koolhaas, who must surely be counted among Rockefeller Center's most awestruck admirers, has written about something he calls Portman's Paradox, wherein the hotel atrium is rushed into America's downtowns as a kind of respirator bringing

2003); Margaret Pugh O'Mara, *Cities of Knowledge: Cold War Science and the Search for the Next Silicon Valley* (Princeton: Princeton University Press, 2005), Langdon Winner, "Silicon Valley Mystery House," in Michael Sorkin, ed., *Variations on a Theme Park: The New American City and the End of Public Space* (New York: Hill and Wang, 1992), 31-60; and Gwendolyn Wright, "The Virtual Architecture of Silicon Valley," *Journal of Architectural Education* 54, no. 2 (November 2000): 88-94.

3. Donald J. Canty, "Rockefeller Center West? John Portman's San Francisco Colossus is Complete, For Now," *AIA Journal* 71, no. 12 (October 1982): 56-63.

artificial light and air to the disappearing city.[4] Portman's Peachtree Center in Atlanta, the first reproduction of Rockefeller Center to be equipped with an atrium if not with a Rockefeller, was the prototype. But Embarcadero Center, it must be said, was its apotheosis. According to Koolhaas, Portman's rediscovery of the atrium, while first giving central Atlanta new life, ultimately accelerated the center's demise via the proliferation of innumerable "ersatz" downtowns at the city's extremities. Downtown was now everywhere.

In the echo chamber called the city, we can thus hear Manhattan itself—with its "culture of congestion" condensed into Rockefeller Center—reverberating in Portman's atria. Or at least we think we can. And we can hear Koolhaas: The city is dead, long live the city. But he too is seeing a ghost. And if Portman's Piranesian imagination aligns him with the metropolitan avant-gardes while Koolhaas, in turn, aligns himself with Portman, the ghost in question is that of the metropolis itself—of New York, of Wall Street, and of mechanized congestion—haunting the ruin called the atrium.

THE RUIN OR, THE REGIME OF THE POTTED PLANT

1.8

1.9

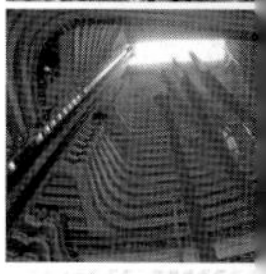

The atrium is a ruin not only because of its Roman origins. In Portman's hands, which are guided by the more supple but equally classicizing hands of Louis Kahn, master of the modern ruin, the atrium also bears witness to the destruction of the *res publica*: the public thing or body as incorporated in the Street and the Market—that, ever since Rome was reinvented by the Renaissance, has locked architecture's soul in an unholy alliance of power, commerce, and civic commitment. To suggest otherwise, as Koolhaas has frequently done in his quest for a "public" realm in which capital and public interest are reconciled, is to smooth over modernity's roughest edges by slightly misreading the signs. Since, along Market Street in downtown San Francisco, the Street as such—Wall Street, the urban Market—had already been replaced in Portman's atrium by the pastoral landscape that overtakes all ruins, announced by the potted plants suspended from its balconies. All that remained was for this landscape to "go public" by moving to the suburbs. In other words, in the fast capitalism of Silicon Valley, the Street was replaced by Nature. And hence the *respublica* was ruined, overgrown in a manner unanticipated by those who understand the multi-national corporation—Portman's phantom client—as merely an abstract, inhuman machine of the sort prefigured in Piranesi's

4. Rem Koolhaas, "Atlanta," in *S, M, L, XL* (New York: Monacelli Press, 1995), 841-843.

prisons and realized in Fritz Lang's *Metropolis*. Since in the atrium, where capital is green, the Street is naturalized and the corporation is humanized.

As an empty shell, the carcass of the metropolis in which the regime of the potted plant and of green capital is incubated, Embarcadero Center thus offers perils—but also freedoms—that are entirely new. In the flickering lights and the glowing, bulbous elevators that are Portman's signature, is the ghost of the machine itself. But this machine is now condemned only to illuminate—to enlighten—a new nature to which, in Portman's case, is affixed the brand name Hyatt.™ So if we find in this corporate hotel a Roman ruin haunted by a ghost from the east—Wall Street, Metropolis, the city-machine—it is only because its earthly inhabitants, its guests, are also ghosts of another sort.

FROM THE STRANGER TO THE RESIDENT ALIEN

Though he probably had mainly the streetwalking Berlin bourgeoisie in mind, in 1908 the German sociologist Georg Simmel identified the "stranger" as the prototypical metropolitan subject, in whom we can recognize without much difficulty the equally distant (yet still gregarious) New Yorker. Simmel's stranger was someone who was near and far at the same time—part of the group but also from elsewhere. Always a potential wanderer, the stranger is "the person who comes today and stays tomorrow."[5] And in the cultural imaginary of Silicon Valley, we might say that this stranger has been transformed into a Resident Alien.

The Resident Alien is an American invention. Bearer of a"green card" that has not actually been green since 1964, the Resident Alien harbors the alienation of Simmel's stranger, at home nowhere and everywhere, but at a global scale. She does so, however, under new economic circumstances that are registered in the 1965 Immigration and Nationality Act Amendments, which changed the criteria for legal immigration into the United States from a preference system based on nationality or race to one based on education and workplace skills. Thus Silicon Valley's technology industry, already well developed by that time, saw an influx of skilled immigrant labor from Asia and elsewhere that continued more or less unabated until the spring of 2001, when the high-technology bubble of the "new economy" headquartered in the Valley burst with unceremonious abruptness.

In the intervening decades, the Resident Alien had become the *flaneûse* of the corporate atrium, which in many Valley firms was

5. Georg Simmel, "The Stranger," in *The Sociology of Georg Simmel*, trans. and ed. Kurt H. Wolff (New York: Free Press, 1950), 402.

decisively infiltrated not only by potted plants but by coffee bars and couches, and supplemented by multi-ethnic food courts. In the atrium, estrangement—Simmel's "blasé attitude"—was thereby converted into a user-friendly sociability that only throws into relief the dislocated nature, the otherness, of the new multi-nationals: both the corporations and the people who work for them. Thus, if many future Resident Aliens still dream of the atrium, the corporate atrium dreams the Resident Alien. And in this dreamspace, this pseudo-public realm—an always-empty social condenser—the Resident Alien becomes to the corporation what the stranger once was to the village: both "them" and "us," at once.

1.11

1.12

1.13

THE ATRIUM PRINCIPLE

Here is an example of how what we can call The Atrium Principle works at Cisco Systems, in the user-friendly, brand-loyal corporate lifestyle that has become know as "The Cisco Way," as practiced in a typical day in the typical life of one Aurora Phillips, an employee at Cisco's north San Jose campus:

> As Phillips worked she didn't need to worry about running errands to the drugstore or the car wash. All material needs were satisfied inside the lettered monoliths [the Cisco buildings]. If she needed breakfast, she could go to the company cafeteria as early as 7 am. Breakfast time at the cafeteria bettered Starbucks, with steaming espressos and rows of fresh-baked pastries. Lunch (and dinner...) could be brick-oven pizza, Asian fusion cuisine, burgers and fries, or a hundred other combinations. Maybe Phillips would need a Cisco T-shirt (though, as with all Silicon Valley companies, free corporate T-shirts were in ample supply). No problem. All and sundry goods could be purchased at McWhorters Express Store in Building J. Money was available at the conveniently located ATM.
>
> Not that she'd have to go down the thickly carpeted stairs or to another building for everything. At the edge of the cubes on Phillips' floor, and in the other alphabetized edifices, stood the break room. Each break room housed one of the fabled refrigerators of many sodas, the free panoply of nonalcoholic beverages.... The sodas often washed down the endless supply of free popcorn, though employees were encouraged to subsist on something other than the free junk food. If Phillips needed some pants pressed, she would go to the break room. The break room also housed dry-cleaning services, for pick-up and return the next day.
>
> A jaunt from Building A to Building L would provide quite a workout, but not as good as the one she could get at the gym housed in Building L. TimeOut, the Cisco gym, offered Phillips and all the other employees the opportunities to use their bodies instead of their minds, with free weights and StairMasters, aerobics, yoga, tai chi, self-defense classes, and massage. Or she could go outside and play [CEO John] Chambers's favorite sport on the basketball courts.

> If TimeOut's health screenings kept her from the doctor, then the monthly dental truck's cleanings could keep her from the dentist. Her car was pampered, too, with onsite washes and oil changes. Cisco provided her with all these perks so that she could spend as much time doing her job as possible.[6]

1.10

In 1981, Reyner Banham was among the first to notice what was happening. Designating the San Jose headquarters of the Qume Corporation by Hawley & Peterson as a Silicon Valley "benchmark building," Banham described it as "two parallel basic boxes with a mall in between." Running down the mall (an atrium roofed in insulating translucent Fiberglas), was "a strip of closely planted *Ficus benjamina* and *Ficus ratusa*, with fountains and pools embracing the commissary and other areas."[7] And so, even as Portman's Embarcadero Center neared completion in downtown San Francisco, the regime of the potted plant was beginning to organize the city's outside–its ex-urbia–from the inside-out. Further, according to Banham, "[b]uried among the shrubbery... you will find little clearings containing glass-top tables and blue-and-chrome chairs, where conclaves of workers will be discussing market strategy, foreign exchange and boyfriends or munching down sandwiches and drinking coffee...."[8]

1.14

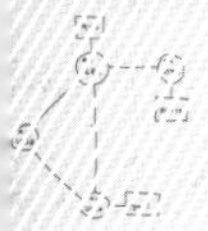

Still, Banham misrecognized such efforts to "improve working conditions" as lending heroic substance to an otherwise public relations-oriented image of environmental sensitivity elsewhere in the Valley, in which "corporate vision has been measured in shrubs and trees."[9] This was not merely an effort to put what Banham called "a new and less intimidating face on an industry whose links to power may not appeal to the current preferences for softer technology and a simpler society."[10] It was the new face of power itself.

6. David Bunnell, *Making the Cisco Connection: The Real Story Behind the Internet Superpower* (New York: John Wiley & Sons, 2000), 92-93.

7. Reyner Banham, "Silicon Style," *Architectural Review* 169, no. 1011 (May 1981): 285.

8. Ibid.

9. Ibid., 288.

10. Ibid.

THE CONTINUOUS INTERIOR OR, FROM WALL STREET TO SAND HILL ROAD

Stretching into the foothills behind Stanford University in Palo Alto is Sand Hill Road. These same foothills have, since the nineteenth century, been the background against which the flight from the city, embodied by Stanford and consummated in the city itself on the *interior* of Embarcadero Center, has occurred. They are the University's collective unconscious and the backdrop for the Stanford Industrial Park, a synergetic synthesis of scientific knowledge and venture capital grown out of the Stanford Research Institute (SRI) that was a secret model for all Valley campuses to come.[11] While for its part the SRI had also been one of three original nodes in the network first known as Arpanet—another kind of continuous interior, the Internet—in which so much of Silicon Valley's crop would later be grown and harvested. So it should not be surprising to learn that pastoral Sand Hill Road is also the home of the fast, green capital— "venture" capital—that has lubricated Silicon Valley's growth since the 1960s. Pseudo-Wrightian office parks nestled into this landscape are said to echo the Bay Area aesthetic that dominates Stanford's campus. Their rustic roofs give shelter to venture capital firms with equally rustic names like Sequoia Capital and Sierra Ventures. In these, sprouting from the classical, ruined monumentality of Wall Street embodied by Portman's urban atrium, is power's new look: casual, relaxed.

1.15

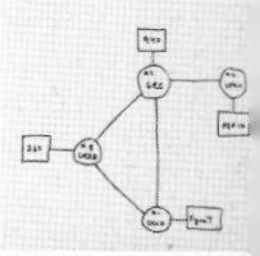

1.16

1.17

1.18

1.19

Venture capital only acquired its abbreviation—VC—at the close of the Vietnam War, when those two letters ceased to designate "Viet Cong" in the American imaginary.[12] As materialized on Sand Hill Road, VC constitutes the landscape—the fields, the rhizomatic grasses—from which spring the ever-changing corporate logos that define the Valley. VC is background. It is scenery. As such, it withdraws from view in favor of the start-ups that have until recently constituted the bulk of its investments, thrusting these out into the glare of the media in anticipation of another inversion of the *res publica*: the Initial Public Offering (IPO). "Going public," as the IPO is called, entails a double reconstitution. First, it entails a bursting forth from the protective shrubbery of the Atrium, and from the enveloping, grassy fields of capital in which the venture is incubated. Second, it entails the consolidation of a corporate identity outside, in the Market and in the Street, that is largely dependent on the communal lifestyle nurtured inside, among the potted plants.

In Silicon Valley, this lifestyle began at Hewlett-Packard in the 1950s with the interactive management style known as "The HP Way," only to be reinvented at Cisco Systems in the 1990s

11. See O'Mara, *Cities of Knowledge*, 97-141.

12. Kaplan, *The Silicon Boys*, 156.

as "The Cisco Way." In both cases, and in every basketball court and coffee bar in between, productivity—or, more importantly for the IPO, the image of productivity—was seen to depend on the socialization of the worker. That is, the image of productivity depended on overcoming the Resident Alien's alienation in the atrium and in the food court. It therefore depended on the internalization of the corporate lifestyle to the extent that there was no longer any distinction between what the Congrès International d'Architecture Moderne (CIAM) used to call Dwelling, Leisure, Work, and Transportation. All was to be integrated, seamlessly and wirelessly, into the unified surface of productive bliss. In that sense, the now infamous "Internet bubble," with which an entire economy was mesmerized in the late 1990s, and in which it thus became encapsulated, was itself a benchmark work of architecture. It was the Atrium itself, the pastoral architecture of green capital and of Sand Hill Road, the architecture of the IPO and of the corporation "gone public," in which the ghost of the *res publica* was doomed to haunt the regime of the potted plant. It was the architecture of the continuous interior.

1.20

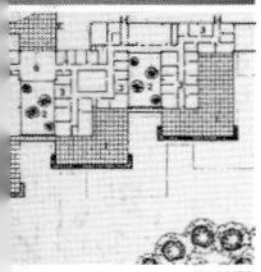
1.21

1.22

1.23

INTERIOR DESIGN

Like all benchmark architecture, the architecture of the continuous interior has its signature architects. Among these is the firm of Hellmuth, Obata & Kassabaum (HOK), headquartered in St. Louis with outposts in San Francisco, Washington D.C., New York, and around the globe. In 1975, having recently finished a project for IBM, HOK completed the Xerox Palo Alto Research Center (PARC) in the Stanford Industrial Park just behind the Stanford campus and not far from Sand Hill Road. Founded in 1970 to create an "architecture of information" suitable to the "office of the future," Xerox PARC hosted the invention of the laser printer (1971), Ethernet networking protocols (1973), the Graphical User Interface (GUI) for use on personal computers (1975), and the first Internet worm (1978), among other output of the information age.[13]

To encourage the creativity necessary to conjure such dream-objects, HOK obligingly provided Xerox with a university-like setting overlooking the actual university. Inconspicuous from the "street" (or from the drive leading to the road that leads, eventually, to Sand Hill Road), the building nestles into the hills of Leland Stanford's former horse farm. Its interior consists of a series of terraced, interlocking clusters and

13. http://www.parc.com/about/history/default.html.

courtyards adorned with the rhetoric of behavioral psychology that, too, would yield a chief maxim of the information age: interact or die. This imperative, which converts the cliché of brainstorming scientists into venture capital of its own, is marked by the presence of informal conversation areas at each cluster corner, complete (by the late 1990s) with video cameras to record the sudden appearance of bright ideas on the whiteboards opposite the couches: the intellectual as property.

To be sure, the stuff on the whiteboards was the very stuff of which Silicon Valley IPOs were made. And so it is no surprise that in late 1979 Steve Jobs, the charismatic cofounder of Apple Computer, toured HOK's building and encountered one of these bright ideas—Xerox PARC's Graphical User Interface (GUI) with its WYSIWYG (What You See Is What You Get) screen. Legend has it that this encounter begat (somewhat illicitly) the Apple Macintosh personal computer,[14] the first PC equipped with a cartoonish "desktop" that permitted users to imagine that they were still manipulating things like "folders," and that the PC was just another piece of furniture that was, like Xerox PARC's couches, suitable for home and office alike. One year later, in 1980, Apple Computer went public.

PCPC

But it was not until 1984 that Apple introduced the Macintosh and with it, re-branded the computer by replacing the impersonal, modular blue of IBM with a happy rainbow of personal choices. Despite histories of technology that push the date significantly farther back, we must insist that the "personal" computer did not "go public"—and therefore did not exist—until 22 January of that year. That was the day of Super Bowl XVIII, a grisly affair interrupted only by the distraction of revolutionary television commercials, among them one from Apple that featured a color-clad woman hurling a sledgehammer at IBM's Big Brother as he is speaking from a screen to an indifferent audience of men in gray uniforms. This was the PCPC (Politically Correct Personal Computer) that succeeded where others had failed in converting the promise of freedom from the claustrophobic corporate box into the guarantee of confinement in the wide open spaces of the continuous interior, populated by Resident Aliens re-branded as "persons" and encouraged by the new markets of the new economy to exercise unlimited personal choice in the food courts and mini-malls of the new corporations. Call this The iMac Principle.

1.24

1.25
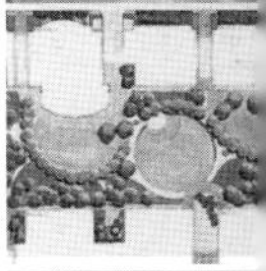

1.26

1.27

14. Kaplan, *The Silicon Boys*, 103.

USERS

In 2002, HOK would undertake a direct application of The iMac Principle in the color-coded lighting emanating from Nortel Networks' Santa Clara campus. Still, back at Apple thinking different did not come so easily. To begin with, the irrepressible homogeneity inflicted on Apple by HOK's older corporate habits had to be offset. To accomplish this, Apple hired four different interior designers to outfit HOK's uniform pods in a diverse array of local identities. Thus did Gensler and Associates, Backen Arrigoni & Ross, Studios Architecture, and John Holey and Associates proceed to "endow each of the buildings' interiors with distinct personalities," as one correspondent put it.[15] The participation of Apple engineers in the "design process" resulted not only in a revolutionary return to private offices in place of cubicles, but also in the return of another repressed model incubated at Xerox PARC, from whom Apple had apparently "acquired" the bright idea of the Graphic User Interface (GUI). At the new Apple, as at Xerox PARC, the rows of offices were interrupted periodically with architecturally "interesting" social spaces equipped, predictably, with couches, coffee tables, and whiteboards. These homes for bright ideas like the GUI were called, with uncanny precision, UDAs, or User-Defined Areas.

1.28

1.29

1.30

Such terminology lays bare the irony of "high-tech humanism," as Langdon Winner has called such well-developed corporate sensitivity.[16] Since in these all-too-humane UDAs, the "human" had become a "user," an addict. This transformation is confirmed by the irrational exuberance of workers at Cisco Systems describing their job during the heyday of the new economy: "It's electronic heroin!" "You're amazed by your own productivity!"[17] Though notably less distinctive than Apple's, by the late 1990s Cisco's interior architecture was feeding the habits of such workers through the concept of "nonterritorial offices": identical, unassigned cubicles. Worker-users were "free" to sit where they liked, when they liked—a non-hierarchical utopia. The theory: again, happy workers = increased productivity. Meanwhile, the more astute managers could always detect the most productive workers in this sea of equality, based on where they were sitting. Since, these workers inevitably had the best seats, having overcome traffic and (rarely, perhaps) hangovers to arrive early, and thus be first in the line of eager programmers entering each morning.[18]

15. Cathy Lang Ho, "Silicon Valley," *Metropolis* 15, no. 3 (October 1995): 70.
16. Winner, "Silicon Valley Mystery House," 39.
17. Bunnell, *Making the Cisco Connection*, 94.
18. Ibid. 91-92.

Meanwhile, back at Apple, utopia came in the form of a village. Gensler and Associates, in their contribution to the continuous interior at Apple's Research and Development Campus, were put in charge of integrating HOK's atrium, with adjoining conference rooms, classrooms, Apple store, and staff café, into the two four-story, 50,000 square foot floor plates on either side. Their response was to extend the pedestrian bridge spanning the atrium into what they called a "Main Street," an offset spine distinguished by vaulted ceilings and "asymmetrical architecture." According to Gensler's own account of the project, this "organizing element" gave unity and orientation to the vastness of the office blocks, from the inside-out. In sympathy with iMacs to come, color-coded accent walls distinguished each floor, while the User Defined Areas (UDAs) engineered "individual creativity." Suites of offices were grouped around each UDA—identifiable in the plan by its architecturally interesting skew. Explicitly theoretical, these whiteboard-and-couch infested spaces were designed, according to their architects, *simultaneously* "to convey a sense of individual empowerment" *and* "a sense of community." [19]

Thus at Apple, interior design was urban design which, in the words of its architects, sought "to create a balance between public and private spaces." HOK went on to duplicate this strategy in the Adobe headquarters in downtown San Jose, a set of three sixteen-to-eighteen story towers linked together on an upper level by a quarter-mile long internal main street called Adobe Way. Meanwhile, just down San Jose's actual Main Street stood the luminous Market Post Tower, golden mirrored home to the MAE West Internet hub, through which passed forty percent of the nation's Internet traffic, making it the second largest network exchange in the world and a kind of downtown for the Internet, another branch of the continuous interior. Encircling this downtown (both virtual and real), were any number of new domestic interiors that celebrated, with zealous determination, the comforts of Main Street and of homeland security. Thus for example, could the soothingly surreal North Park Apartment Village in north San Jose (not far from Cisco) offer four "community choices" in the form of four trees—The Cypress, The Oaks, The Pines, and The Laurels—designed for "smart living" among the potted plants of Silicon Valley's new landscape.[20]

Adobe Systems Inc. had moved its headquarters to this repopulating, renovated downtown at the southern end of the Valley—newly equipped with a technology museum and other value-added

1.31
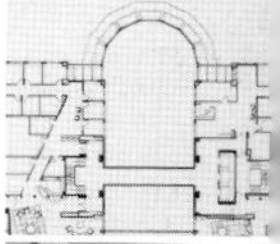

1.32

1.33

1.34

1.35

19. Arthur M. Gensler, *Developing the Architecture of the Workplace* (New York: Edizioni Press, 1988), 88.

20. http://www.northparkapartments.com.

amenities—after its co-founder and president, Charles Geschke, was kidnapped in the parking lot of its previous offices in suburban Mountain View. Their San Jose campus was Portmanesque in its interiority, with a fearsome security apparatus that converted the parking garage below into the first line of defense against would-be kidnappers, in a beguiling demonstration of corporate insecurity. And as with Portman's atrium in downtown San Francisco sixty miles away, public was private and "community" meant paranoid consumers parading down Main Streets of all shapes and sizes. The autonomy—the interiority—of the Enlightenment individual, modernity's Engineer or the free-wheeling *flanêur*, had long since been invaded by a soft new collective called the Corporation. This process in turn gave birth to a new pseudo-public realm, the continuous interior that extends from the atrium, outward to the highway and inward to the User-Defined Area and to networks of all kinds, in Silicon Valley and beyond.

THE DEVELOPER OR, VIRTUAL REALITY

Prior to designing spaces for Apple's users to "think different," Gensler and Associates had developed a related strategy of serial differentiation to service another central figure in Silicon Valley's urban mythology lodged in the unconscious of Portman's atrium: the Developer. In this case, the developer's name was William Wilson Associates, the largest such firm in San Mateo County (at the northern edge of the Valley) at the time. The site was 65.8 acres on the eastern side of Interstate 101 in Redwood City. The project: 1.2 million square feet of office space, distributed in five buildings, ranging in height from nine to sixteen stories, and in gross area from 200,000 to 310,000 square feet each. Here was another form of flexibility calibrated, literally, to the ups and downs of the market, which in this case turned out to be the software industry. The development, which was planned in the late 1980s and completed in stages through the early 1990s, was called Centrum, with Wilson partnering with Aetna Insurance to form Centrum Associates. On 7 April 1989, Centrum Associates announced that it had leased the first two of the virtual (i.e., yet-to-be-built) buildings to Oracle Corporation.[21] Thus did Centrum, a speculative office park with an off-the-shelf visionary name, materialize in advance the corporate vision called Oracle that was previously distributed in smaller offices throughout the Valley. As it did so, Centrum—designed by Gensler, architects of

21. "Oracle Selects New Headquarters Location," *PR Newswire*, 7 April 1989.

the continuous interior, with Peter Walker and Martha Schwartz as landscape architects—was also transformed from office park to campus. The difference in terminology being crucial, since a landscaped office complex with multiple tenants is a "park," while a similar complex with a single tenant is a "campus." And it was through the market and the market alone, that Centrum officially became a campus.

The buildings themselves were as visionary as the name. Five clusters, each consisting of a combination of cylinder and block wrapped entirely in mirrored glass with horizontal concrete bands marking the floors, fanned out along a fourteen-acre artificial lake. At one end was a hotel complete with restaurants, with a fitness center and a child care center opening into the landscape. Running from low to high beside this exotic piece of paradise (a "lagoon," as the press release put it), these buildings were machines for renting, with their internal, quantitative variations in available square footage offering potential tenants flexibility in space planning and occupancy. This same strategy extended to the financial negotiations that converted the virtual park into a virtual campus for five thousand real and virtual (i.e., yet-to-be-hired) employees. Confronted with the real-time growth of corporate vision in the form of Oracle's stock price and therefore its space needs, William Wilson Associates president William Wilson declared: "We had to stay flexible."[22]

1.36

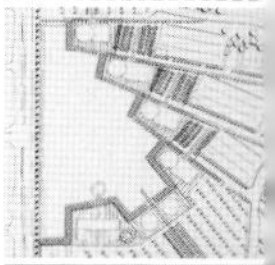

1.37

1.38

1.39

The deal, which took over a year and a half to complete, was for Oracle initially to occupy two of the five planned buildings, the first in October 1989 and the second in August 1990, for a total of 530,000 square feet of space for their new headquarters. In that sense, the serial differentiation of the elegantly rising volumes could be understood as materializing, in "real" space, the equally real virtuality called Oracle that was represented by the letters ORCL on the NASDAQ stock exchange. Oracle's process of going public began when it acquired those letters in 1986, and continued for almost ten years as it occupied its new campus, an architectural IPO rising from low to high out of the grassy fields of speculative development coupled with venture capital—paradise lost and regained on a daily basis. John Hamilton, William Wilson vice president, supplied the architectural theory: "We made sure we could meet [Oracle's] *projection* of personnel, functional, and financial considerations."[23] In other words, the Oracle campus was an architectural *project* in every sense of the word. Like the corporation it now housed, it was a dream, a hallucination.

22. "William Wilson Negotiates Largest Highrise Lease in California," *Business Wire*, 7 April 1989.
23. Ibid. Emphasis added.

BENCHMARK

1.40

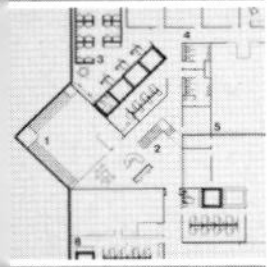

1.41

1.42

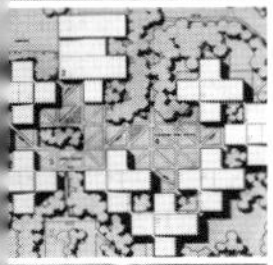

1.43

1.44

Gensler's Centrum/Oracle complex was also a Silicon Valley benchmark that could be added to the list of notable buildings in the "Vale of Chips" compiled by Reyner Banham a decade earlier. Indeed, when the name Oracle was affixed to one of its cylinders, it helped to extend the virtual boundary of the Valley further north, back toward San Francisco, establishing a kind of visual threshold for reverse-commuters (driving from city to suburb) with its height. It became a landmark in a city without landmarks—a landmark without a city—and thus a new kind of monument. Its blank iterability also extended a tendency exhibited by two other buildings on Banham's list. "Neat, silvery smooth and as slickly styled as an advanced computer" was how Banham had described the IBM Santa Teresa research facility designed in 1974 by another architectural acronym, MBT Associates.[24] This earlier computer architecture adhered rigorously to what Banham called the "Eliot Noyes / Museum of Modern Art vision" long identified with IBM: the sleek, minimalist box. Its site plan was composed of a series of nine modular, cross-shaped clusters, distributed around color-coded courtyards. Locked in a planning grid that was drawn into the landscape by Peter Walker, these buildings still dreamed distantly of New York—the gridded metropolis that held the fragments of modernity together even as it tore them apart. Whereas their color-coding anticipates The iMac Principle, if only by revealing that each unit is essentially the same.

Two years later, Gensler and Associates set the architecture of computers free from the grid in Silicon Valley. They did so with the first piece of literally "digital" architecture: a slick, low black box built in Santa Clara for the Digital Corporation in 1976. Banham described the building as "the rock-bottom image… a dark crystal on a green velvet mount," announced by a prominent, tasteful sign.[25] Still, what appears here to be a *reductio ad absurdum* of Robert Venturi and Denise Scott Brown's "decorated shed" turns out to be nothing of the sort. At Digital there is no "shed" to decorate, only two floating signifiers—the sign and its building—adrift on the lawn. And there is no grid—not even a Las Vegas-style "strip"—to integrate this box and its logo into anything like a city, which must therefore be sought elsewhere.

These three objects—MBT's modular, patterned IBM complex, Gensler's Digital box, and their later crescendo of cylinders at Centrum/Oracle—also share an aesthetic commitment to the seamless surface. They are all blanks, or a series of blanks,

24. Banham, "Silicon Style," 284.
25. Ibid., 285.

interrupted only by the lightest of traces. As such, they reinvent architecture's relation to modern technology by replacing the visual expression of mechanical assembly with its explicit *concealment*. We know these objects as "high-tech" precisely because their technical contents are invisible. Their blankness is that of the microprocessor, an aesthetic effect vaguely echoed by local lore associating Oracle's cylinders with the cylindrical stacks of early disc drives (or today, with stacks of blank DVD's). These inert images, these blanks, are the very architecture of information as well as its opposite, the architecture of entropy, simultaneously.

Each blank is also a mirror, which is ultimately the source of their resolute urbanity. Each is surrounded by an architecture of parking on which it depends. Like the buildings themselves, these striped asphalt lots and ramped garages are most empty when they are completely full—rows and rows of abandoned technological shells, machines whose "users" have exchanged one interior for another, the car for the cubicle or, as at Apple and elsewhere, the upholstered comfort of the User Defined Area. As mirrors, the empty architectural shells adjacent to the empty cars capture the urban exterior in a No Stop City of microscopic detail. Their floor plans seem magically derived from circuit boards and computer chips, those vast cities collapsed into every PC. While together, they form a Continuous Monument, a hall of mirrors in which the modern metropolis is exhausted by sheer extrapolation, a *mise-en-abîme* of technological progress.

SHELL AND CORE

1.45

1.46

Developers have taken to referring to the design of such boxes as "shell and core." A kind of *Existenzminimum* of green capital, "shell and core" designates the architectural results of a mini-max equation: minimal investment for maximum return. Thus on the outside is the empty shell ("tilt-up" is preferable for "speed of erection") and on the inside, the hardened core, the dried-up residue of mechanization: elevators, restrooms, machine rooms, and duct chases. Everything else is flexible, including the financing. Floor plates are calculated not on the basis of optimal accommodation of known uses, but on optimal accommodation of the unknown. This is the architecture of market-based "performance": the architecture of strategic neutrality. Inside, the modulated, temporalized "space" of modernism has been replaced by lines of spatialized time: time-to-market, length-of-lease, lifecycle cost, capitalization, rate-of-return, and planned obsolescence.

As mirrors of the market and as illegitimate offspring of Sand Hill Road these shells thus force our attention back onto green capital itself. That is, they force our attention back onto the landscape, the rhizomatic fields: on the interior, cubicles and potted plants; on the exterior, parking lots and lawns.

There is some evidence that Gensler thought they had found a new kind of city at Centrum/Oracle. And there is some evidence that they may have been right. Centrum/Oracle's mute monoliths are in fact held together by the landscape out of which they rise, in which the metropolitan grid is replaced by an extension of Digital's plush, green lawn, which includes the tree-lined "lagoon" trimmed with Walker and Schwartz's grassy geometries. Built on landfill with a drainage slough running through it, this Oz follows the planning precepts of the garden city, with an "urban core" (the buildings) concentrated along the artificial lakefront complete with "willow walk," and a "rural fringe" along the slough. Walker and Schwartz merely connected the two with poplar allées.[26]

But this city again turns out to be a village, in which global and local are collapsed into a corporate community that seeks at every turn to overcome the mirrored abstraction of "shell and core" and of green capital with a new form of figuration—to put a face on the faceless networks of the information age. On the nightly business news, that face is that of a father, the CEO. The significant difference is that in Silicon Valley's mythology, this Oedipus remains an adolescent. As such, he likes to play. "Serious fun," rather than the all-too-tragic seriousness of Greek myth, is his management strategy. At Cisco, this takes the form of basketball courts. While at Oracle, the fitness club is supplemented by an exercise course in which vigorous visionaries run circles around one another by running around the campus, in circles. In Silicon Valley, paradise lost is paradise regained, as a playground. The languor of corporate golf, with its class associations, has thus been replaced on these lawns by a pseudo-egalitarian "fitness," with its reduction of the corporate body to sheer biology. The transgressive pleasure of "eating oysters with boxing gloves, naked, on the nth floor"[27] has been channeled into the utilitarian efficiency of cross-programmed relaxation.

In that respect, the greatest innovation on this and many other fronts in the battle for Silicon Valley's architectural and urban soul has been achieved by the San Francisco head-

26. "Centrum, Redwood City, California," *Process Architecture* 85 (October 1989): 142.
27. Rem Koolhaas, *Delirious New York: A Retroactive Manifesto for Manhattan* (New York, Oxford University Press, 1978), 128.

quarters of Studios Architecture. Since, if there is another subsequent benchmark to add to Banham's list, it would be the former Charleston campus of Silicon Graphics Inc. (SGI), designed by Studios in collaboration with the SWA Group (landscape architects) and completed in 1997.

First, some background: In 1881 a New York physiologist named George Beard identified a syndrome afflicting the burnt-out "brain-workers" of the modern city as "American nervousness." Twenty-two years later, Simmel diagnosed the "blasé attitude" exhibited by the typical inhabitant of the modern metropolis as a psychosomatic defense mechanism against an excess of external sensory stimuli. By the late twentieth century, such urban pathologies had migrated to Silicon Valley and exurbias worldwide, in the form of road rage, chronic fatigue syndrome, and a generalized *stress* that did not distinguish between the pressures of work and the pressures of the family, since as with CIAM's categories, these domains were slowly merging.[28] Thus did Studios/SWA respond, at SGI, with an architectural antidote to the permanent deadline and compulsive happiness: exercise rooms, meditation chambers, peaceful gardens, and—again—recreation areas.

As Banham had already implied about the potted plants in earlier atria (and, we can add, the white noise machines in earlier office landscapes), such amenities were inducements to higher productivity through a balance of concentration and relaxation. This was both a logistical and aesthetic project. Logistical, since it entailed flexible work hours and time off for recreation. Aesthetic, since it entailed a replacement of the modern Machine with a postmodern Nature.

For example: While Le Corbusier had famously identified modern architecture with the automobile, urging architects to take a closer look at the new sports cars, the designers and users of still newer machines at SGI apparently could not tolerate looking at their own well-maintained cars for very long. Therefore, at the SGI complex what looks like a campus-like arrangement of deconstructively decorated sheds organized around a courtyard is actually an enormous artificial mound. Under the mound is a parking garage: employee parking. In the automobile city, there must be no automobiles in sight. Instead, there must only be grassy lawns and landscaped knolls. The stress-inducing view of the parking lot is thus replaced with the relaxing view of shrubbery. Nature (the mound) swallows Machine (the car).

1.47

1.48

1.49

1.50

28. See George Beard, *American Nervousness, Its Causes and Consequences: A Supplement to Nervous Exhaustion* (New York: Putnam, 1881); Georg Simmel, "The Metropolis and Mental Life" (1903), in *The Sociology of Georg Simmel*, trans. and ed. Kurt H. Wolff (New York: Free Press, 1950), 409-424; and Juliet Schor, *The Overworked American: The Unexpected Decline of Leisure* (New York: Basic Books, 1991).

But there are complications. The original (first) nature, in the form of the land that lay underneath, was apparently contaminated with the residue of the industrial age to the point of emitting methane. So Studios/SWA buried it and the automobile under a new (second) nature, piled high to reinforce the isolation of this neo-medieval citadel called SGI, with its reconstituted community formed around multiple coffee bars with built-in whiteboard countertops. The Resident Alien was nowhere to be seen within all of this well-being, not because she was not there but because she had been rendered invisible—naturalized. The tumultuous global city in which she was born had been converted, at SGI, into a global village—a machine for thinking (different), wrapped in a warm and fuzzy green blanket.

1.53

1.54

FROM SEAGRAM TO SGI

The blanket itself embeds this thinking, as it eases into its surroundings. The "density bonus" built into the zoning deal that made the entire complex possible required SGI to "give back" a certain percentage of its reclaimed land to a nonexistent public, as well as to connect their campus to Shoreline Park, adjacent. In that sense, this campus must be seen as a migration westward of changes made to the New York Zoning Resolution in 1961 to allow additional building height in exchange for plazas below, on the model of Ludwig Mies van der Rohe's Seagram Building. The difference was that the empty, windswept plaza had become an empty, breezy park, with travertine and water exchanged for grass and trees. In return, SGI was allowed to build an additional 160,000 square feet of office space in a cluster of six buildings that were all different and therefore all the same. Color-coded stair towers punctuate the expressive Studios design, in which torqued skins and leaning trellises persevere in announcing that the urbane anonymity and elegant monotony of Seagram had been conquered by sheer will. The architecture of business, like its inhabitants, had become "interesting" and playful.

Its site, too, had acquired contour and definition, making up in agitation what it lacked in nuance. Unable to sit still, SGI's fields flowed in two directions simultaneously. As at Oracle, one side of the campus addressed itself to the new urbanity of the corporate neighborhood, with its low-slung tilt-ups and rangy parking lots. There, both site and buildings straightened out, lined up. In contrast, the other side was a parade of informality. There, curves and angles cut the volumes into their hill while absorbing the bouncy rhythms of the adjacent park. In the middle of the whole affair, at the crest of the hill, was the official Commons Area, a diminishing cascade of rotated squares that organized every blade of carefully mowed grass into a ruthless theater of corporate togetherness forced out into the open. From here landscape was pure gradient: fading in one direction into the street, in another into the park, in another into tall unkempt, grasses, and in still another, into the old nature of a dry estuary reaching in from the bay. This last was a rough hewn, virginal territory that completed the transition–from green to rough, in the manner of a golf course. Call this gradient of relaxation, this mound of parking topped off with manicured precision that dissolves at its edges, The Golf Course Principle.

THE (EXIT) SIGN

1.51

1.52

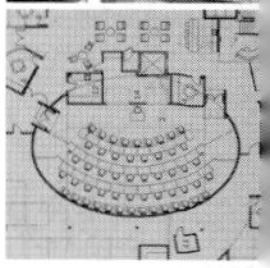

In 1999, at the height of the new economy enthusiasm, Studios completed the interior design of a 110,000 square-foot headquarters for the online financial services company E*Trade in Menlo Park. Again, a "public boulevard" designed to provide "opportunities for impromptu meetings between disciplines [e.g., bankers and software engineers] and the cross-fertilization of ideas" within the company.[29] Again the coffee bars. And among the signs circulating in front of the well-caffeinated symbolic analysts staring at E*Trade's screens was COMS, the NASDAQ symbol for 3Com, for whom Studios had just completed Phase III of their corporate campus in nearby Santa Clara. Like the others it was, according to its architects, "conducive to the productive enjoyment of work." Again a "pedestrian village" on a landscaped podium with cars below. And again a "contemplative environment" spinning off a well-stocked corporate cafeteria that opened onto the crest of a landscaped knoll.[30] That same year, Studios also began work on the interiors of the corporate headquarters of the Internet service provider Excite@Home in Redwood City just west of Interstate 101, not far from Gensler's Oracle. A collection of four shell-and-core buildings designed by HOK for "flexibility and rapid growth" again nourished by coffee and corporate food, this campus was again organized atop a grassy crest, at the center of which was written into the pavement the company sign: @.

1.55

1.56

Occupied in 2000, by December 2001 this new home for Excite was empty, abandoned as the company dissolved into the post-bubble, post-9/11 brave new world of corporate consolidation and increased military spending. Irrational exuberance had become homeland security, and Excite's giddy efforts to convert the Internet into a

1.57

1.58

29. *Studios Architecture: Selected and Current Works* (Victoria, Australia: Images Publishing, 2002), 98.
30. Ibid., 76.

home had given way to the return of the repressed "homeland" that had been lurking within the global village all along in the form of Excite's chief competitor: AOL, or America Online. Stripped of Excite's corporate logo—formerly visible to all time travelers speeding (or creeping) into the future down Interstate 101—shell and core had proven itself as an exit strategy. All that remained was the @ sign written into the landscape, an exit sign leading to an off-ramp, a potential line of escape from a digital future increasingly dedicated to securing the home called the nation.

1.59

1.60

1.61

By early 2003, Silicon Valley had a twenty-five percent vacancy rate, the highest in the United States. The pastoral lawns and empty parking lots of green capital were now littered with signs reading "For Lease" juxtaposed with other, blank ones from which, as at Excite, colorful logos had been erased. But the poignancy of this scene should not be misread as a morality tale, in which corporate greed gets its just deserts as the global economy undergoes one of its many pseudo-natural "corrections." No, its poignancy lies in its displacements, since what the signs themselves had erased was the city itself, not by converting it into a simulacrum, but by converting it into a home, a village—global, corporate, or otherwise. In the subsequent erasure of the logos, the city had thus reasserted itself in its paradoxical emptiness: the empty parking lots vividly revealed that this had always been a city of empty shells, of worker-consumers desperately following the signs leading toward a happy future of corporate togetherness, but always having to return, day in and day out, to their own isolation. This is the Multi-National City (MNC). And in it, floating atop a sea of parking like an island unmoored from its geological foundations, architecture drifts.

1.62

1.63

1.64

FROM HARDWARE TO SOFTWARE

But even fake nature abhors a vacuum. Thus in July 2003, Google Inc. announced that it would take over SGI's Charleston campus, while SGI consolidated into its Crittenden Technology Center nearby. The relocation was completed by August 2004. On 18 August 2004, Google went public.

Google's founders became billionaires on the simple premise that searching the Internet should be simple. But just as important to the IPO's success was the public impression that these were happy people working happily and productively in a happy place where the company motto, number six on their list of "Ten things Google has found to be true," was "You can make money without doing evil." In practice, this amounted to offering mass-customized, income-generating advertisements only to users who have declared their interest in a product by initiating a search. Among the other Google truths were "Focus on the user and all else will follow" (No. 1), and of course "The need for information crosses all borders" (No. 8).

But of particular relevance to the MNC was Google truth number nine: "You can be serious without a suit." Here was the not-so-secret relationship between the user-friendly architecture of Silicon Valley and its promises of economic success with a clear conscience. Not only, as Google's official philosophy reminds us, because of the ubiquitous lava lamps and rubber balls, or because the company chef used to cook for The Grateful Dead and thus represented—for northern California—the heights of hedonism. But also because "[i]n the same way Google puts users first when it comes to our online service, Google Inc. puts employees first when it comes to daily life in our Googleplex headquarters." [31] Thus at Googleplex, the former home of the formerly friendly SGI, all is well.

CVRP

There is at least one exit ramp along Interstate 101 that still beckons. This is recently completed Bailey Avenue exit at what is known as Coyote Valley, seven miles below San Jose at the southernmost extremity of Silicon Valley. There, the two fault lines and their accompanying ridges converge so tightly as to produce a kind of geological and geographical terminus to the sprawling technopolis. The exit leads to IBM's Santa Teresa research facility designed by MBT and designated by Banham as Silicon Valley's first architectural benchmark. And were it not for bursting bubbles, the exit would also have given access to —and been paid for by—a new campus in the making for decades, designated by public officials and developers as the Coyote Valley Research Park, or CVRP.

Coyote Valley marks the end of Silicon Valley's arrow of progress, its very tip, the cutting edge, the vanguard, the avant-garde. It is also a Silicon Valley-in-miniature, and a terminus for other dreams from other times. This makes it a bottleneck in time, a point at which progress gets stuck in traffic and bends its arrow back, into a feedback loop. In 1964 Oceanic California, a subsidiary of Castle & Cooke and the developer of Sea Ranch, planned an exuberant "New Town San Jose" in Coyote Valley. The project was eventually abandoned. In 1984, Tandem Inc. was scheduled to begin construction of a new corporate campus in Coyote Valley. Again, the plans were abandoned. In 1985,

1.65

1.66

1.67

1.68

1.69

1.70

1.71

31. http://www.google.com/corporate/tenthings.html.

one year after introducing the PCPC, Apple announced its own plans to build a campus of the future there. Again: abandoned.

In 1998, Coyote Valley Research Park LLC was formed. Investors included Divco West Properties, Gibson Speno, Westbrook Partners, and Cisco Systems. That same year the group acquired a 688-acre parcel in north Coyote Valley. The consortium planned to develop the land into a new, full-service campus for 20,000 worker-consumers. Cisco would then purchase this campus from the group, more than doubling its Silicon Valley office space. The deal was estimated to be worth $1.3 billion.[32] Designed by Devcon Construction in collaboration with Cisco, the campus was to be composed of thirty-eight virtually identical buildings of up to six stories in height, configured in loose compliance with the village-generating protocols of the New Urbanism. The Environmental Impact Statement generated by the San Jose planning department described the resulting clusters linked by a "Main Street" as "neighborhoods."[33]

But on 24 October 2001, facing mounting losses, Cisco announced that it had dramatically scaled back its commitment to the project, indicating its intention to buy only fifty-five to one hundred thirty-five acres of the land without any immediate plans for construction. In exchange for release from the original agreement, Cisco refunded the consortium of investors at what was called a "reasonable rate of return." Divco West Properties, Gibson Speno, and Westbrook Partners thus made a profit on the failed deal while maintaining control of future development.[34] Renderings of the proposed design, which had been posted on the consortium's website, vanished. But the architecture of the campus had been realized nonetheless, not in the form of soon to be abandoned shell-and-core structures, but in the form of images constructed, circulated, and abandoned as capital consumed itself, in circles.

32. As reported in Peter Grant, "Coyote Valley Investors Gain from Cisco Deal," *Real Estate Journal: The Wall Street Journal Guide to Property*, 31 October 2001, http://homes.wsj.com/columnists_com/bricks/20011031-bricks.html.

33. "North Coyote Valley Campus Industrial Area Project DEIR," http://www.ci.san-jose.ca.us/planning/sjplan/eir/northcoyote/project.html.

34. Grant, "Coyote Valley Investors Gain from Cisco Deal."

1 FROM **NEW YORK** TO **SILICON VALLEY**

FEEDBACK

Coyote Valley Research Park 2003

→ In January 2002, the New York-based firm of Martin/Baxi Architects (M/BA) took up the abandoned Cisco project, having already imagined the partial erasure of Oracle, 3Com, Intel and other signs in anticipation of a new architecture. By chance, plans had also been in preparation should Cisco find itself in need of an architectural alternative to corporate happiness. Spreadsheet analysis had shown that a mere shift in the numbers—doubling the allowable FAR from .25 to .5—could double the return on investment. All that had to be overcome was a fear of heights, since such a doubling would require taller buildings.

At the time, the tallest building in Silicon Valley was eighteen stories. Zoning, which reflected aesthetic preferences regarding density and height, precluded anything more. The objections raised by environmental and community groups to the original Cisco/Devcon plan, with its six-story structures, were equally symptomatic, since greater density would be more efficient at an urban and regional scale, and thus more ecologically sound. But back in New York, something had happened that had everybody talking about tall buildings, office space, and the real estate market. In response to the destruction of the World Trade Center, architects worldwide were already preparing various architectures of the future to symbolize anticipated military triumph for an implied presidential client. Embarrassed by architecture's newfound "relevance," M/BA— following in the footsteps of Portman, who had commissioned himself to relocate Rockefeller Center in San Francisco—decided instead to commission itself to relocate the World Trade Center to Coyote Valley.

The result was a continuation of the Silicon Valley timeline, in another series of spreadsheets that described a line of forty buildings, rising from six to forty-six stories and totaling fifteen million square feet, equal to the amount lost in lower Manhattan. The continuously varying line derived from a genome made up of three building types, each of which was subjected to parametric variation, from minimum to maximum. By virtue of such variation, every building, as well as every floor of every building, was different (The iMac Principle). One of the three types was prototyped specifically for Silicon Valley. It consisted of an imploded box of indeterminate functionality encapsulated in its own atrium, with potted plant—a finite, wireless world from which no exit was necessary, where the corporate lifestyle could be fully consummated, and where Work, Dwelling, Leisure, and Transportation were one (The Atrium Principle).

The overall proportions of each box were a function of its position in the quantitative array. Each of the sides of the interior volume housing the floor plates was folded gently inward in mirrored symmetry. These folds were echoed in slight ripples in the second skin, which enclosed the atrium which enclosed the interior volume. Together these two skins produced an environmental buffer zone around the building's perimeter equivalent to a double-skin enclosure that enabled passive heating and cooling of the interior space. In turn, the center of the interior volume was interrupted by a twisted vortex—a void drawn through the entire building. Together with the tapering twist of this vortex, the variable geometries of the building's folds ensured that the size and shape of each floor plate was different, with different spatial proportions and different degrees of access to natural light, which entered most directly through the vortex deep inside the building.

The vortex and the folds also acted structurally, meeting the ground plane which, in turn, rose into smaller, structural mounds as it passed into the building. The entire assembly was held together by thousands of small-scale framing members joined at thousands of points, in a redundant network in which no two members were the same—a three-dimensional, flexible cage made possible structurally by finite-element analysis, and punctuated only by vertical service cores. Likewise for the double layer of glazing that formed a doubled-up, mass-customized curtain wall, with a transparent outer layer and mirrored inner layer, in which workers living 24/7 inside the building could see their idiosyncratic individuality reflected on the outside in multi-faceted, multi-national splendor.

Each of the landscaped mounds on which the buildings sat was of similarly different dimensions and proportions, as was each of the forty property subdivisions, thus allowing for variation in area that could be subleased in the event of another economic "correction." And so these continuously differentiated buildings were scattered across Coyote Valley, each matched to a mound and to a subdivision based on buildable area—a three-dimensional spreadsheet. Parking was under the mounds, with landscaping proceeding from artfully manicured greens at the crests to state-of-nature roughs at the valleys (The Golf Course Principle). Circulation was arranged in one-way circles extrapolated from the Bailey Avenue interchange that had been conjured in anticipation of the defunct Cisco campus (The Entropy Principle). The result? More sprawl, but at ever greater densities that turned Silicon Valley's history back into itself.

Spinning in such circles this decentralized, scattered center remained a campus without a name: a faceless system that incorporated all of the possible logos of world trade into its hyper-differentiated blankness. But it was also an exit, a little piece of nondescript utopia that refused to yield to the pressures of domestication. Its seamlessness was forever interrupted by its own abstraction in which —as with its predecessors—was also reflected the abstraction, the unassimilable difference, of the Resident Alien: a stranger who comes today and stays tomorrow, both "them" and "us" at once. Within this abstraction there remain still more counter-futures to be discovered, futures in permanent suspension, futures that cannot be traded, that are not reducible to the closure of market speculation and the longing for a home. Call this utopian realism.

1

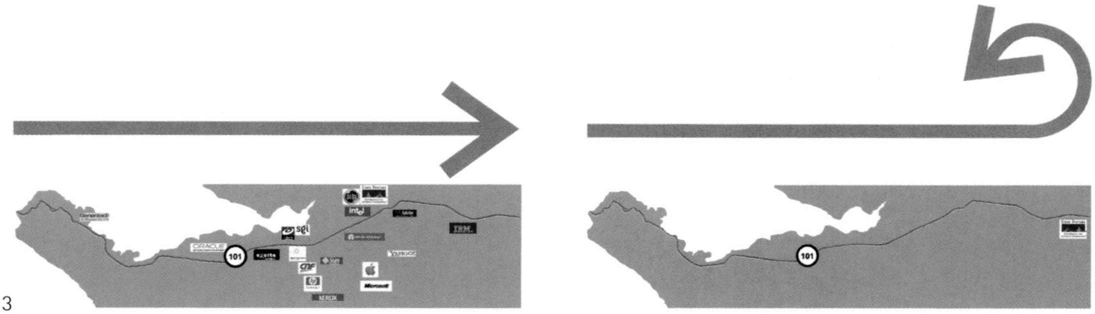

2, 3

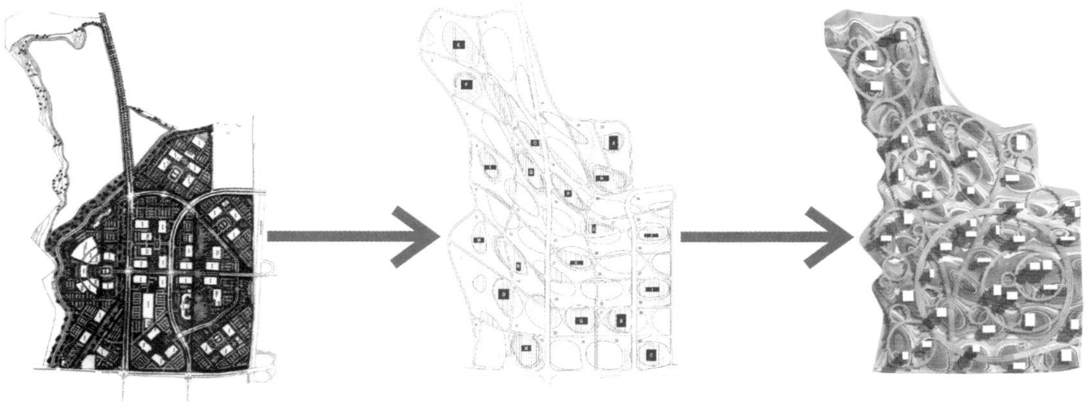

4

CVRP2003

[1] Coyote Valley history, from Castle & Cooke (1964) to Tandem (1984) to Apple (1985) to Cisco (2000) to...
[2] The Arrow of Progress. Logos along Interstate 101, Silicon Valley, 2003.
[3] Feedback. Cisco CVRP as turning point along Interstate 101. Silicon Valley, 2003.
[4] From Cisco/Devcon (2000) to M/BA (2001) to M/BA (2003).

1

2

3

CVRP2003

[1] Formerly 3Com, 2001.
[2] Top: Formerly Oracle, 2001. Bottom: Formerly Intel, 2001.
[3] Rebuilding the World Trade Center in Silicon Valley (a test).

1

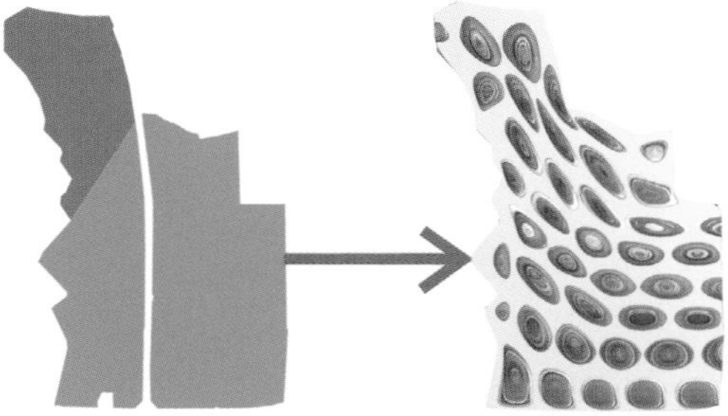

2

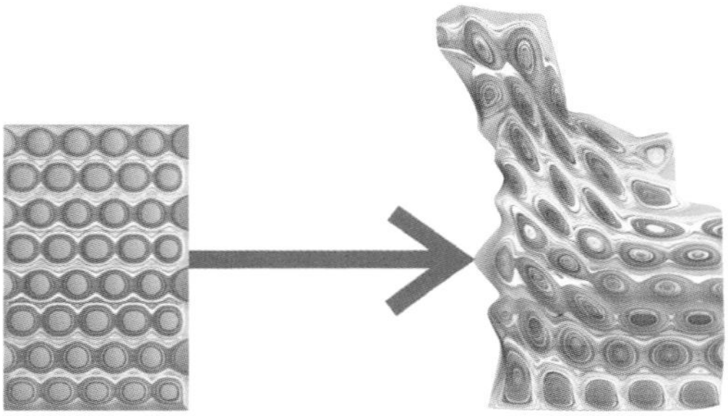

3

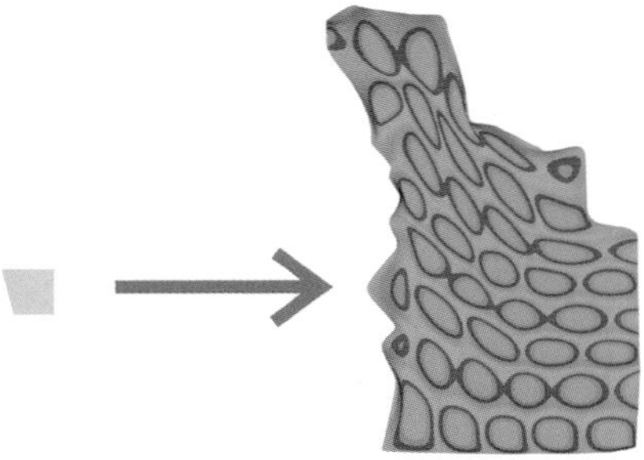

4

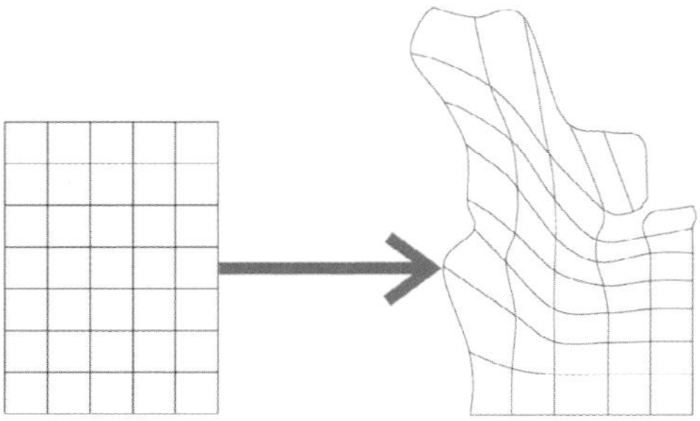

5

The Golf Course Principle.
[1] From green to rough, in the lawns and plazas of Apple, Excite@Home, and M/BA's CVRP.
[2] Drainage. [3] From green to rough. [4] Rebuilding the World Trade Center in Silicon Valley (site comparison).
[5] The iMac Principle (property subdivision), from grid to gradient).

1

2

3

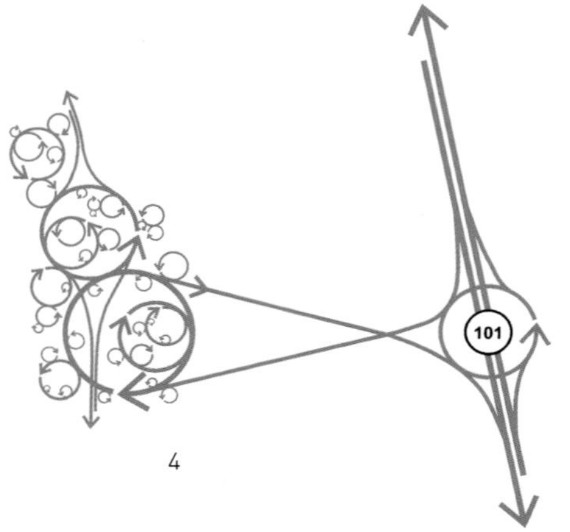

4

CVRP2003

[1] The Entropy Principle (circulation, in circles).
[2] The Entropy Principle (scatter).
[3] Circulation, in circles.
[4] Circulation, in circles, and Bailey Avenue interchange (Interstate 101).

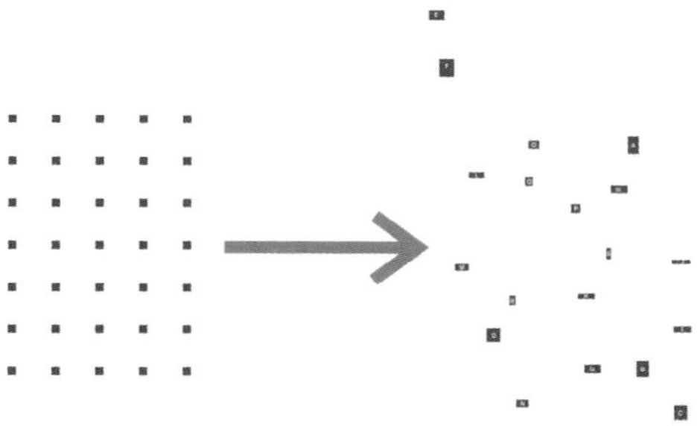
5

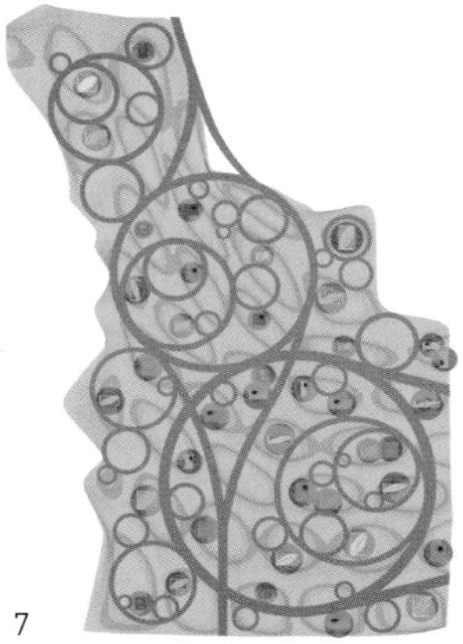
7

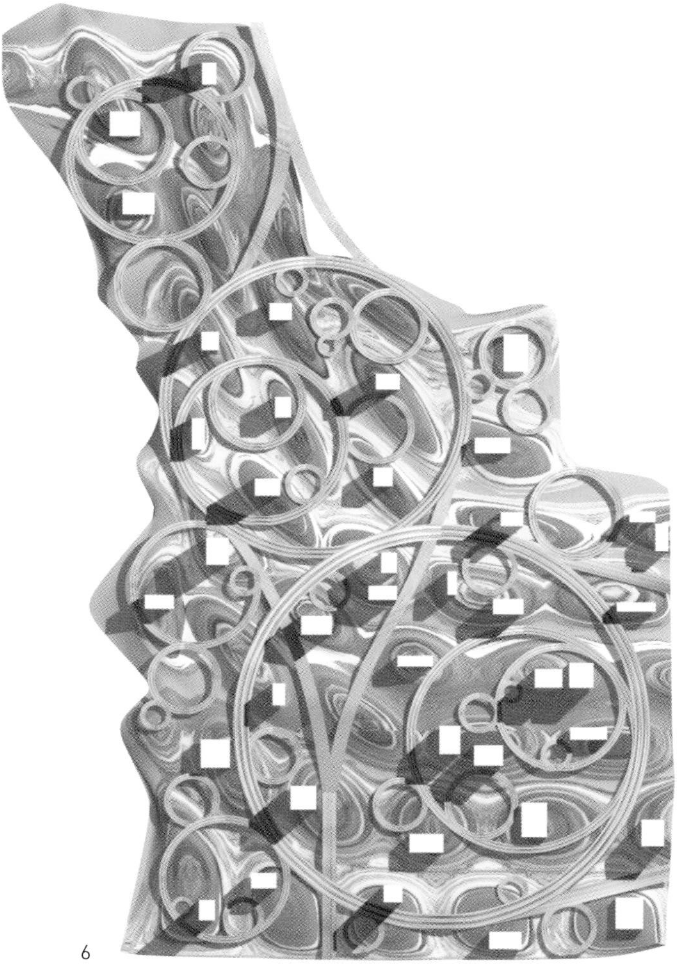
6

8

9

[5] Buildings (scatter). [6] Site plan.
[7] Roads, parking, buildings, landscape.
[8] Roads, parking, buildings.
[9] Buildings, color-coding.

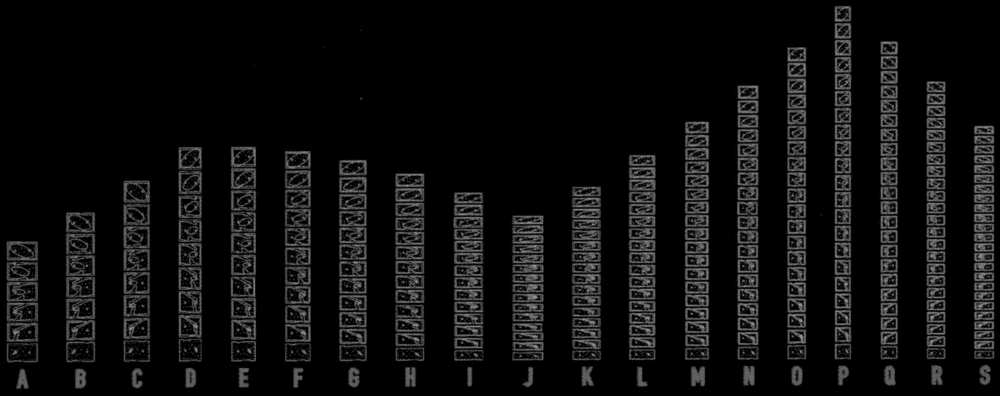

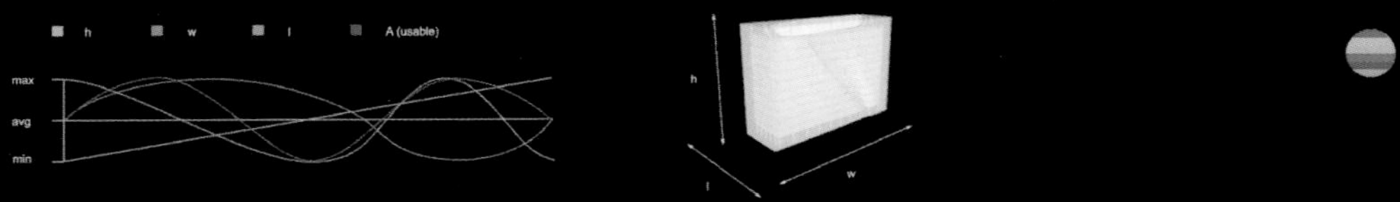

	A	B	C	D	E	F	G	H	I	J	K	L	M	N	O	P	Q	R	S
h (stories)	6	7	8	9	10	11	12	13	14	15	16	17	18	19	20	21	22	23	24
h (usable)	5	6	7	8	9	10	11	12	13	14	15	16	17	18	19	20	21	22	23
w (ft)	210	224	238	252	266	280	294	308	322	336	308	280	252	224	196	168	140	112	84
l (ft)	336	308	280	252	224	196	168	140	112	84	98	112	126	140	154	168	182	196	210
h (ft)	84	98	112	126	140	154	168	182	196	210	224	238	252	266	288	294	308	322	336
w (inner)	182	196	210	224	238	252	266	280	294	308	280	252	224	196	168	140	112	84	56
l (inner)	308	250	252	224	196	168	140	112	84	56	70	84	98	112	126	140	154	168	182
A (sf usable)	280,000	329,000	370,000	401,000	420,000	423,000	410,000	376,000	321,000	241,000	294,000	339,000	373,000	395,000	402,000	392,000	362,000	310,000	234,000

plan

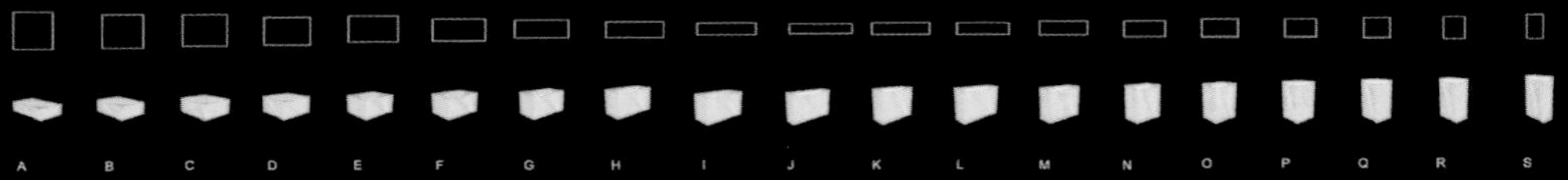

1

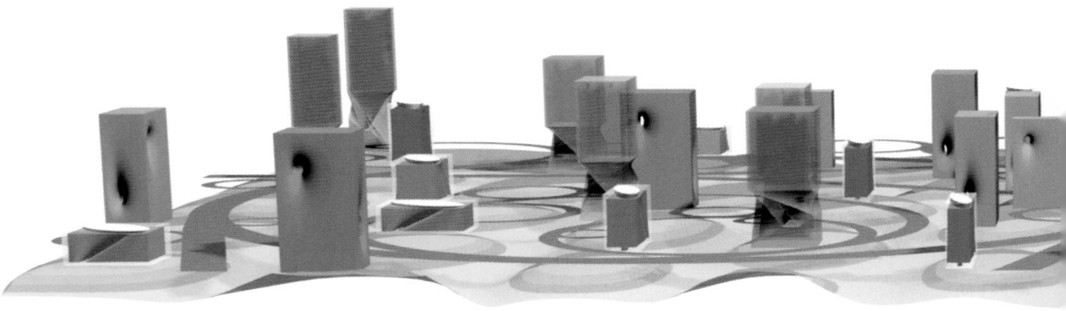

9

CVRP2003

[1] The iMac Principle, genome spreadsheet, plans (first version).
[2]The iMac Principle: Color-coding in iMacs, HOK's Nortel Networks lobby (sideways), and M/BA's proposed CVRP genome.

2

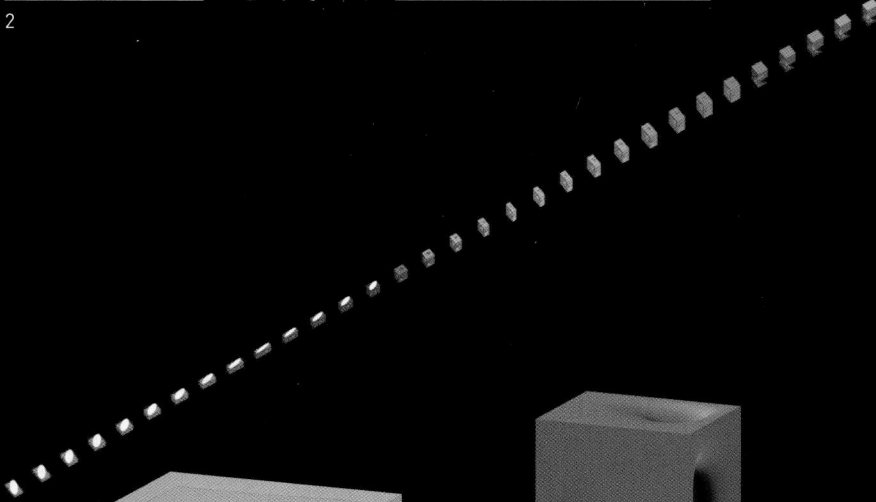

3

4

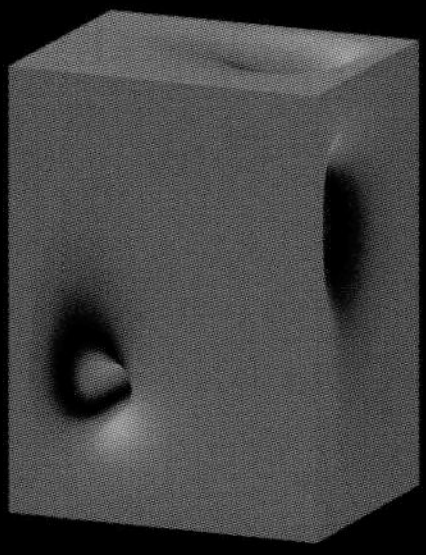

5

6

7 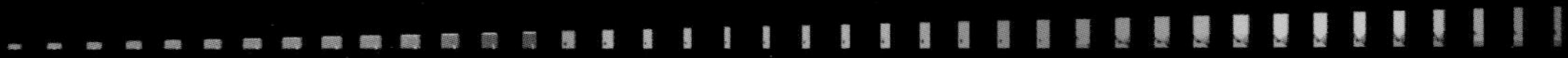

8 

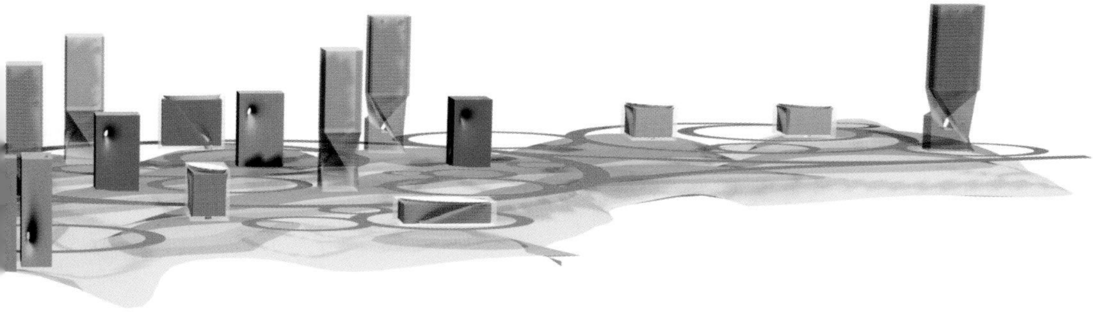

Genome:
[3] Axonometric.
[4] Prototype A.
[5] Prototype C.
[6] Prototype B.
[7] Elevation.
[8] Plan.
[9] Genome, redistributed.

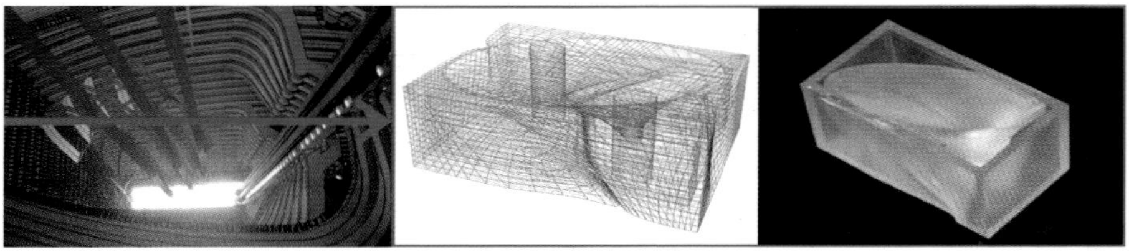
1

2

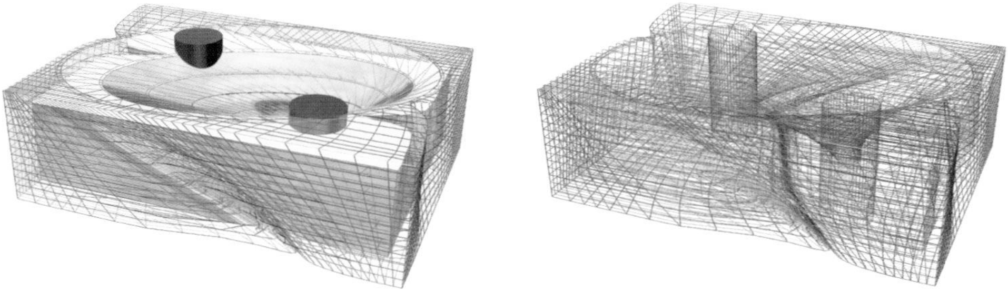
3, 4

5

CVRP2003

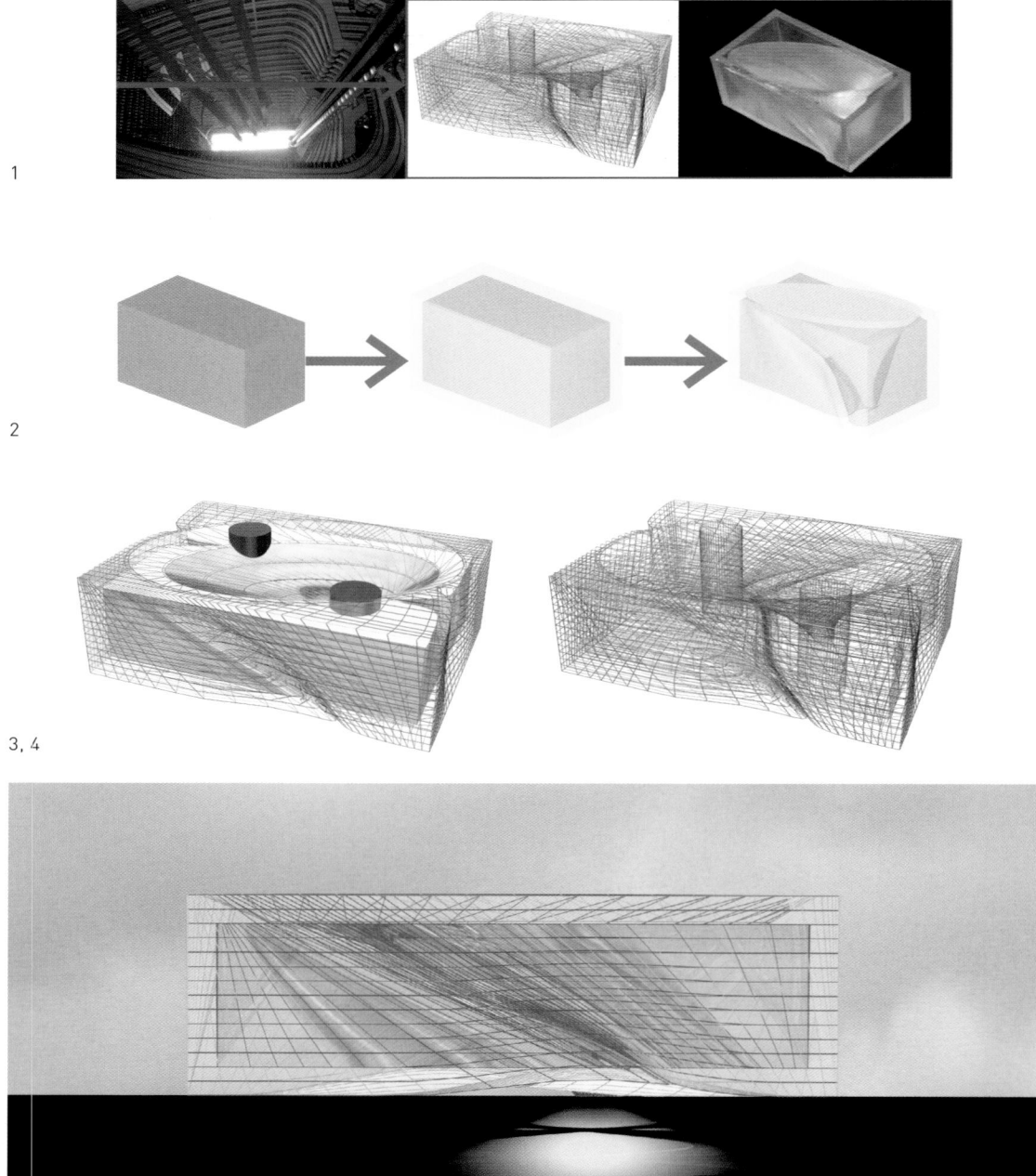

[1]The Atrium Principle. Re-use and inversion of Portman's atrium in the Peachtree Center in Atlanta, with M/BA's inside-out atrium shown in wireframe isometric and in a "reverse positive" model.
[2] The Atrium Principle (inside-out).
[3] Prototype A. [4] Structure,
[5] Façade with parking below.

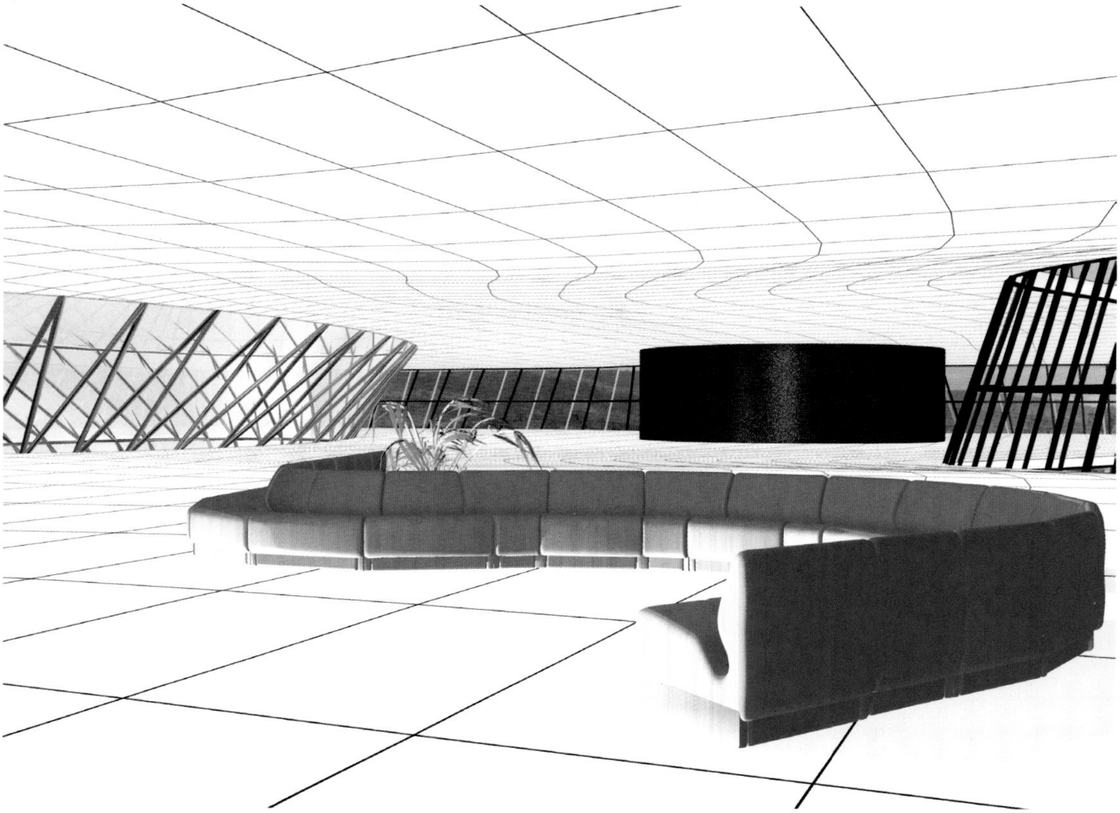

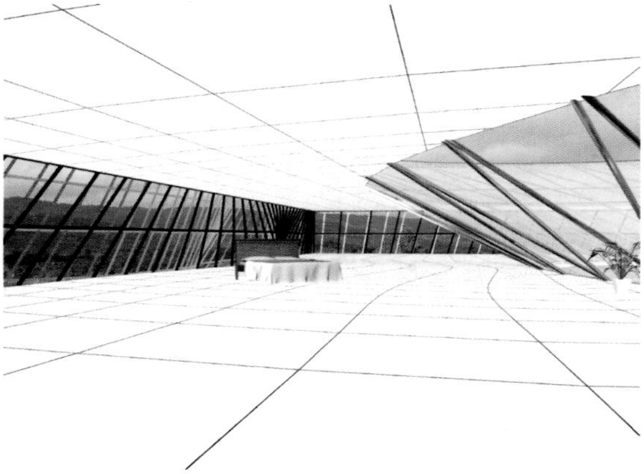

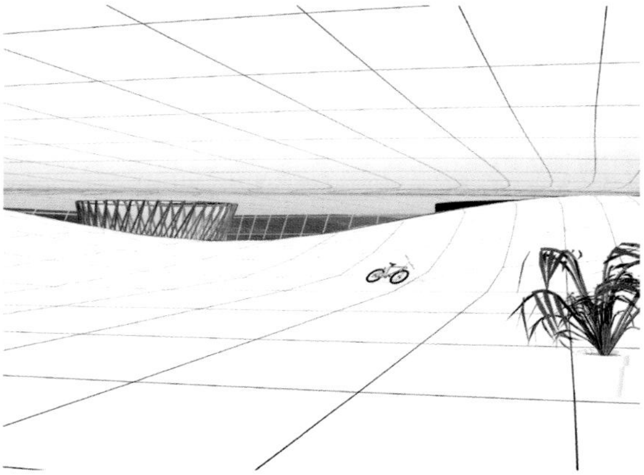

Interiors.

1

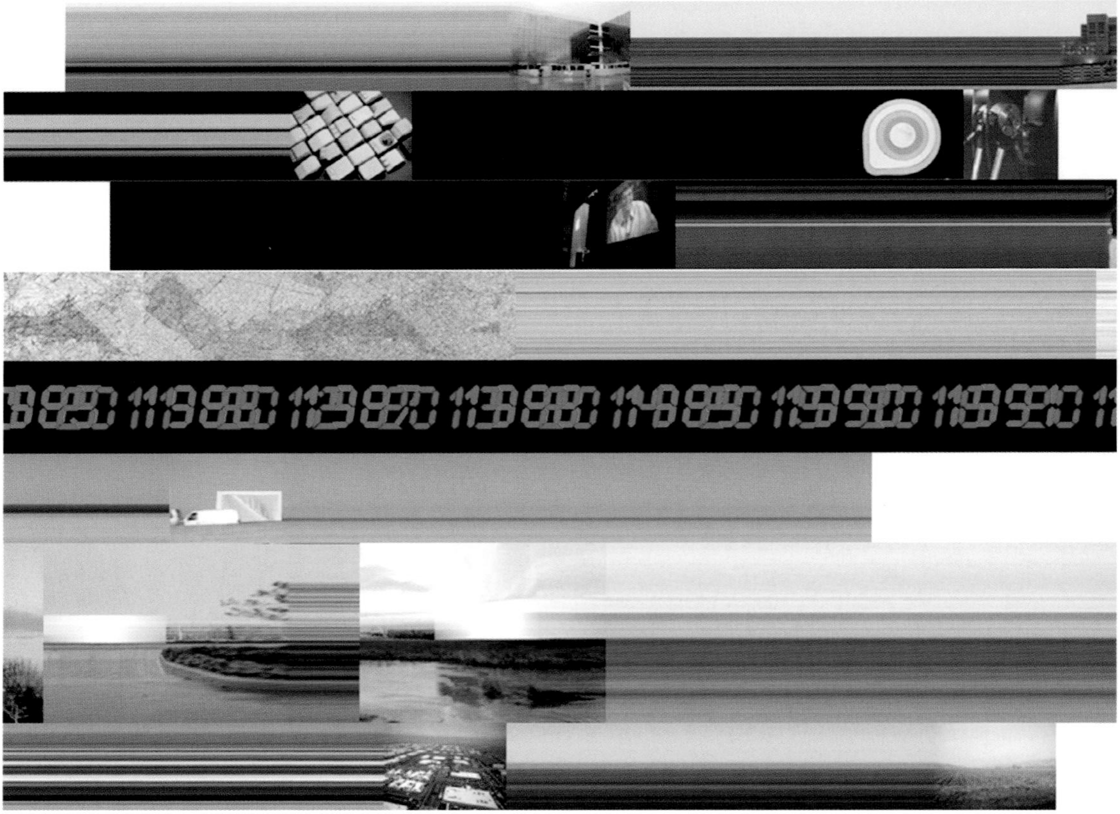

2

CVRP2003

[1] Cisco to CVRP. Buildings and landscapes along Silicon Valley highways,
including M/BA's proposed Coyote Valley Research Park (CVRP).
[2] Remix. Digital projection remixing historical material and M/BA's possible futures, from 1950 to 2050.

Prototype A.

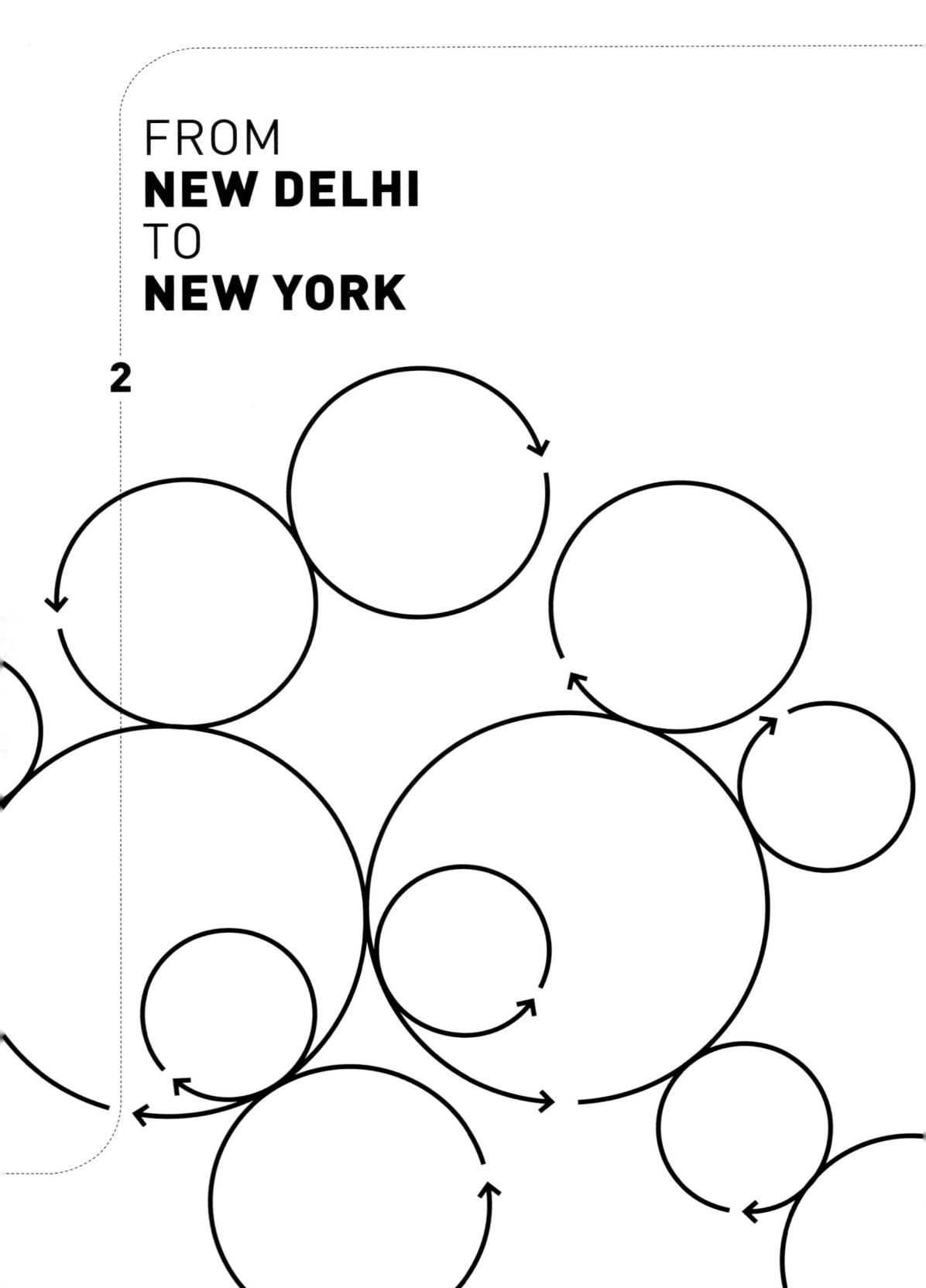

FROM **NEW DELHI** TO **NEW YORK**

2

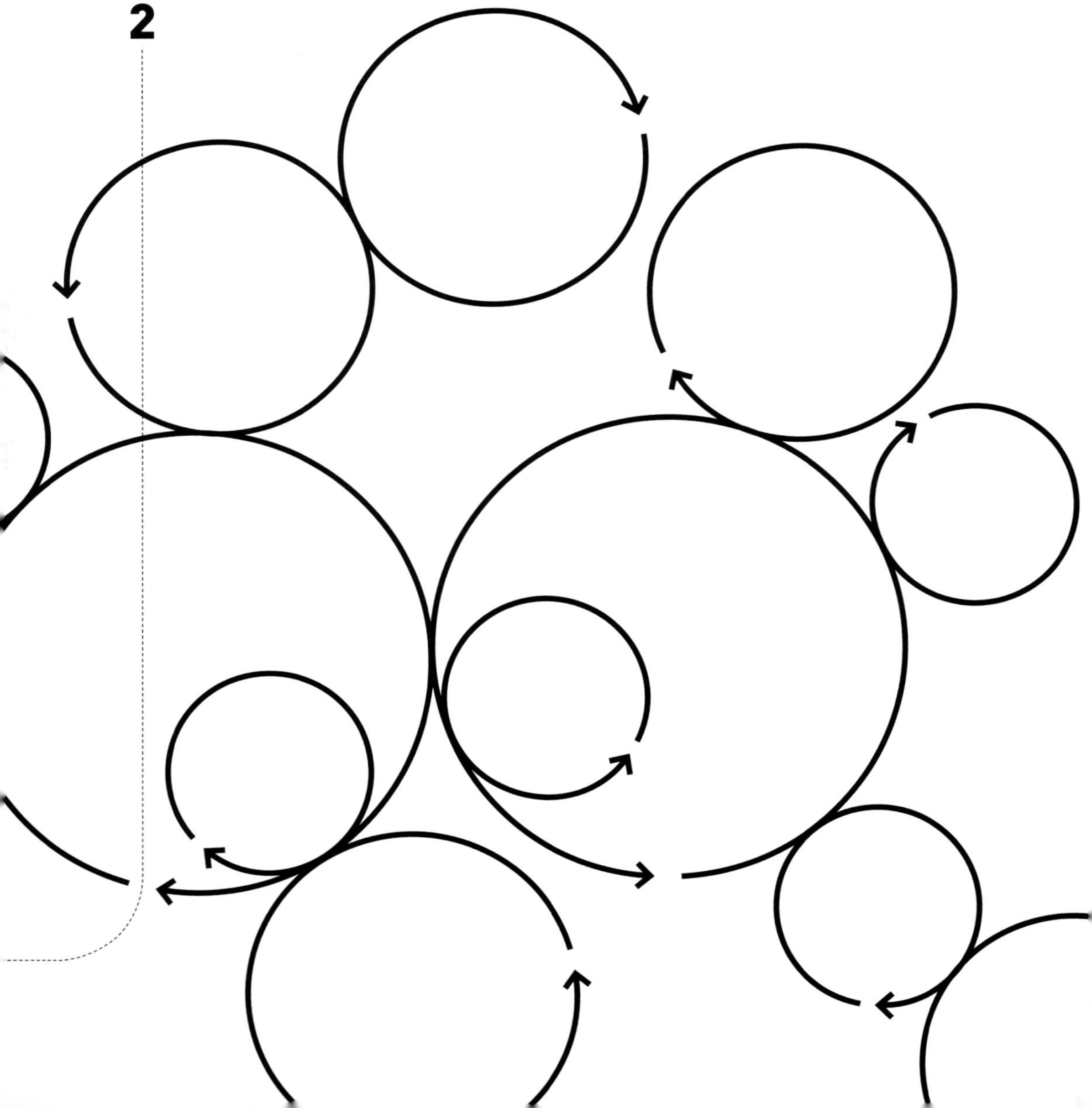

We do not know *what* a particular building signifies. We only know *that* it signifies, after the fact. For example: three months after the events of 11 September 2001 there was a smaller, unrelated attack on a former headquarters of modernity's most extensive empire. On 13 December 2001, unidentified militants attacked a meeting of the Indian parliament taking place in the circular Parliament House in New Delhi. The building, known under the British Raj as the Council House, was designed by Sir Herbert Baker and completed in 1927. At the time of the attack, it was controlled by the Bharatiya Janata Party (BJP), the Hindu nationalist party that held a regular parliamentary majority from 1998 until 2004. Then Prime Minister Atal Bihari Vajpayee compared the attack to the 9/11 events in New York, and his government implicated Pakistan. India and Pakistan lurched toward nuclear war, which was eventually averted through negotiations. In retrospect this attack, like 9/11, appeared all the more real for its symbolism. Especially since the BJP had risen to power in the aftermath of an even more vivid piece of architectural iconoclasm when, on 6 December 1992, militant Hindus flattened the Babri Masjid, a sixteenth century mosque in Ayodyha, setting off riots in which thousands died.

When it was built, the New Delhi imperial complex, designed by Sir Edwin Lutyens in collaboration with Baker, had been hailed as a happy, conciliatory synthesis of western neoclassicism and the "Indo-Saracenic" style. An amalgam of motifs, including *chattris* (pavilions) and *jhallis* (carved stone screens) cribbed from the palaces and fortresses of northern India's earlier Mughal rulers, it still stands as a monument to empire as such. Yet the construction of New Delhi, with its geometric, axial plan drawn as if from scratch, was also the result of the British Raj withdrawing its official seat from Calcutta, a site of intensifying civil unrest, to a site near Shahjahanabad ("Old Delhi"), the former seat of Mughal rule. It seems the British imagined that this move, together with a regionally inflected architecture, would bring them closer to the hearts and minds of their colonial subjects.[1] But the many peoples that made up British India lost their patience, and at midnight of 14 August 1947 the twin states of India and Pakistan were born.

2.01

2.02

1. Suhash Chakravarty, "Architecture and Politics in the Construction of New Delhi," *Architecture + Design* 2, no. 2 (January-February 1986): 76. See also Thomas R. Metcalf, *An Imperial Vision: Indian Architecture and Britain's Raj* (Berkeley: University of California Press, 1989); and Norma Everson, *The Indian Metropolis: A View Toward the West* (New Haven: Yale University Press, 1989).

EMPIRE REDUX?

On 5 January 2003, *The New York Times Magazine* cover read, boldly: "The American Empire (Get Used to It)." Inside was an article titled "The Burden," by Michael Ignatieff, which argued that by virtue of its military might, "the United States rules a new kind of empire" which had been attacked on 9/11.[2] And whether or not this was actually true, the *Times Magazine* had already proposed an answer to an architectural question that was implied by Ignatieff's hypothesis: what does empire look like?

The answer took the form of a "study" published in the *Magazine* on 8 September 2002, with commentary by the *Times* architecture critic Herbert Muschamp. Titled "Thinking Big: A Plan for Ground Zero and Beyond," Muschamp's article celebrated a group of hypothetical projects for the former World Trade Center site and its environs that had been hastily designed by a lineup of star architects accompanied by a few younger upstarts. The study proposed a kind of open-air museum of contemporary architecture, laid out in full accordance with the precepts of the New Urbanism complete with reconstructed "streets," and populated with set pieces executed with futurist élan. Muschamp's text resolved the apparent contradiction—neo-traditionalist planning dressed in avant-garde attire—by declaring: "The product envisioned by the study is a recast cultural identity for 21st century New York: a revised mythology of our place in the era of globalization."[3] In other words, New York's cultural identity—its mythology—was to remain progressive, even as it reorganized itself along the lines of the suburbs created a century earlier as an antidote to the instabilities that "progress" implied. Thus architecture and urbanism were shown to be two (different) sides of the same coin.

THE SURGE

Referring to the "outpouring of images and emotions" in the debates over what should be built on the site, Muschamp wrote: "Fantasies of new buildings became a form of recovery: signs of the city's resilience in the face of unprecedented enemy assault."[4] Architecture's job in a post-9/11 New York, then, was apparently to boost spirits on the homefront while the boys and girls in Washington prepared a counteroffensive. But there were exceptions.

2. Michael Ignatieff, "The Burden," *The New York Times Magazine*, 5 January 2003, 22.
3. Herbert Muschamp, "Thinking Big: A Plan for Ground Zero and Beyond," *The New York Times Magazine*, 8 September 2002, 55.
4. Ibid., 46.

For example: the *Times* showcase included a disarmingly sober contribution by Rem Koolhaas and his colleagues Joshua Ramus and Dan Wood in the New York office of OMA (Office for Metropolitan Architecture). An upside-down office tower growing progressively wider toward the top rather than at the base, "giving extra space to the more desirable and expensive upper floors,"[5] it frankly acknowledged the economic interests that had underwritten New York's modernity since the nineteenth century. It also exhibited a striking silence with respect to these interests. For his part, Muschamp was unable to remain silent, feeling obliged instead to speak against the crassness of developers, on behalf of New York's cosmopolitan multiculturalism and the "relative sophistication of our cultural appetites" which he saw embodied in the *Times* study. With no hint of irony, he declared: "We are one great polyglot aspirational surge."[6] Indifferent, perhaps, to the bloodthirsty aspirations of this "surge," the accompanying images of architecture thus answered the question of what the new empire might look like: "progressive."

TRADITIONS

Still, despite the momentary delusion of those Americans who had responded in unison to the events of 9/11 with the implausible claim that "we are all New Yorkers," it was unclear where the headquarters of new imperium would be. While New York was still the leading candidate, there were others. There was Washington, for one—home of the battle-scarred Pentagon building and the crusading White House. And then there was the pious, traditional "heartland" itself—red in tooth and claw—that would re-elect George W. Bush in 2004.

EAST-WEST

These two apparently unrelated developments—the dismantling of earlier empires and the assembly of others—had already intersected on the far east side of Manhattan beginning in 1946. This was the year when, symbolically, New York went multi-national.

On 10 December 1946, John D. Rockefeller, late of Rockefeller Center, purchased a piece of land on the East River in Manhattan from William Zeckendorf for $8.5 million and donated it to the newly formed United Nations. Wallace Harrison, who had previously worked for both the Rockefellers and Zeckendorf, acted as

5. Ibid., 53.
6. Muschamp, "Thinking Big," 58.

a messenger between them, sealing the deal in a restaurant with a hastily sketched plot plan.[7] From this surreptitious beginning, Harrison went on to lead an international team of architects to design the new UN headquarters.

2.03

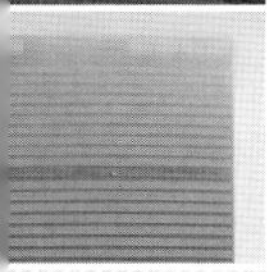

2.04

GROUND ZERO

With a nod to Le Corbusier, the UN designed by Harrison et al collected the various organs of the new, international body into a poised and graceful composition of discreetly articulated shells. Among these organs was the Trusteeship Council which, according to the UN Charter, was intended to "promote the political, economic, social, and educational advancement of the inhabitants of the trust territories [former colonies], and their progressive development towards self-government or independence as may be appropriate to the particular circumstances of each territory and its peoples and the freely expressed wishes of the peoples concerned...."[8] And although India was never in the custody of the Trusteeship Council, the neoclassical monumentality left behind by the British Raj in New Delhi was also left behind by the architecture of the United Nations. In its place rose a new monumentality—a modernist promise of universal rights, of transparent governance, and of a level playing field; a new beginning, from scratch: a ground zero on the East River.

2.05

2.06

2.07

FOLLOW THE MONEY

The UN Secretariat, New York's first truly curtain-walled skyscraper, was the screen on which the city's future was projected. Its gridded patterns were quickly transferred back to the corporate clients (including the Rockefellers) with whom it originated, as the corporation took over from the state as architecture's principal patron. What is more, as a string of well-branded monuments to the new, corporate imperium began to appear just west of the UN along Park Avenue—Lever House, Seagram, Union Carbide—it seemed only a matter of time before lower Manhattan, with its increasingly obsolete "cathedrals of commerce," would give way to midtown as the city's—and the world's—corporate headquarters. At minimum, the skyline circa 1960 testified, like a bar graph with twin peaks, that Manhattan was becoming multi-nodal. Whereas, in one more turn of the

7. George A. Dudley, *A Workshop for Peace: Designing the United Nations Headquarters* (New York: Architectural History Foundation and Cambridge: MIT Press, 1994), 21-28.
8. *Charter of the United Nations*, Chapter XII, Article 76b. For full text, see http://www.un.org/aboutun/charter/.

screw, as downtown doubled up in midtown, midtown's monuments were reproduced downtown. This took the form of a mutation in the architectural genome that recombined the United Nations with Rockefeller Center, resulting in a bifurcation that yielded the Chase Manhattan Bank headquarters on the one hand, and the World Trade Center on the other.

WHISKEY (AN INTERLUDE)

On the midtown skyline one building stood out, sort of. The whiskey-colored Seagram Building was designed as a corporate home for the House of Seagram, through the collaborative efforts of Ludwig Mies van der Rohe and Philip Johnson, and completed in 1958. It has been said that its peerless plaza was single-handedly responsible for catalyzing the 1961 change in New York's zoning laws, which enabled builders to build higher in exchange for leaving a bit of open space below. In 1980, the House of Seagram sold this plaza and its accompanying building to the Teachers Insurance and Annuity Association College Retirement Equities Fund (TIAA-CREF), who bought it to add to their growing real estate portfolio. In 2000, TIAA-CREF sold the building in turn to RFR Holdings LLC, whose architecture collection by then also included Lever House. Meanwhile, the Seagram Building's originality had been confirmed by its reproducibility, not only in the many "lesser" curtain-walled variations in Mies's own *oeuvre*, but in the form of the much lamented "copies" that rapidly infiltrated the New York skyline, including Gordon Bunshaft's Union Carbide Building a few blocks south.

Completed in 1960, the Union Carbide headquarters was a fifty-two story slab set back thirty-three feet from the sidewalk, backed up by a twelve-story annex facing Madison Avenue to the west. At its base was a proto-atrium, in the form of an expansive two-story lobby. Like Seagram, this building eventually proved to be a mere module in the open circuits of exchange. In 1982 Union Carbide sold the building to Manufacturers Hanover and took up residence in a "horizontal skyscraper" designed by Kevin Roche in Danbury, Connecticut, which in turn became an outpost of Dow Chemical when that company bought Union Carbide in 2000. Meanwhile, in 1991 Manufacturers Hanover merged with Chemical Bank, and what was once the Union Carbide Building became the Chemical Bank Building. Shortly thereafter Chemical merged with Chase, precipitating another name change.
And finally, in 2000 Chase merged with JPMorgan, which abandoned its neo-Egyptian atrium-equipped headquarters on Wall Street—also designed by Roche and eventually sold to Deutsche

2.08

2.09

Bank—to take up residence in what became (after 9/11) the very patriotic and very secure JPMorgan Chase Headquarters on Park Avenue—formerly just Chase, formerly Chemical, formerly Manufacturers Hanover, formerly Union Carbide.

2.10

2.11

2.12

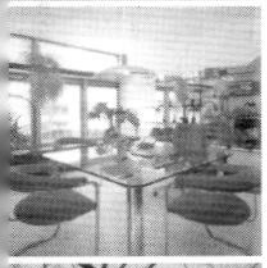
2.13

2.14

CRYSTALS

→ Meanwhile, after carefully analyzing the SOM building in New York, Roche produced its alter-ego in the suburbs. In recognition of the ineluctable logic of the continuous interior, this new building had swallowed its parking garage, from which Carbiders would be disgorged from their cars deep inside the horizontal bar, in close proximity to their offices. Like its predecessor, Union Carbide's new Danbury headquarters was a modular building, though its crenellated plan yielded a giant, crystalline snowflake-like fractal that—unlike Bunshaft's anonymous, urban, original Miesian copy—was made up of a set of modules *each a little different*. These in turn were fitted out in still more finely differentiated systems of interior furnishings, selected by each employee from a variety of fourteen different options as an expression of his or her individuality—his or her personality, even—within the diverse corporate family: a global village for a multi-national corporation, in Connecticut.

More or less simultaneously, Roche also oversaw the displacement of another piece of New York's mid-century multi-national landscape—this time just across the street. As early as 1966, at the request of the Ford Foundation, Roche had prepared plans for the expansion of the United Nations complex on First Avenue just opposite the original buildings. The client for the new complex was global: the United Nations Development Corporation (UNDC). Roche therefore proposed a small world: two mirrored crystalline towers connected by a multilevel concourse. As built in 1985, the visionary concourse was replaced by a utilitarian bridge, but the crystal world above remained.

WORLD TRADE

→ Rewind back to 1946, the year the United Nations project was begun. That same year, New York State set up a "World Trade Corporation" to promote international commerce in order to move more goods through the industrial Port of New York and into the new markets opened up by the war. Although no architectural plans were made, studies were undertaken for the construction of about a million square feet of office space scattered in twenty-one buildings throughout the city. The idea lay dormant until 1956, when the Chase Manhattan Bank under its president, David Rockefeller, decided to move its headquarters to a site in lower Manhattan near Wall Street. Gordon Bunshaft of Skidmore, Owings & Merrill (SOM) was to be the architect. And so "Little Rockefeller Center," as the project became known, brought with it the tower-in-the-plaza model originating at Seagram, and replaced Rockefeller Center's inward focus with an outward glare.

Also in 1946, Rockefeller founded the Downtown-Lower Manhattan Association (DLMA) in order to encourage further development in the Wall Street area and thus shore up his investment. SOM were hired to develop a one hundred-block plan for the revival of the entire financial district. The earlier, unbuilt World Trade Center (WTC) scattered through the city was consolidated in a single complex of large buildings. By 1960, this World Trade Center called for five to six million square feet of office space to be located on a site on the east side of lower Manhattan south of the Brooklyn Bridge. SOM's original scheme for the site amalgamated the United Nations Headquarters with that of Lever House: a set of modernist slabs—banks, offices, and a "world trade mart"—poised on a podium, on which also sat an ovoid object reminiscent of the little dome atop Harrison's UN Assembly building: the relocated stock exchange.

2.15

2.16

2.17

But the capital necessary to realize such megalomania was unavailable. Later that same year (1960), the Port Authority of New York and New Jersey inherited the project from the DLMA and hired the architect Richard Adler to study it further. Adler produced a more detailed scheme that was presented in a report to New York Governor Nelson Rockefeller and other officials in 1961, a year that also saw a proposal for the Port Authority to take over the Hudson and Manhattan transit tubes (now the PATH trains) that connected the city to New Jersey. A piece of legislation that linked this infrastructure with the World Trade Center project failed, however, largely because the east-side location of the Center promised little direct economic benefit for New Jersey. But by late 1961, the World Trade Center project had been revived on a new, west-side site directly over the train termini and thus connected much more directly with the tunnels. New legislation was approved and Adler prepared studies of the new site in which a number of the basic urban planning decisions were made.

TOWERS, OR PUBLIC RELATIONS

It was also around 1961 that the idea of a one hundred-plus story skyscraper was apparently first entertained by the Port Authority's public relations department. Indeed, in a historical echo of things to come after the WTC's demise, by mid-1962 the question of public relations for the project had gained a sufficiently high priority within the Port Authority that Adler, a relative unknown, was relieved of his duties and a national search was launched to find an aesthetically more ambitious architect to re-package the project in a distinct and recognizable image. Among the candidates were Mies (too old), Philip Johnson (not enough experience with skyscrapers), SOM (perpetual insiders), Walter Gropius, and Minoru Yamasaki (a.k.a. "Yama"), who had recently completed a number of important institutional commissions.[9]

2.18

Yama was chosen. His office began working closely with the various technical departments within the Port Authority, as well as with the New York firm of Emery Roth & Sons, who acted as associate architects responsible for overseeing detailing and construction. The design eventually built, which was distinguished by the doubling of its towers (each the tallest in the world), was publicly unveiled in 1964. The scheme overtook the Pentagon as the world's largest office complex, providing ten million square feet of largely speculative office space. Construction of a slightly modified version began in 1966, and in 1970 the World Trade Center concourse opened, with the lower ring of buildings, (Numbers 4, 5 and 6) complete. The first tower, No. 1 World Trade Center, which was the first to be hit on 11 September 2001, opened in 1973. Building No. 2, the second to be hit but the first to fall, opened in 1976, completing the first phase of the project.

PLAZAS

Meanwhile, having failed at the World Trade Center, SOM kept itself busy on other projects nearby. Prominent among these were the smooth, extruded trapezoid of the Marine Midland Bank headquarters (1967) just to the west of the Chase tower, and the ponderous headquarters of US Steel one block further west at 1 Liberty Street (1972), directly across from the twin towers. Together the three—Chase, Marine Midland, US Steel—formed a string of corporate monuments with adjacent plazas to rival

2.19

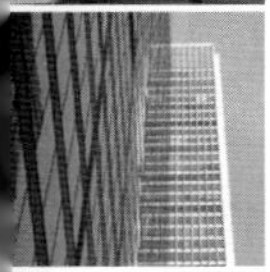
2.20

2.21

2.22

9. See Eric Darton, *Divided We Stand: A Biography of New York's World Trade Center* (New York: Basic Books, 1999), 114-117; and Anthony Robbins, *The World Trade Center* (Englewood, FL and Fort Lauderdale: Pineapple Press and Omnigraphics, Inc., 1987), 19-27. On the history of the World Trade Center, see also Angus Kress Gillespie, *Twin Towers: The Life of New York City's World Trade Center* (New Brunswick, NJ: Rutgers University Press, 1999).

those on Park Avenue (and later, on Sixth), while cutting a swath through the city fabric that reunited the World Trade Center —realized under the gubernatorial aegis of David's brother, Nelson Rockefeller—with its secret sibling Chase Plaza (or "Little Rockefeller Center") at the other end.

THE CONTINUOUS INTERIOR, AGAIN

2.23

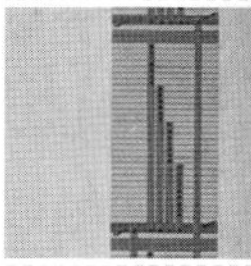

But where the windswept plazas of Chase and its neighbors poignantly established a sequence of ground zeros—a series of empty planes haunted by the ghosts of vanished urban crowds—the World Trade Center decisively relocated these crowds to the suburbs. This relocation was accomplished underground, in the PATH trains and subway lines connected to the shopping concourse below the infamous plaza. These connections converted the twin towers into a node in a network, a continuous interior singularized in the daily ritual of a typical commuter: from house to car to train to concourse to lobby to elevator to office, and back again.

Like its predecessor the United Nations, the World Trade Center was therefore not— strictly speaking—in New York. But where the UN's territorial dislocation was secured by the fence running round its perimeter that marked off, physically and juridically, an island of international territory exempt from the city grid and its laws, at the World Trade Center the dislocation occurred from the inside out. Not only was it possible for an out-of-town office worker to occupy the towers daily without ever entering Manhattan's streets; not only was the Center owned and operated by the bi-state Port Authority, an agency also responsible for the region's airports; not only did its scale, its abstraction, its empty plaza render it an alien craft stranded in the grid. The World Trade Center was also never exactly *in* New York because it was never really a center.

PLANES

2.24

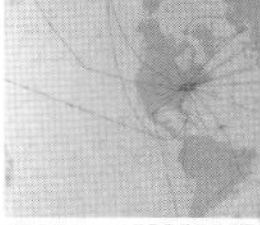

An early Port Authority press release for the project showed the virtual axes of business travel as dotted lines on a globe traced by airplanes uncannily headed directly toward the towers. At the level of imperial fantasy, this was a mid-twentieth century version of all roads leading to Rome. As such, it was also a magnification of the urban axes inscribed into New Delhi that converged on the monumental center of British rule. Still, the very presence of these airplanes on the Port Authority's diagram indicated that things were being pulled apart even as they were being linked together. If the World Trade Center was to serve as an icon, a monumental destination, it would only do so by doubling itself up, by multiplying. Thus, at the center of world trade was a gap, a space between—between towers, between cities, between nations, between worlds—that was forever traversed by the continuous interiors of global business and yet, forever opened up.

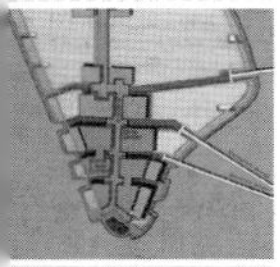
2.25

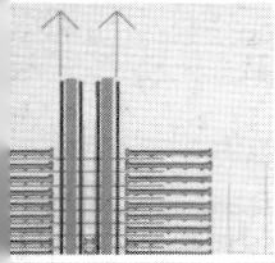
2.26

2.27

TREES

The theory for all of this was supplied by the Regional Plan Association of New York (RPA), in a document titled *Urban Design Manhattan*, a manifesto attached to the RPA's Second Regional Plan of 1969. Disguised as a defense of the "forgotten man"—the pedestrian—the plan actually proposed an amalgamation of midtown and downtown into a single, multi-nodal Central Business District (CBD) organized around what its authors called "Access Trees," or infrastructural hubs located at major transit interchanges that channeled office workers efficiently through the circuitry of the continuous interior. In the Access Tree, "roots, trunks, branches and leaves and the fluids moving along these paths" became "underground trains and platforms, the stairs, ramps, and elevators, corridors, offices and the people who use them."[10]

At the center of each cluster, sunken below the street, was an open-air "mixing chamber." But this was no homecoming for the pedestrian, no return to the nineteenth century stroll along the boulevards. Since, in the century that separated Charles Baudelaire's dandified perambulations from the white-collar conformism of *Urban Design Manhattan*, and the Parisian arcades from New York's Access Trees, the *flanêur*—Baudelaire's aimless urban wanderer—had become a commuter. And the Access Tree was above all else a machine for commuting, a regional transportation system extrapolated into corridors and elevator banks that converted its inhabitants into abstract "fluids" pulsating through prescribed channels, like the equally abstract, equally fluid personages pulsing through the channels on the television sets that awaited them at home, at the other end of their confinement. And like the television set, the mixing chamber was a valve. Through it, channels passed, their fluids flowing momentarily together, then separating again.

Emboldened by the pastoral vision of their arborescent model, the bureaucrats at the RPA demonstrated its applicability to the CBD with a case study in midtown. Quoting Le Corbusier,

10. Rai Y. Okamoto, Frank E. Williams, Klaus Huboi, Dietrich Kunkel, Carlisle Towery, and C. McKim Norton, Stanley B. Tankel, Boris Pushkarev, and William B. Shore, *Urban Design Manhattan* (New York, Viking Press, 1969), 31.

Sant' Elia, and Eugène Hénard, they imagined a densification of Manhattan's west side equivalent to "66 additional Time-Life Buildings" by the year 2000.[11] To illustrate, these were drawn in a repetitive, gridded array worthy of Ludwig Hilberseimer, on thirty-three blocks between Eighth and Eleventh Avenues, from Forty-Fifth to Fifty-Fifth Streets, with two forty-eight-story Time-Life Buildings per block.

The diagram thus extrapolated the blank repetition of Wallace Harrison and Max Abramovitz's "XYZ" Buildings—immediately adjacent to Harrison and Abramovitz's earlier Time-Life Building on Sixth Avenue—into an urbanism of its own. A decade later Rem Koolhaas would decry these buildings in a "postmortem" appended to *Delirious New York* as "Manhattanism unlearned… simple extrusions of the site," while also noting (with hopeful circularity) that after XYZ comes A again—a return to origins and, presumably, a reawakening of the rather more delirious Rockefeller Center model.[12] Koolhaas's wishful thinking notwithstanding, in its XYZ repetitions, as in the Rockefeller-backed WTC that followed their lead, Rockefeller Center's lively delirium was in fact exhausted. So much so that Peter Blake would later accuse Harrison of murder—of having perpetrated (with accomplices) what Blake called a "Slaughter on Sixth Avenue."[13]

2.28
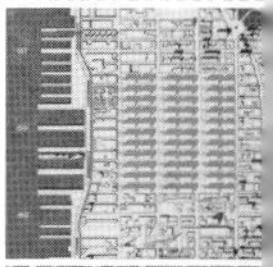

2.29

2.30

2.31

But the RPA planners were quick to add that their diagram should not be taken literally, warning that the Time-Life module was merely representative, and that "future buildings will vary in size… and are neither expected nor desired to be located in the diagrammatic arrangement" shown.[14] So what did the planners actually have in mind? Their "Form Response Diagram" shows the Hilberseimer field converted into a cluster of Access Trees grown up around a multilevel "mixing chamber" at Tenth Avenue and Forty-Second Street, and connected to other similar clusters in the CBD: around Penn Station, around Grand Central, and around Rockefeller Center, with other, smaller clusters at Tenth Avenue and Fiftieth Street and Tenth Avenue and Thirty-Fourth Street. In this vision, which was no less probable than the construction of two one hundred-ten-story towers downtown, the CBD had become a network. This network was organized by an infrastructural diagram that illustrated existing and potential movement systems connecting the CBD to itself and to its periphery at a variety of scales and speeds: pedestrians above and below grade, crosstown shuttles, subways, automobiles,

2.32

11. Okamoto et al, *Urban Design Manhattan*, 11.

12. Rem Koolhaas, *Delirious New York: A Retroactive Manifesto* (New York: Oxford University Press, 1978), 240.

13. Peter Blake, "Slaughter on 6th Avenue," *Architectural Forum* 122, no. 3 (June 1965), 18-22.

14. Okamoto et al, *Urban Design Manhattan*, 68.

commuter and regional rail lines, all supplemented by a hypothetical "gravity vacuum tube" system underground.

The net result of all this networking was a displacement, a decentralization of the Central Business District not externally, but internally. Now distributed into a system of linked-up but separate centers with megastructural office complexes atop transportation hubs and shopping concourses, the RPA's imaginary CBD was both more and less dense at the same time. Its sixty-six new Time Life Buildings were redistributed throughout midtown in different shapes and sizes, grouped in clusters of five to fifteen, but also split apart to such a degree that it was necessary to invoke the science fiction of "gravity vacuum tubes" to hold them all together. In fact, in the fertile imaginations of the RPA bureaucrats, the CBD was spinning uncontrollably on its axis, sending parts of itself flying off into space, centrifugally, even as it gathered itself together into ever tighter, ever denser concentrations, centripetally.

And the first thing to go with all the spinning was the ground itself. Here we can hear *Urban Design Manhattan* crying out: all the slaughters, all the dead bodies, all the commuters, all the windswept plazas past and present (from Chase to the WTC to...) are to be swept up into this new vortex, this new field of networked forests, the urban jungle, reborn! And more: the jungle will be multilevel, since—in a beautiful tautology—the erosion of the ground plane and the erasure of the empty plaza by multilevel "mixing chambers" was to be both the cause and the effect of reforestation. But which comes first, the roots or the tree? Public infrastructure or private development? No comment. Still, it was a forthright dream, vividly captured in diagrams of hyperconnection to the suburbs and beyond. And the city thus imagined was quite literally groundless—not because it had no base in so-called reality (these were sober bureaucrats), but because it was all too close to the new realities of the city. There, on the ground, urban space had given way to the continuous interior, an ungrounded, uprooted, displaced space in which even trees the size of skyscrapers had difficulty taking root.

2.33

2.34

THE CITI IS (NOT) A TREE

→ Witness Citicorp. The World Trade Center may well have been the first realization of the Access Tree principle, if not its secret inspiration: a super-connected infrastructural machine complete with "mixing chamber" (the underground PATH escalator bank) that secured its isolation from the surrounding city. But the complex that followed the Access Tree diagram more faithfully, and certainly belongs among is progeny,

2.35

2.36

was midtown's Citicorp Center. It was an imperfect realization, to be sure (only one tower, not a cluster), but a realization nonetheless.

2.37

2.38

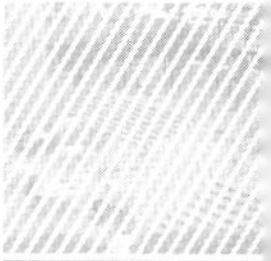

Designed by Hugh Stubbins and completed in 1977, Citicorp Center represented a commitment, on the part of Citibank and its holding company Citicorp, to a near-bankrupt city threatened by the erosion of its tax base as corporations and their constituents fled to the suburbs. But it also represented a penetration of extra-urban space back inside, deep into the heart of the metropolis. A suburbanization of the CBD that was made possible by the Access Tree strategy, Citicorp Center consisted of a sixty-five-story skyscraper, square in plan, lifted off its base by four colossal columns poised at the midpoints of each of its sides. Incorporated into this base was an eight-story atrium, a shopping mall equivalent in content if not in size to that located below the World Trade Center's plaza. At Citicorp, however, mall and plaza switched places, with the open space required by zoning incentives allowing extra height now sunken below street level. Through this "mixing chamber" a subway station poured its commuters into the building's atrium and from there, to their respective cubicles above. The continuous interior—which at the World Trade Center and its predecessors had left the plaza behind as a windswept, negative monument to an impossible collectivity—had now incorporated a fragment of the suburban "outside" into itself. This incorporation was echoed by the ominous staircases leading down from the street—points of no return for the streetwalking *flanêur*, and for the modern metropolis itself.

Meanwhile, on the roof, pitched at forty-five degrees toward the south, one hundred units of luxury residential condominiums were projected, in a Manhattan-style version of terraced, hilltop housing. But an uncooperative market forced the conversion of the building's signature crown to a mere solar collector, which itself never saw the light of day due to an MIT study that deemed it unlikely to be cost-effective after all. So Citicorp's slant, which some have read in the tradition of seventies supergraphics as the peak of a giant number "1," turned out to be just as arbitrary as the signifiers floating in the form of dollar signs through bank's global channels on a daily basis. "Space-age architecture," its architect Stubbins called it.[15]

But as at the WTC downtown, in place of a "center" for Citicorp there were only gaps, holes, *dis*placements. Indeed, Citi*bank* was actually headquartered one block further west, in a curtain-

15. Dianne M. Ludman, *Hugh Stubbins and His Associates: The First Fifty Years* (Cambridge, MA: Stubbins Associates, 1986)

walled tower designed by SOM at 399 Park Avenue. Citi*corp*, which did relocate to the new building, was set up in 1961 as the First National City Overseas Investment Corporation to accommodate the bank's subsidiaries and affiliates overseas, which were managed on a country-by-country basis. During the late 1960s and 1970s, the bank also diversified its business into other investment arenas. Among these was real estate. Citicorp Center itself was primarily a real estate investment that began with the secret, systematic acquisition of parcels comprising an entire urban block by No Name Realty (yes, really), an entity invented for the purpose of concealing the company's interest in the land to keep prices down.[16]

2.39

1968: THE MATRIX

Beginning in late 1968, a year marked by international protests against an increasingly abstract, increasingly diversified "system," Citibank formally abstracted itself into a diversified, decentralized system under what was known as "matrix management" in order to control its newfound complexity. By the late 1960s Citibank was doing business in dozens of countries, and its president and future CEO Walter Wriston had his eyes on an increasingly global financial market. Dissatisfied with the capacity of so-called relationship banking—business relationships cultivated over time with local clients—to respond to such ambitions, Wriston sought the advice of the management decentralization guru Peter Drucker, who suggested decentralization. Drucker also suggested that Wriston hire the consultants McKinsey & Company to obtain the same advice. Thus was born Citibank's "matrix," a decentralized scheme in which the bank was reorganized into six business divisions: corporate, commercial, retail, operations, overseas, and investment management.[17]

In the matrix, there was movement—movement of employees, managers, and capital across the different business sectors and across national borders. In place of "relationships," the bottom line became the bottom line: profit and loss. And so, even as Citibank/Citicorp sought to center itself in midtown in New York's new Central Business District (CBD), it spun itself off locally and globally. The lubricant for all the spinning was capital. Specifically, it was international finance capital lubricated by petrodollars and by the liquidation of the Bretton Woods Accords, which had formerly restricted the scope of inter-

16. Philip L. Zweig, *Wriston: Walter Wriston, Citibank, and the Rise and Fall of American Financial Supremacy* (New York: Crown Publishers, 1995).
17. Ibid., 242-273.

national banking by regulating currencies pinned to dollars that were pinned, in turn, to gold. By all accounts Citibank was first and most aggressive in accelerating this deregulation, embarking on a program of "Third World" lending that would lead, eventually, to a debt crisis in which Citi's rhizomatic (as opposed to arborescent), matrix-like overextensions would be shown to have been as much geopolitical as financial. But in the meantime, during the late 1970s as it built its Access Tree in midtown, Citibank/Citicorp would proliferate across borders of all kinds, decentering and recentering around ever-mutating topologies: industry-related alliances, service to and competition with other MNCs (multi-national corporations), regional hegemonies and counter-hegemonies, and so on.

THE ATRIUM, AGAIN

But if Citibank's chief rival with an equally metropolitan name—the Rockefeller-led Chase Manhattan Bank—had long ago relocated from midtown to downtown, Citicorp's vision of midtown was also in the process of relocating: inside.

In 1983, two towers could be seen rising on adjacent blocks on Madison Avenue. At Fifty-Seventh Street was the IBM Building, designed by the modernist Edward Larrabee Barnes. While at Fifty-Sixth Street was the AT&T Building, designed by the post-modern Philip Johnson and completed in 1984. The pairing repeated another, earlier one, when Eero Saarinen designed—simultaneously—suburban laboratories for IBM and for AT&T's research wing, Bell Laboratories. The latter building was among the first to incorporate what would become the corporate atrium: an "X" drawn across the plan dividing the building into quadrants while bringing the outside in, in the interest of programmed relaxation. However, the apotheosis of the internalized atrium is arguably to be found just a few blocks west from the UN on Forty-Second Street, in the Ford Foundation Headquarters. Completed in 1968 by Saarinen's successor firm, Kevin Roche John Dinkeloo and Associates, the Ford Foundation housed a veritable forest designed by the landscape architect Dan Kiley, who had also consulted on Saarinen's effort at Bell Labs.

Meanwhile just a little further west, on Madison Avenue, the reverse was happening. Skyscrapers were sprouting atria on the outside—extensions of themselves that systematically swallowed up the "public space" (or zoning incentive) formerly known as a plaza. In order to do so, the towers were politely lifted up off the ground plane a bit—not as heroically as at Citicorp, but decisively nonetheless. At IBM, a void was cut out at one corner, leaving the tower to cantilever perilously above, while the AT&T

2.40

2.41

2.42

2.43

2.44

2.45

2.46

2.47

2.48

2.49

2.50

2.51

2.52

2.53

2.54

2.55

Building perched atop an outsized classical colonnade. Slipped underneath and adjacent were two glass enclosures: at IBM, a bamboo-filled, triangulated "winter garden" (the missing corner moved one block south?), and at AT&T a vaulted passage so overscaled (to match the building's Chippendale top) as to render any comparison to earlier arcades a little strained.

So where Citicorp sunk its zoning-required plaza to bring it closer to the subway lines underneath, in the absence of infrastructure these other two monoliths internalized theirs, thus rehearsing the street-level defeat that had already occurred two decades ago in the string of empty plazas downtown. Also in 1983, these two were joined by the Trump Tower one block west, designed by Der Scutt with Swanke Hayden and Connell, whose pseudo-gilded atrium (complete with waterfall) was linked mid-block with its more restrained neighbor at IBM. Thus, what Chase-Marine Midland-US Steel-WTC were to the plaza, IBM-AT&T-Trump were to the atrium. Where at Citicorp and at the WTC the continuous interior could still be imagined as full of commuters circling to and fro, here it was empty, even when filled with people. Absent infrastructure—the bridges, tunnels, and subways that displaced the CBD even as they supplied it with requisite "fluids"—the corporate atrium could only replace Access Trees clustered outdoors (as foreseen by the RPA planners) with potted plants and furniture, indoors. The Trump Tower took this one step further, by incorporating a triangular stand of trees into its cascading exterior terraces. But already at IBM, the Access Tree had become a stand of domesticated bamboo, while at AT&T, it was cut off, cut down, and converted—remorselessly—into a giant grandfather clock.

WORLD FINANCE

Still, perhaps New York's most famous trees remain the sixteen *Washingtonia robusta* palm trees from the Mojave desert embedded in the marble floor at Cesar Pelli's World Financial Center atrium, which is officially called the Winter Garden and forms the symbolic heart of lower Manhattan's most complete piece of suburbia to date, Battery Park City. Pelli had established his atrium-building credentials as early as 1977, when he successfully converted the Museum of Modern Art into a faux-suburban shopping mall, with an income-generating residential tower attached. Begun in 1981 (while the MoMA expansion was under construction) and completed in 1988, the World Financial Center (WFC) was a collaboration between Pelli, various executive architects, the landscape firm of M. Paul Friedberg and Associates (atrium and plaza), and the client, Olympia & York

Equity Corporation. It consisted of four towers ranging from thirty-three to fifty-four stories, arrayed around the glass, steel, marble, and palm atrium. Each tower was given a different, "distinctive" top. North to south: ziggurat, pyramid, hemisphere, and truncated pyramid—each top, like its tower, a little squat. Hovering immediately above and behind them was the World Trade Center.

The complex was built on 13.5 acres of landfill and housed a total of about 6.5 million square feet of space, six million of it office, the rest retail and "public." Olympia & York (O&Y) invested $1.2 billion in the project. Having overextended itself in its enthusiasm for post-urban, post-modern waterfront developments with further adventures at London's Canary Wharf and elsewhere, O&Y paid the price with a monumental restructuring in 1992 that reinvented the firm under the reassuring name of Brookfield Financial Properties. Still, the WFC—and in particular, the Winter Garden—had become lodged so deeply in the imaginary landscape that is called New York, that the first piece of architecture to be rebuilt (literally, faithfully, uncannily) following the events of 11 September 2001 was Pelli's atrium.

OFF CENTER

2.56

2.57

Meanwhile, the proliferation of "centers" downtown found an echo across the river, spinning off another Pelli on the shores of Jersey City, with its own (projected) atrium ("The Terraces"). This was the Goldman Sachs Tower, designed by Pelli in collaboration with SOM and completed in 2004.[18] It was a key monument in what *New Yorker* architecture critic Paul Goldberger called a new "Shanghai on the Hudson." It also resulted in a face-off of Pellis—the World Financial Center looking west, Goldman Sachs returning its gaze in near-axial alignment, eastward. Here, straddling the Hudson, the city became a hall of mirrors, in which the "center"—tower-plus-atrium—is endlessly reflected, back in and back out.

But during construction, an internal rebellion broke out amongst Goldman Sachs employees. Apparently, many were not ready to abandon the company's existing headquarters at 85 Broad Street (SOM, 1984) or other buildings nearby, and decamp to New Jersey. Relocation plans were revised. By mid-2004 for the most part only back-office and support functions and those who performed them had made the trip across the river to Jersey City, which had become the New York metropolitan area's version of

18. Paul Goldberger, "The Sky Line: Shanghai on the Hudson," *The New Yorker* 80, no. 21 (2 August 2004): 76-78.

back-office parks like those in Shanghai, or in India's IT sectors in Bangalore, Gurgaon, and elsewhere. And like their counterparts across the globe, these new worlds-without-qualities on the Jersey shoreline were given meaningful, upwardly mobile names, again with no hint of irony: Newport (with its Southampton and East Hampton Towers) and Harborside.

Meanwhile, to accommodate recalcitrant executives and their constituents, Goldman Sachs hired Pei Cobb Fried to design a new office building in lower Manhattan just opposite the one in Jersey City. It was to be located in Battery Park City, next to Pelli's four original towers, in a further mirroring of Pelli's mirrors. Renderings were released in May 2004: Two million square feet, including six 75,000 square foot trading floors (each equipped with one thousand shouting traders), and a tree-lined street. No atrium.

But all was not lost. More monuments to an uncertain future were on New York's internal horizon, though they had moved back up to midtown again. Among these was one designed by Pelli at 731 Lexington Avenue (between Fifty-Eighth and Fifty-Ninth Streets). This building was known as the Bloomberg Tower, in honor of New York mayor Michael Bloomberg's eponymous empire, Bloomberg LP, whose headquarters it now housed. Between Bloomberg's slender fifty-five story spire and its adjacent seven-story shopping complex was something called One Beacon Court, a neo-baroque *exterior* "public space" equipped with vehicular drop-off and glass canopies. The first thirty floors of the tower itself were dedicated to offices. While upstairs on floors thirty-one to fifty-five was something special: one hundred luxury condominium apartments—Citicorp's forgotten residential dream realized, five blocks uptown.

2.58

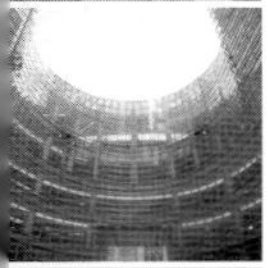
2.59

TWC

2.60

Even so, Bloomberg's polite mixture of uses—luxurious living above, only slightly less luxurious working below, with convenient shopping next door—was only a shadow of what was rising simultaneously just a few blocks west on Fifty-Ninth Street, at Columbus Circle. This was the former AOL-Time Warner Center, which changed its name after old media and new media went their separate ways, following the irrationally exuberant merger of America Online (AOL) and Time Warner Communications in early 2001. On 19 September 2003 Time Warner officially dropped the "AOL" from its name and from its stock symbol, which returned to the original "TWX." And so the new building nearing completion in midtown became just the Time Warner Center (TWC), under which name it opened to great fanfare in early 2004.

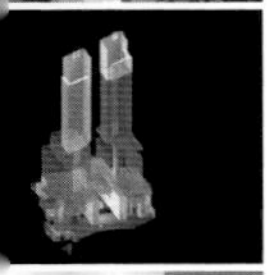
2.61

2.62

Though like its comrades it was hardly at the “center” of anything, the TWC was more than just a building. Designed by David Childs of SOM (future architect of Ground Zero), with the Related Companies as developer-clients, it was at least seven buildings rolled into one. Each of its two angular glass towers contained multiple functions served by multiple lobbies and multiple elevator banks. In the north tower, luxury hi-rise living sat atop a luxury hotel, which in turn sat atop a speculative office building. In the south tower, residential condominiums were crossed with Time Warner’s new headquarters featuring CNN’s new studios, in which news anchors sat poised against the dramatic backdrop of a new New York outside. Below, in the six-story base out of which the two towers sprang, was an arching interior “street” (by any other name a shopping mall). Above the “street” and below the towers was a string of gourmet restaurants and an acoustically isolated building-within-a-building designed by Raphael Viñoly to house “Jazz at Lincoln Center,” whose geographically inaccurate name signaled more than just a little uncertainty as to the cultural cachet offered by its actual location atop a shopping mall.

2.63

2.64

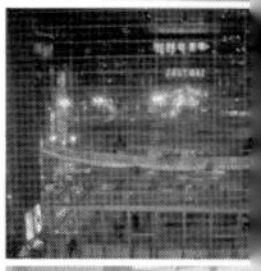

2.65

2.66

Viñoly’s outward-looking auditorium was separated from Columbus Circle by an exquisite filigree of hyper-transparent glass extending down to street level. Designed by the artist-engineer Jaime Carpenter, this veil confirmed the TWC’s real project: to absorb the street into the atrium through an act of sheer architectural will. The TWC’s near-invisible glass wall well-nigh accomplished this, as it opened the atrium/mall’s interior “plaza” to the renovated Columbus Circle outside, and onto a vista that also took in Bloomberg’s tower a few blocks further east on Fifty-Ninth Street. Inside, it was abundantly clear that the relaxed shoppers passing casually through were—properly speaking—no longer in Manhattan, or at least not in the Manhattan that spawned Koolhaas’s “culture of congestion” and other, associated deliria.

But neither were they merely in the anesthetic suburbs transplanted back into the city, via the circuitous routes followed by the continuous interior and its atriums. They were, as the saying goes, in their own world. As such, they were rootless. Like the signs drifting across the building’s “street” façades (inside and out), they floated. As did the building itself, despite architectural efforts to anchor it to a non-existent “context” by way of a plaza-less street wall clad in wafer-thin slabs of granite. What is more, the TWC decisively cut off the roots of the Access Tree envisioned for the site by the RPA planners twenty-five years earlier.

Thanks in part to the efforts of preservationists concerned with the shadow that a larger building would have cast over

Central Park, the project had been scaled down since its initial conception in 1985, which had taken the form of twin post-modern towers designed by Moishe Safdie in association with Emery Roth & Sons and the developer Mortimer Zuckerman of Boston Properties. Thus the new, shrunken complex–irony of ironies–was no longer subject (by virtue of its reduced bulk) to the requirement that the builders "give back" something to the general public in the form of a renovated subway station immediately below, which would have been tied into the larger complex above in the tradition of the Access Tree.[19] This, in the end, was not a building designed for those who ride the subway.

Even more than its predecessor the WTC, which literally floated on the banks of the Hudson in a structural "bathtub," the TWC was a boat set adrift on the global seas. Below it lay what was left of the old city. While on this boat was, in theory, an entire world, *the* entire world–a perfect Noah's Ark of hermetically-sealed living, working, leisure, and circulation all tangled up and wrapped in a glass skin outside, and a multicolored, themed "environment" inside. Conceivably, a new race of multi-ethnic globe-trotting condo owners could now stay at home, content to procreate upstairs and sustain themselves downstairs, moving in a continuous, closed loop from elevator to elevator along the way–a Silicon Valley-like commute in microcosm, wrapped in mahogony veneer and stylish stainless steel.

Most melodramatic of all, however, was that the contextualist TWC explicitly revisited and repeated the secret origin of the WTC's twin towers–Emery Roth's doubled-up residential towers (the San Remo and the El Dorado), which were themselves doubled up by Irwin Chanin's double twin towers (the Century and the Majestic), all on nearby Central Park West. In doing so, the TWC nearly succeeded in neutralizing the dreaded emptiness–the allegedly meaningless neutrality–of the WTC's plaza, by replacing it with meaningful "experiences" to be had browsing possible lifestyles in the new exurban interior, alongside the potted plants.

But is it possible that the "elsewhere" embodied by the TWC might also be tinged with a hint of something else despite itself–an escape from the stifling imperatives of contextualism at the height of its powers, or perhaps even a liberation from meaning through sheer exhaustion? And might this inadvertent utopia even harbor, by virtue of its tangible otherworldliness, hints of real collectivity, as when the elevator doors close and all are stuck in either: 1. A Sartrean hell of unwanted and unwelcome intimacy, or 2. An actual public space? Or, again, are the possible contours of such collectives–formed temporarily

19. Charles Linn, Alan Joch, and James S. Russell, "The Making of AOL Time Warner Center," *Architectural Record* 191, no. 6 (June 2003): 86-94.

in the deepest interior of the continuous interior—already limited by who is allowed out of the subway, past the security guard, and onto the elevator in the first place?

WAR

While all of this was going on in midtown, plans were afoot to "rebuild" the emptiness full of people that was the World Trade Center, downtown. And this time around, all involved were determined that the result be, well, meaningful. The failure of the six schemes first proposed for the site by Beyer Blinder Belle and Peterson/Littenberg, with their strained allusions to New York's "history" (in the form of Rockefeller Center look-alikes), had momentarily opened the door to other possibilities. That door was promptly closed, however, even as the Lower Manhattan Development Council (or LMDC, which controlled the site) issued an emergency plea for more "innovative" designs. Since, this call for innovation was also a call to arms. As transparent as the glass veil stretched across the TWC's atrium, the newly closed door on New York's future concealed nothing behind its "progressive" veneer, as a panic-stricken nation embarked on its zealous crusade, its "war on terror."

Enter Daniel Libeskind, a lone *auteur* competing against five other teams selected by the LMDC. Each of the resulting schemes had its merits. But with the possible exception of the blank mega-grid offered by New York's "home team"—Peter Eisenman, Richard Meier, Charles Gwathmey, Steven Holl—one after the other they managed to reach new, unbearable heights of architecture made meaningful. In the end however, none could compete with Libeskind in satisfying the tendency towards Disney then under construction at the Time Warner Center and slowly drifting downtown. The group of young digerati called (yet again without irony) the United Architects may have come the closest, despite their poor showing in the polls. At minimum, their twisting, crystalline "cathedral" (as they called it) managed to produce an unholy alliance of spirituality and marketing in tune with various fundamentalisms—Cass Gilbert's "cathedral of commerce" meets Philip Johnson's Crystal Cathedral—second only to Libeskind's surge of aestheticized aggression. Either way, the "war on terror" had found its avant-garde.

THE CENTRIPETAL / CENTRIFUGAL SPIRAL

Unable to withstand the pathos downtown, other architects looked to Silicon Valley for an antidote. Was it possible that clues to the future of cities could be found *outside* the "city"? Or was this mere nostalgia for the recently burst bubble of the new economy? Jersey City and its doubles were also considered: Queens West (just east of SOM's lonely Citibank Tower Queens), Brooklyn's Metro Park (SOM again), the new suburbs (complete with HOK football stadium) being contemplated on Manhattan's far west side, and even the office landscapes in White Plains (a new back-office magnet) as well as those near Princeton. Pinpointed on a map, these sites formed a spiral of decentralization that again somehow twisted back inward. With each successive wave of suburban development came a new concentration of towers and their accessories on Manhattan's little island: in the 1950s, Park Avenue; in the 1960s, Sixth Avenue; in the 1970s, the WTC, Citicorp, and friends; in the 1980s, the World Financial Center (WFC), AT&T, IBM, etc.; and after an incubation period in Silicon Valley during the 1990s, the (AOL)TWC.

Extended further still, this corporate spiral—centripetal and centrifugal at once—passed through the new information landscapes of IT parks worldwide, in which Silicon Valley's hallucinatory dream was being dreamt anew. But for the moment, all roads still led back to Rome, or at least to lower Manhattan. Like those civil defense diagrams drawn since the 1950s that had Wall Street, street of dreams, at the center of an atomic bulls-eye, or the world map dreamed up by the WTC's planners that already showed the flight paths of airplanes headed toward the towers, this spiral diagrammed the irresistible, gravitational force-field of that black hole called Ground Zero. It was there that empire's dreams lay smoldering, and it was there that coming nightmares were being prepared.

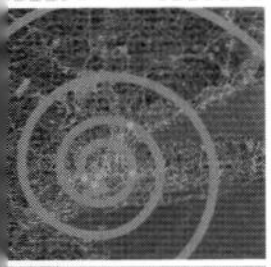
2.67

2.68

NUMBER ONE

Immediately prior to 9/11, Martin/Baxi Architects (M/BA) had been collaborating with Patrice Derrington (who would later become the LMDC's Vice President for Corporate Finance) on another project in lower Manhattan. This was the addition of a rooftop penthouse to a nineteenth century office building overlooking Battery Park, whose near-mythic address—No. 1 Broadway—was enough to make it a landmark. There, under the legal constraint not to alter the existing exterior shell of the building, M/BA applied The Atrium Principle already developed in Silicon Valley: a small rooftop structure was emptied of its contents and wrapped in glass shell, with access from behind under a pair of monocoque shells. The iMac Principle also found modest application, with each piece of tinted, reflective glass just a little different—gradually less reflective and less tinted, from east to west—in a gradient of opacity and reflection behind which emerged the shell of the original structure. This superimposition also produced a south-facing double skin that acted as an environmental buffer zone through which heated air could be circulated passively.

But most importantly, this small penthouse had no program. Designed as both an amenity and an investment for an investor who had recently acquired the building, the space deliberately oscillated between conventional office, executive conference suite (rentable), event space (rentable), and unofficial *pied-à-terre* (personal). Such programmatic indeterminacy was structurally necessary given the economics of investment. All had to be as fluid as possible while remaining usable during an unspecified interim period, in anticipation of the increased value of the property by virtue of its prime location in a slowly transforming lower Manhattan. Then suddenly one bright blue morning, No. 1 Broadway was covered in the gray dust of what used to be the World Trade Center. The future of lower Manhattan was now uncertain, and the project was over before it began.

A REPORT

2.69

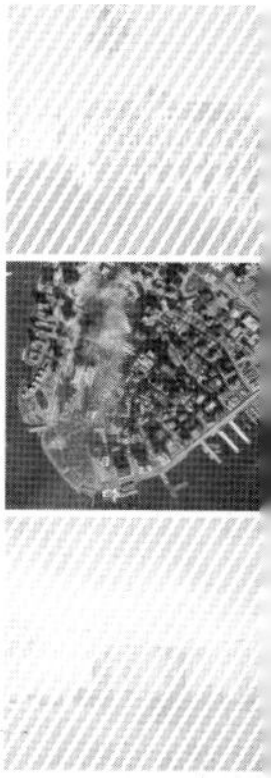

During the months that followed, Derrington, now at the LMDC, co-authored an internal LMDC document titled "Revitalization Strategy for Lower Manhattan," which was issued in 2002 but never received wide circulation.[20] The report, which was based on a study by McKinsey & Company, gestured appropriately to the economic jargon that underwrote the tendency toward Disney, as income-generating office space was already being reduced to make room for the exertion of architectural finesse, mainly in the form of themed memorial "experiences." But the LMDC's "Revitalization Strategy for Lower Manhattan" actually recommended just the opposite: extreme commercial density, without apology.

In a chart that distilled the report to its essence, three development scenarios were compared. The first "base case" scenario was essentially to restore lower Manhattan to its status as a "second CBD" prior to 9/11 by rebuilding ten to twelve million square feet of office space, with five thousand new housing units and two million square feet of retail. The second scenario, favoring "residents and tourists," described the direction already being pursued by the LMDC, despite all the fanfare about office towers: nudging lower Manhattan gently toward the suburbs, by building far less office space (five to six million

20. Lower Manhattan Development Corporation Department of Corporate Development and Economics, "Revitalization Strategy for Lower Manhattan," internal report, December 2002.

square feet) than was destroyed, and far more (high-end) residential space (seventeen thousand units), with 2.5 million square feet of retail. Compared to the break-even "base case" of the first scenario, it was projected that this formula would cost the city $6 billion in lost revenue and twenty-five thousand jobs.[21]

By mid-2004, as the cornerstone for the ostentatiously named Freedom Tower was being laid with Republican ceremony, this was roughly the scenario on the boards, minus the residential space. The main tower, designed by Childs (with Libeskind relegated to a supporting role) provided only 2.6 million square feet of office space. Add the other office tower designed by Childs just off-site—No. 7 World Trade Center—with its 1.65 million square feet, and you still get only 4.25 million square feet. Only an eleventh-hour judgment in an arcane court battle suggested that higher densities remained possible, by holding that what is called "9/11" actually occurred twice (two planes + two towers = two "events"), thus entitling WTC leaseholder Larry Silverstein to twice the insurance money and theoretically at least, twice the building. Still, in the interim, a process of Disneyfication had been set in motion that left Silverstein and his dollars to contend with all of the "culture" already cluttering the site—memorials, museums, and so on.

The third development scenario contemplated and, in this case, advocated in the LMDC report envisioned lower Manhattan as a "Global Downtown." For this, fifteen to eighteen million square feet of office space were proposed—one and one-half times as much as in the original WTC—with seven thousand new housing units and 2.5 million square feet of retail. This was a "build it and they will come" scenario, premised on upgraded connectivity to area airports already being planned, and new state-of-the-art technological infrastructure to support the round-the-clock needs of global business. The return on investment was projected as a net gain of $13 billion in revenue for the city and fifty thousand new jobs. In the harsh language of economic development, Ground Zero was thus seen as raw material for a reinvigorated global city through investment in high-rise density, a strategy that was also defended in the *New York Times* a month later by the inventor of the "global city" concept, Saskia Sassen. According to Sassen, "The geography of the global economy consists of both world-spanning networks and… concentrations of resources, as provided by about 40 global cities. New York remains at the top."[22] In other words: the centripetal/centrifugal spiral—or, a headquarters for a multi-national empire?

21. Ibid., 22.

22. Saskia Sassen, "How Downtown Can Stand Tall and Step Lively Again," *The New York Times*, Sunday 26 January 2003, Arts & Leisure, 35.

2

FROM **NEW DELHI** TO **NEW YORK**

FEEDBACK

World Trade Center 2003

In a late entry to the LMDC competition for "innovative" designs for the World Trade Center site, Martin/Baxi Architects (M/BA) utilized the numbers from the LMDC report, but increased the total built area of the site by one-half again, to twenty-four million square feet. This area was distributed in an upside-down WTC/TWC, with Ground Zero now elevated 1,640 feet in the air, to become a park. Supporting it were three towers rather than two. Move the Time Warner Center (TWC) downtown. Add a tower. Turn it upside down. What do you get? A "rebuilt" World Trade Center (WTC). Thus also were two earlier, exemplary proposals combined: Koolhaas's upside-down tower featured in the New York Times study, and Bernard Tschumi's dissenting Tri-Towers of Babel, completed after Tschumi withdrew from the same Times study.[1] The difference was that it was the sober 1970s rather than the delirious 1920s that were revisited in M/BA's upside-down WTC, with three tapering towers each matching the height of the original twins: 1,360 feet, with minimum footprints touching down on the original "ground." Supported on this tripod was a stack of twenty ground zeros, with park on top. The top heavy volume formed a roof over the entire site, making the construction of the "Freedom Tower" impossible. Otherwise, the street level was left open, allowing the tendency toward Disney to take its course. Spiral ramps at the foot of each tower quietly descended into a massive parking garage filling the underground "bathtub," which was penetrated by infrastructure from the sides and by elevators from above.

The floor-to-floor heights of the towers varied within algorithmically controlled limits to yield a barcode-like section: every floor a different height, and by virtue of their tapering volumes, every floor a different width and breadth. Same difference. Shooting through the center of each tower was a cylindrical, structural void, a hole instead of an atrium, open to the sky 1,640 feet above. Around its perimeter were glass elevators scaling the heights of the hollow core. Half of these elevators ran express from the parking garage/PATH/subway station to a sky lobby running the full width and breadth of the

one hundred-eleventh floor—the first of the twenty ground zeroes in the sky. From there, commuters, tourists, shoppers, and residents could catch the other half of the

1. Bernard Tschumi, *Tri-Towers of Babel: Questioning Ground Zero* (New York: Columbia Books on Architecture, 2003)

elevators surrounding the three cores and travel back down to individual floors below (having added a thought-inducing additional two minutes to their journey). Or, they could drift across the sky lobby through a field of elevators leading upward and eventually to the park at the top. In all, an upside-down Access Tree.

The upper branches (or roots?) of this tree passed through a cloud of structure: a massive, cantilevered space frame that extended the structural logic of El Lissitzky's utopian *Wolkenbügel*, or horizontal skyscraper, into the third dimension. But unlike Lissitzky's project, this structural cloud had no hierarchy, no major and minor elements. Instead, thousands of small framing members of constant thickness and variable length were joined in a dense, redundant network—a three-dimensional mesh. Rhythmically undulating ceilings dipped down at frequent, parametrically regulated intervals to meet the floors and thus to make a structural connection. Structurally, this cloud was thereby connected to itself internally at thousands of points, like a sponge. Functionally, the dips in the ceiling yielded service spaces, duct chases, private rooms, circulation zones, and so on.

And like the interrupted No. 1 Broadway project, this WTC had no program—not because program was nothing, but because it was everything. In a city in which some of the most desirable properties are in old, disused warehouses, the possible uses of these vertical open spaces were constrained only by their architectural and infrastructural particulars. These particulars included the variable relationship between shell and core in the towers below, and the variable relationship between ceiling and floor in the "ground" above. And like New York itself, this WTC was provided with a full gradient of exposure to natural light, by virtue of the three mirrored glass vortexes that sprang up from the three holes in the towers. As a result, despite the repetition of its perimeter, each ground zero was a little different, penetrated by three voids that grew a little bigger as they climbed upward, yielding an appropriately variable set of interior landscapes in which sat an appropriately variable set of potted plants.

The only piece of program—if you could call it that—that was specified was the rooftop park. It was another ground zero interrupted by the three mirrored vortexes which had now grown together, nearly touching at their tangent points. The rest was a great lawn, planted with three great spirals of genetically identical trees (clones) that overlapped one another to form a moiré. Differences would become evident only as each tree grew differently in this harsh environment.[2] It was an authentically public garden operating according to its own internal laws, majestically elevated above the ground and literally supported by the architecture of finance, but accessible only through the topological tangles of its Access Trees, in which public elevators pierced through the deepest recesses of private space.

Below all of this, on the underside of the stack of ground zeroes, was a memorial. It consisted simply of the two original tower footprints projected upward into the volume hovering above, forming two upside-down voids. The horizontal surface through which these voids passed was covered in a gridded sheet of fluorescent lighting. Thus, pedestrians stranded in the abject theme park formerly known as lower Manhattan could gaze upward at Ground Zero, reflected in a glowing, luminous ceiling with two black holes where twin towers used to be, and remember a better future.

2. Here M/BA was inspired by Natalie Jeremijencko's work with cloned trees distributed through the San Francisco Bay Area (in close proximity to Silicon Valley) to test the effects of environment on growth. Jeremijencko is also the author of a row of live, upside-down trees at the entrance to Mass MOCA.

1

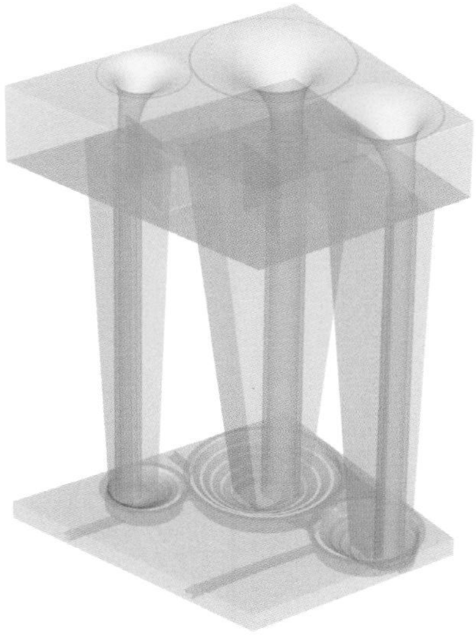

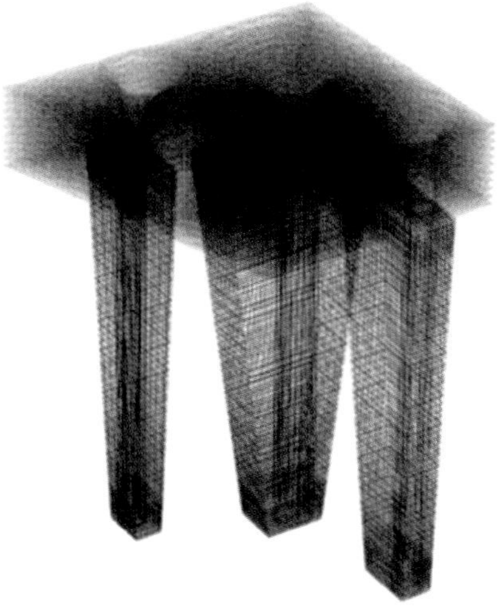

2, 3

WTC2003

[1] Axonometric.
[2] Axonometric x-ray.
[3] Structural cloud.

1

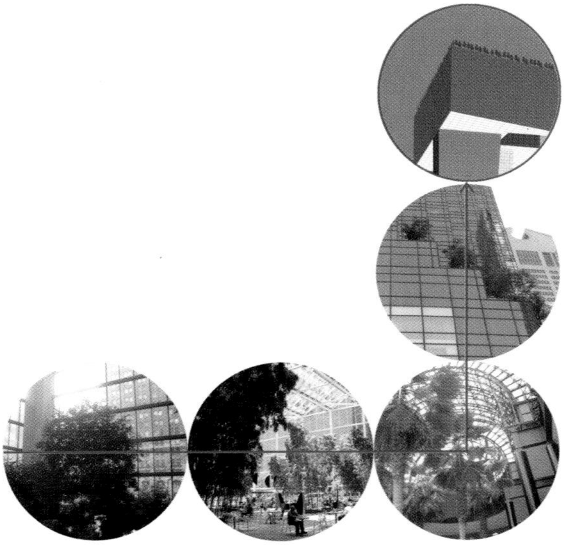

2

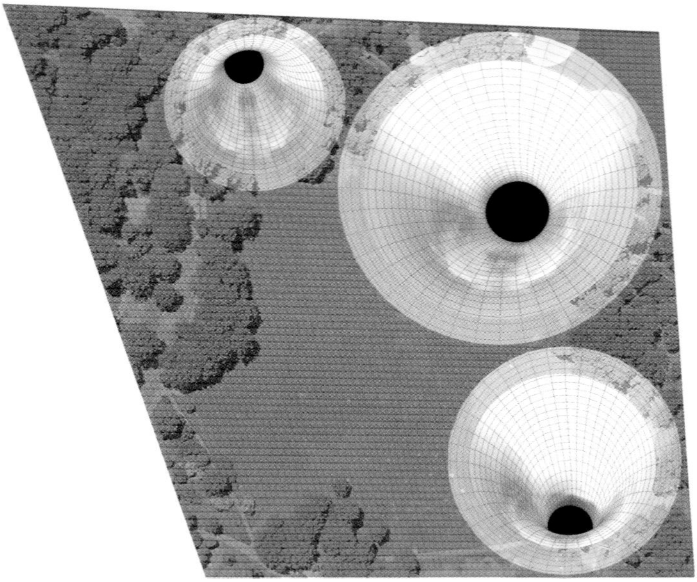

WTC2003

[1] Green Buildings. "Nature": from atrium (IBM, Ford, WFC) to terrace (Trump) to roof (M/BA).
[2] Roof plan: Park with genetically modified trees and inside-out atria.

1
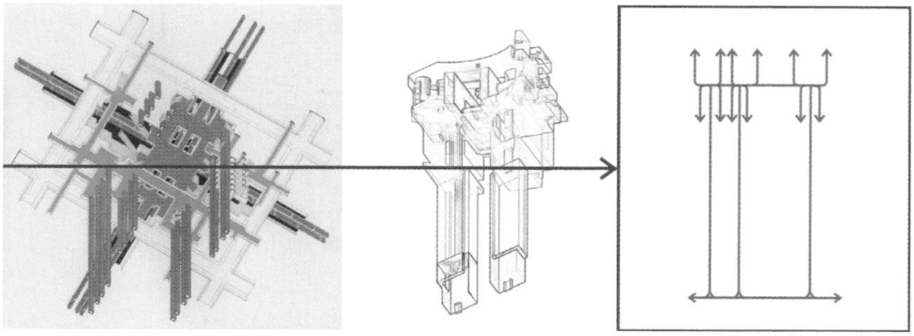

2
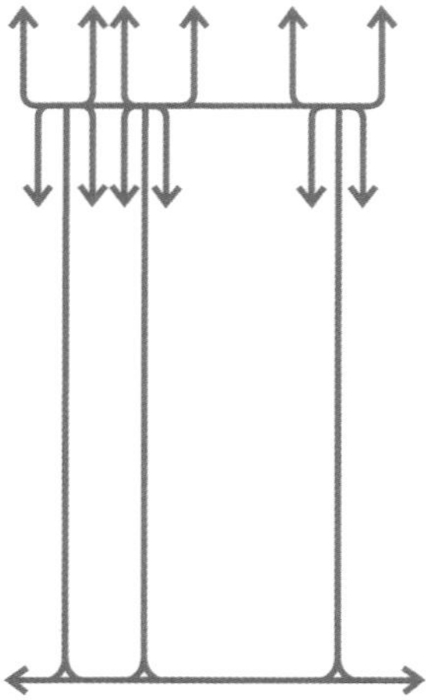

3
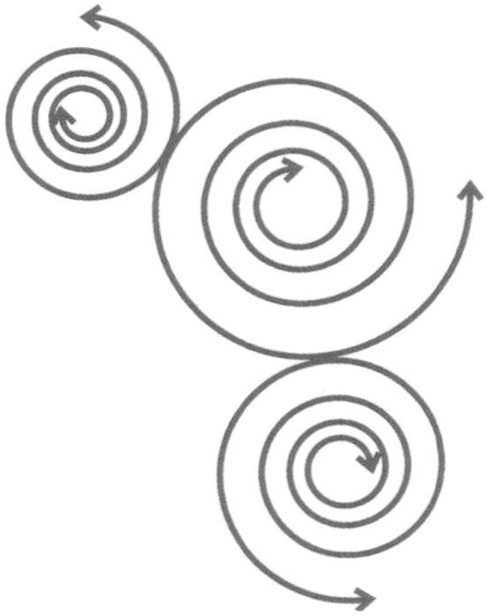

[1] Trees, Upside-down. Re-use and inversion of *Urban Design Manhattan*'s Access Tree. L to r: UDM's Access Tree (upside-down), SOM's Time Warner Center (upside-down), and vertical circulation in M/BA's WTC (right-side-up).
[2] Upside-down Access Tree (vertical circulation).
[3] Site circulation at street level and below.

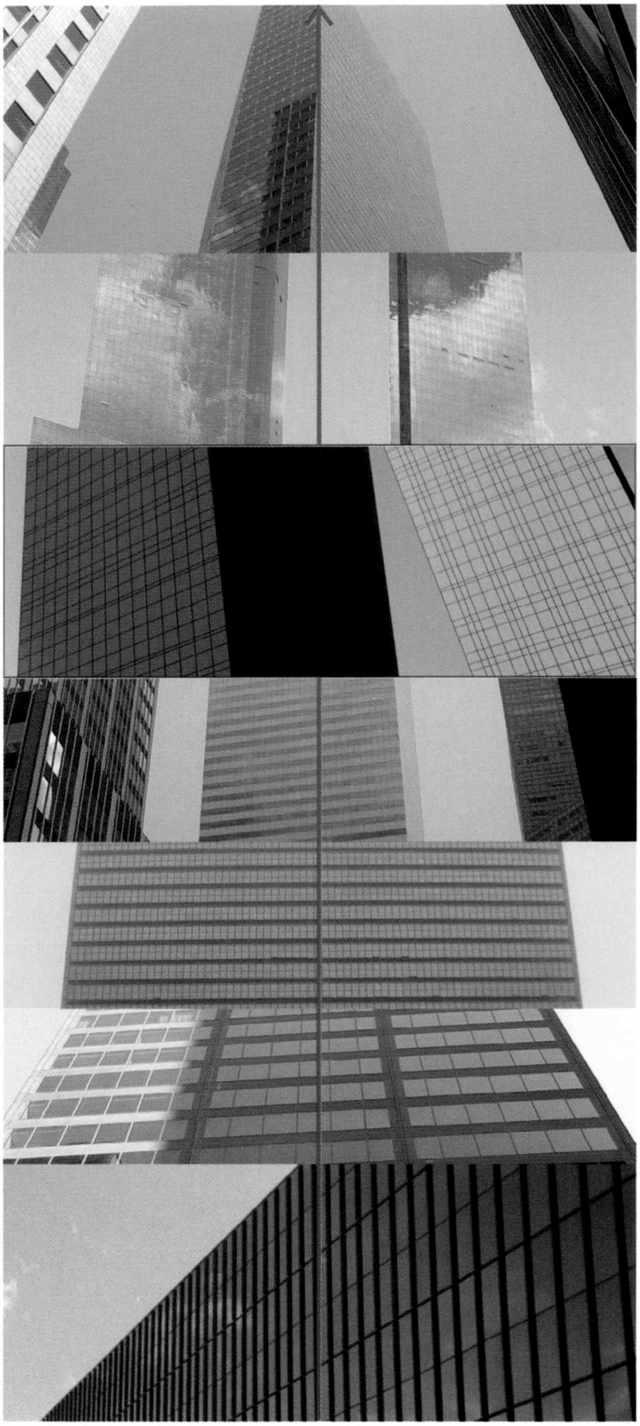

WTC2003

Curtain Wall Samples. Curtain walls in and around New York, including M/BA's WTC.

Futures Reflected: Manhattan's past (Pelli's WFC) and possible future (M/BA's WTC) as reflected in Jersey City.

WTC2003

View from street.

View, with Downtown Athletic Club (center).

WTC2003

9/11 memorial.

From Street to Sky. Looking up in New York, including M/BA's WTC.

WTC2003

View from Jersey City.

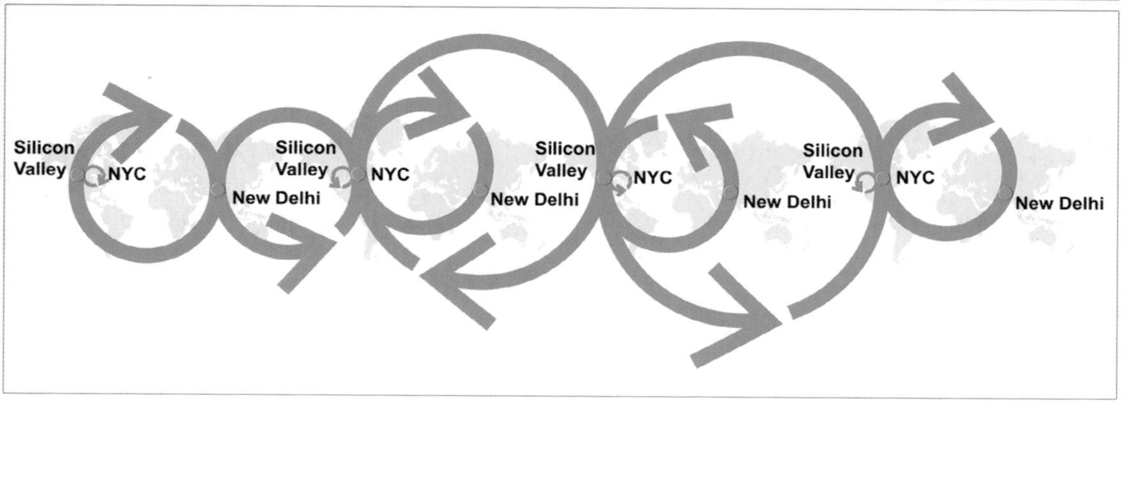

Remembering the WTC. Modified Port Authority press release (1964), and round trips.

FROM **SILICON VALLEY** TO **NEW DELHI**

3

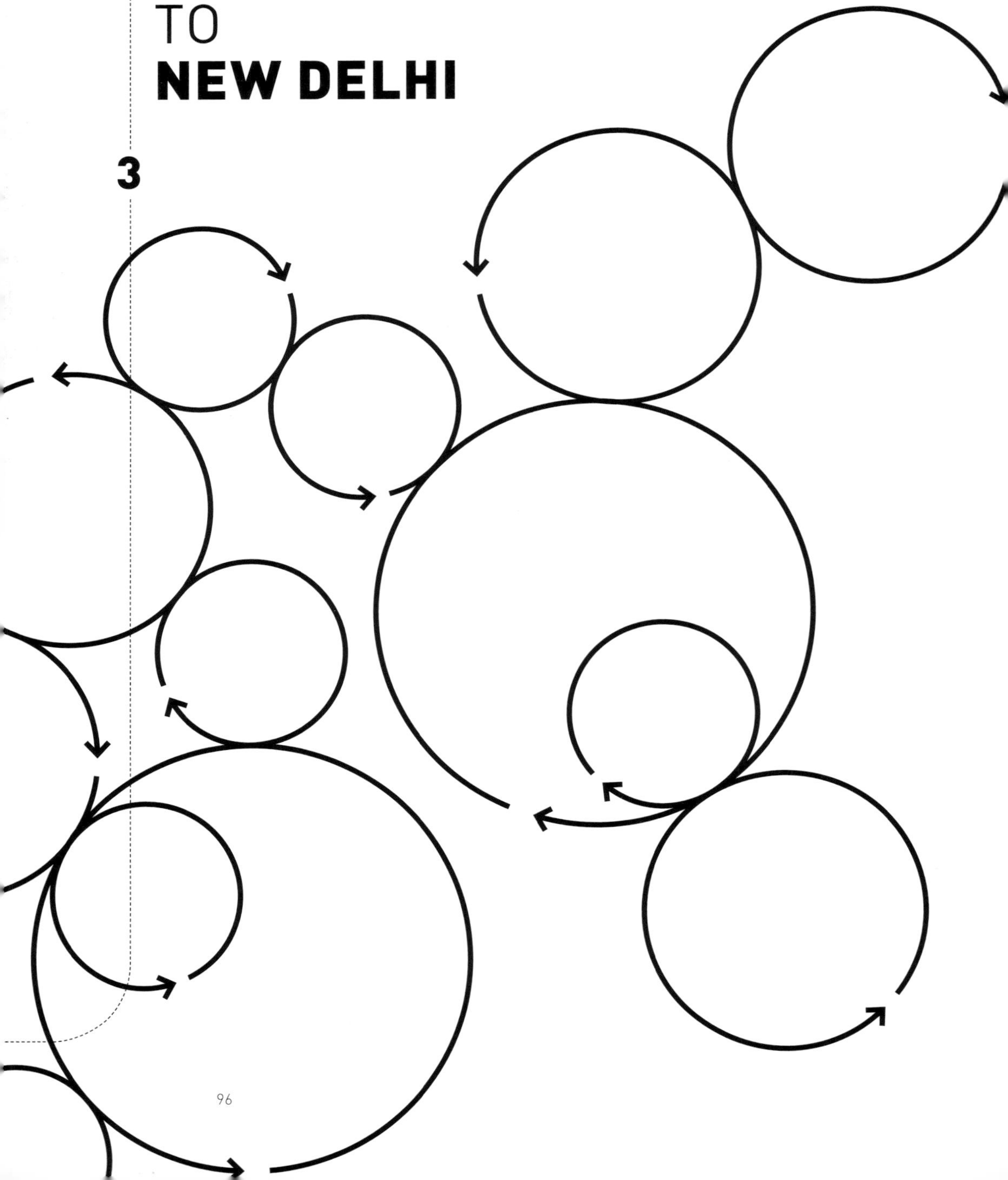

A mirage: Out on an open plain, eighteen kilometers from the postcolonial grandeur and congestion of central Bangalore in southern India, stands the International Tech Park, Ltd. (ITPL). Its sleek stone surfaces give form to what, back in Silicon Valley, is called "outsourcing," an arrangement served by a system of flexible, skilled labor that is called, in India, "body shopping." ITPL was designed by Singapore-based RSP Architects Planners & Engineers (Pte.) Ltd., and built in stages from 2000 to 2004. It consists of five buildings with five different names: Discoverer, Innovator, Creator, Explorer, and Inventor. Stake holders in the original development included Tata Industries Ltd., the Government of Karnataka, and a consortium of Singapore-based investors.

3.01

3.02

WORLD CLASS

The 28-hectare full-service ITPL campus was advertised by its managers as a state-of-the-art "World in a Park," complete with mall, health club, and a residential complex nearby. A testimonial by one Fran Feldman, a general manager at America Online India (an ITPL tenant), summarizes its attractions:

3.03

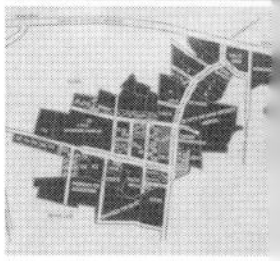

> In our quest to expand our ability to provide world class customer service to our 36 million members worldwide, AOL chose ITPL in Bangalore as the site to set up our largest call center outside of the United States. We enjoy the state of the art facilities and the quiet atmosphere of the beautifully landscaped Tech Park as well as the additional facilities located in the basement which provide our teams additional outlets for food, fitness, shopping and fun.[1]

This little piece of India's "Silicon Plateau" reportedly sprang from a 1992 meeting between then-Indian Prime Minister P.V. Narasimha Rao and Singaporean Prime Minister Goh Chok Tong. Though a public/private venture, it was inspired in part by the Indian government's systematic investment in the information technology industry, under the Software Technology Parks (STP) Scheme of 1991, which was the result of a policy white paper written in 1986 titled "Computer Software Export, Software Development and Training." Under STP, software firms that did a one hundred percent export business were entitled to five years of tax-free existence. And in New Delhi, bureaucrats often dream in block letters. So by 2004, there were forty-one official information technology (IT) centers scattered throughout the country administered by Software Technology Parks of India (STPI), under the Indian government's Department of Electronics (DOE). In parallel with the Electronics Hardware Technology Park Scheme (EHTP), STPI offered services, support, and financial

1. http://www.intltechpark.com/about_itpl/testimonials.htm.

incentives to companies devoted to increasing India's high-tech exports, a project that is officially described as "encouraging, promoting and boosting the Software Exports from India."[2]

3.04

3.05

DIGITAL (PARK)

Not far from ITPL, in Bangalore's recently developed Electronics City (Phase 2), is a campus called Digital Park. Its name is in keeping with Bangalore's reputation as the ultimate garden city—so designated by its former British rulers, who should know, since they invented the garden city. Designed by architect Karan Grover in accordance with an "ecology friendly theme," and built to accommodate 4,200 employees, Digital Park, like ITPL, consists of five buildings with five different names, this time themed according to five elements: Earth (Prithvi), Water (Jal), Space (Akash), Air (Vayu), and Fire (Agni). The ecological theme further extends to the campus infrastructure, which is said to recycle every drop of relatively scarce water that passes through it. Bird watching (on site) is encouraged. Opened in 2002, it became the home of Hewlett-Packard GlobalSoft Ltd., formerly Digital GlobalSoft Ltd., which was once a subsidiary of Digital Equipment India Ltd., which was the Indian subsidiary of Digital Equipment Corporation (DEC) until 1998, when that company was acquired by Compaq Computer Corp., which in turn was acquired by Hewlett-Packard in 2004. In memory of this history perhaps, the signs atop the complex of ecologically themed buildings in Digital Park continued to carry the original Silicon Valley company's straightforwardly mythic name: Digital.

3.06

3.07

EUPHORIA IN THE CAFETERIA

Like its Silicon Valley counterparts, as well as the even more pastoral campuses of its indigenous neighbors in Electronics City (Phase 1)—the Indian software giant Infosys and its competitor Wipro—Digital Park's environmental friendliness extended to in-house coffee, tea, and dining. The following anonymous composition, titled "Euphoria in the Cafeteria," celebrates the social life on campus:

All work and no coffee break,
Dull software engineers you'll make!
So move out from the office interior,
And head for the cafeteria!

So, what will it be? Coffee or Tea?
Anything's fine, to break the monotony![3]

3. "Digital: A Trusted Partner," http://www.koramangala.com/korabuz/y2k2/sept1r.htm.

Such corporate lyricism is a reminder that there is more than technology being produced here and in other digital parks around the world. And where Digital's environmentally sensitive ethos and its happy cafeteria represent efforts to reinforce employee identification (and loyalty) through what is called "internal branding," in Bangalore and beyond such hospitality also extends to the customer, who is more often than not another corporation.

Thus did Bangalore-based Sundaram Architects Pvt. Ltd. provide Infosys Technologies Ltd. with a prominently placed Corporate Care Center containing eight conference rooms for customer consultation, and an "experience theater" in which the history of software could be experienced in front of what was once the largest video wall in Asia. Unwilling to settle for a mere cafeteria, Infosys also provided its employees—known internally as "Infoscions"—with a building by Sundaram Architects called The Food Court, which actually housed three food courts, a gymnasium, an Infosys company store (which also sells selected Microsoft products), and a bank, with a curvilinear swimming pool outside. The company likes to claim that four thousand quadratic equations were "crunched" to produce its parabolic concrete-shell roofs, which shade stylistically in the direction the Brazilian communist and architect of concrete shells, Oscar Niemeyer.

NRI

3.08

An NRI is a Non-Resident Indian. Often, the NRI and the Resident Alien are the same person. Familiar denizens of Silicon Valley's atriums, after the Valley's economic bubble burst in 2001 many NRIs returned to India. Many went to Bangalore. And more than a few wound up eating lunch (and sometimes dinner and sometimes breakfast) in The Food Court at Infosys. There, on 13 November 2002, the lucky ones would have been able to meet Microsoft Chief Software Architect Bill Gates on his first visit to India. "It was long overdue," said his Indian counterpart, Infosys co-founder N. R. Narayana Murthy.[4]

3.09

Meanwhile, on any given day aspiring NRIs who are—by definition—not (yet?) Resident Aliens can be seen in the waiting room of the United States embassy in New Delhi, waiting. Obtaining a US visa is a grueling and often humiliating process. Still, it is done. But it is not done inside the actual embassy building. Rather, waiting for visas takes place in an ancillary building on the embassy grounds. The embassy building itself, hidden behind layers of security both physical and virtual, is reserved for

4. Amy Waldman, "Bill Gates Finds a Seattle in India," *The New York Times*, International, 14 November 2002, 1.

those in the foreign service whose duties include doing whatever it is that embassy workers do, other than denying visas.

Despite the barricaded streets surrounding it, the US embassy remains something of a landmark in New Delhi's lush diplomatic neighborhood. Once the United States' largest listening post in Asia, from an architectural point of view the building, which was designed by Edward Durell Stone and completed in 1954, stands as the monumental achievement of a postwar turn toward modernism in the US State Department Foreign Buildings Operations office (FBO). The first of many embassies designed under this regime, Stone's project was subject to a directive issued by a special board advising the FBO on architectural matters:

> To the sensitive and imaginative designer [an embassy commission] will be an invitation to give serious study to local conditions of climate and site, to understand and sympathize with local customs and people, and to grasp the historical meaning of the particular environment in which the new building must be set. He will do so with a free mind without being dictated by obsolete or sterile formulae or clichés, be they old or new; he will avoid being either bizarre or fashionable, yet he will not fear using new techniques or new materials should these constitute real advance in architectural thinking.[5]

3.10

3.11

3.12

3.13

Stone was hardly one for the "bizarre or fashionable." To prove this, he provided the State Department with a glass box set on a plinth. Inside, the box was penetrated by a courtyard-as-tropical water garden (though the local climate is technically semi-arid). Outside, it was wrapped entirely in a patterned screen of perforated terrazzo block. In keeping with the FBO directive, Stone designed the screen as a gesture to that same local climate, but perhaps also to an image of the "East" lodged in his (and his clients') imaginary, reinforced by what he called the "oriental opulence" of the gold-leafed colonnade surrounding it. Like the imperial headquarters built by Sirs Edwin Lutyens and Herbert Baker in New Delhi three decades earlier but with significantly less subtlety, this was a piece of architectural diplomacy—an effort to convince whomever would listen that the US was a good neighbor, by wrapping a corporate glass box in a sensitive skin.

In the old days, entry to the US embassy was gained on axis, across a grand lawn with circular reflecting pool and fountains, up a grand stair and under the colonnaded porch. Today, visitors are forced to skulk off-center toward to a militarized guard's booth in front of a threatening wall, only to be dispatched round the back to the outbuilding housing future NRIs

5. Pietro Belluschi, FBO Architectural Advisory Committee memorandum, 27 January 1954, quoted in Jane C. Loeffler, *The Architecture of Diplomacy: Building America's Embassies* (New York: Princeton Architectural Press, 1998), 124-125. Also quoted in Edward Durell Stone, *The Evolution of an Architect* (New York: Horizon Press, 1962), 138.

waiting indefinitely for visas. Those fortunate enough to be invited up the steps are greeted by a grim, well-armed Marine standing inside a bulletproof glass booth, inside Stone's glass box inside the perforated terrazzo shell. In late 2002, conspicuously taped to the Marine's booth, was a "Wanted" poster: Osama Bin Laden. Directly across from him hung an awkwardly grinning triumvirate—President, Vice President, Secretary of State. A face-off.

IIC

3.14

As a measure of Stone's success, perhaps, an alter-ego to the US embassy and its aggressive regionalism was soon to be found in the more genteel regionalism of the India International Centre (IIC), which opened in 1962. For starters, its patrimony traces back to New York and San Francisco, rather than to Washington. Funded by the Rockefeller Foundation (in the wake of that family's contribution to the United Nations headquarters), the IIC was designed by Joseph Allen Stein, an American architect from Berkeley who had become head of the new architecture school in Calcutta a few years earlier. Stein would go on to design the Ford Foundation headquarters next door in 1968, even as Kevin Roche was completing his own, more famous Ford Foundation in New York in 1967.

A conference center and forum dedicated to international cultural exchange, the IIC's architecture exudes a cosmopolitan optimism that lands softly on its site adjacent to Lodhi Gardens in central New Delhi. Again there are screens, verandahs. But now they are rendered in a more "local" material: blue glazed tile crafted in Delhi. Still, the paradox of identity is inescapable. Unlike the UN, which laid claim to modern architecture's supposed universality, the "international" nature of the IIC was to be secured by its site specificity, which extended to its users to the degree that, as the inaugural brochure put it: "...the Centre will be a forum for the exposition of the cultural patterns prevailing in the different parts of the world by the men and women most competent on the subjects—nay, embodying in themselves each such pattern."[6]

6. India International Centre Inaugural Souvenir, 1962, quoted in Stephen White, *Building in the Garden: The Architecture of Joseph Allen Stein in India and California* (Oxford: Oxford University Press, 1993), 146.

CHANDIGARH.COM

Meanwhile, back in Bangalore, The Food Court at Infosys was hardly the first ghost of an earlier, heroic modernism to haunt that city's subtropical landscape. In 1977, work was begun on the Bangalore campus of the Indian Institute of Management (IIM), designed by Stein's future partner, Balkrishna V. Doshi, and completed in 1985. The IIM acronym was already known to those following modern architecture's international meanderings in the 1960s, when Louis I. Kahn designed an IIM campus in Ahmedabad, which was begun in 1962 but completed only after Kahn's death in transit in 1974. Doshi had worked in Paris on Le Corbusier's plans for Chandigarh and, after setting up his own practice in Ahmedabad, he assisted in bringing Kahn to India to design the IIM. Doshi's own Bangalore IIM was an ode to Kahn, with its iterative, cubic spaces fabricated from the modest means of raw concrete, with local granite block in place of Kahn's mythic brick. But it was even more overtly modeled after Fatehpur Sikri, the sixteenth century Mughal imperial compound inhabited by Akbar and his court. Simultaneously princely and prosaic, Bangalore's IIM thus telescoped the precolonial with the postcolonial—royal gardens and local granite—in an environment that scrambled Kahn's hierarchies into episodic spatial sequences interwoven with plantings, all designed for a new class of managers who would eventually manage the country's entry into the "new economy" growing up nearby in the new, digital gardens of Bangalore's technology parks.

3.15

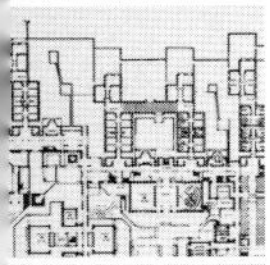
3.16

3.17

3.18

3.19

3.20

3.21

Yet the persistence of Kahn notwithstanding, the most visible of modern architecture's ghosts haunting India's modernity remains that of Le Corbusier, whose spirit still roams the verdant avenues, monumental halls, and modest housing of Chandigarh, capital of Punjab, which now does double duty as the capital of neighboring Haryana as well. Chandigarh still embodies the possibility of building entire cities—entire worlds, even—from scratch. And it was of this city that its prime sponsor, Prime Minister Jawaharlal Nehru, could declare with a politician's tact:

> I do not like every building in Chandigarh. I like some very much, I like the general conception of the township very much but what I like above all, is this creative approach not being tied down to what has been done by our forefathers and the like but thinking out in new terms, trying to think in terms of light and air and ground and water and human beings, not in terms of rules and regulations laid down by our ancestors.[7]

7. Jawaharlal Nehru, "Mr. Nehru on Architecture," *Urban and Rural Planning Thought* 2.2 (April 1959): 49, as quoted in Vikramaditya Prakash, *Chandigarh's Le Corbusier: The Struggle for Modernity in Postcolonial India* (Seattle: University of Washington Press, 2002), 19.

In practice, these new terms were first laid out by Albert Mayer and Matthew Nowicki, and after them by Le Corbusier, assisted by Pierre Jeanneret, Jane Drew, Maxwell Fry, M. N. Sharma, A. R. Prabhawalkar, B. P. Mathur, Piloo Moody, U. E. Chowdhury, N. S. Lambda, Jeet Lal Malhotra, J. S. Detghe, and Aditya Prakash, all of whom together extended to Nehru an open hand in symbolic, concrete solidarity.[8]

In contrast perhaps, among the offshoots of Bangalore's corporate gardens illegitimate heirs to Chandigarh's sparkling, technologically enhanced future—is the one hundred-eleven-acre Chandigarh Technology Park (CTP), located just outside of the city and anchored by an Infosys campus. Another golden opportunity for bureaucratic abbreviation, CTP, like its Bangalore counterpart ITPL, was developed under the STPI scheme and administered by the Department of Information Technology (DIT), Chandigarh. But other, equally fantastical names were not far behind, and on 20 May 2004, Denver-based Quark, Inc. broke ground nearby on a forty-six-acre campus—a home for seven thousand new Quarkians (yes, that's right, Quarkians), complete with multiplexes and shopping. Chandigarh was chosen over Bangalore in part for a "quality of life" deemed attractive to engineering talent in short supply even in India. The move was led by future Quark CEO Kamar Aulakh, himself a graduate in engineering from Chandigarh's Punjab University, who made sure the new campus would be state-of-the-art. Thus could Quark boast to prospective employees of its India Development Center (IDC):

> A modern, 21st-century office, Quark takes every care to ensure that the workplace is energetic and lively. It is a "flat" organization without archaic, bureaucratic designations. The Quark culture is designed to help individuals realize their true potential in a comfortable environment. Employees are known as "members" of their departments, and there are no superficial barriers between one employee and another. Quark is committed to making every employee feel at home. This is reflected in almost every aspect of the work culture—from the fresh, clean architecture of its glass building to the elegant interiors, and from the relaxed dress code to the well-stocked pantries and cafeterias.[9]

In explaining to these prospective employees "Why Chandigarh?", Quark further emphasized the benefits of a planned city with modern amenities and comparably low levels of air pollution. But the company also felt obliged to apologize for the city's relative lack of historical attractions. So instead of its shabby modern architecture and the not-so-shabby utopia it imagined, the environmentally-friendly Quark chose to emphasize

8. The names of those who assisted Le Corbusier on Chandigarh are given in Prakash, *Chandigarh's Le Corbusier*, 14.

9. http://www.quarkindia.com/careers/lifeatquark/workculture.html.

Chandigarh's greenery. According to the company, the city possesses an abundance of "theme-based gardens and parks," including Leisure Valley (running through the center of Le Corbusier's plan), the Rose Garden, the Terraced Flower Garden, and the Botanical Garden. There is also Sukhna Lake, surrounded by a "golf course of national repute" and winter home to "exotic migratory birds" from Siberia, among other wildlife.[10] All of which suggested a science fiction vision of ecotopian bliss, in another kind of city in another kind of universe parallel to Le Corbusier's. The Quarkians called this Quark City.

A five thousand acre office-cum-residential township, Quark City, with Quark's IDC as its anchor, was expected to bring twenty thousand new jobs to the Chandigarh area, thereby overcoming that city's previous shortcomings in attracting IT companies, despite Le Corbusier's best efforts in laying the technological groundwork. Thus could Quark, Inc. proudly boast of the projected economic impact of its proposed new city:

> A messiah in the form of an MNC may yet usher affluence and advancement to the region while providing an international platform that the enterprising people of the region had been waiting for.[11]

The MNC had arrived.

3.22

AN ERROR

Le Corbusier, who no doubt would have preferred to be recognized as Chandigarh's first messiah, also waxed lyrical about the city's natural setting. There are many stories told about his adventures there, but perhaps the best is told by Le Corbusier himself, under the title "Birth of the Legend":

3.23

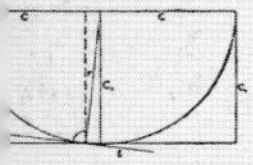
3.24

3.25

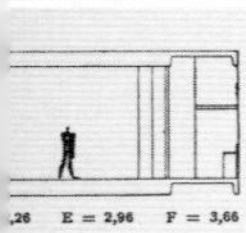
3.26

> On 28th March, 1951, at Chandigarh, at sunset, we had set off in a jeep across the still empty site of the capital—[P. L.] Varma, [Maxwell] Fry, Pierre Jeanneret and myself. Never had the spring been so lovely, the air so pure after a storm on the day before, the horizons so clear, the mango trees so gigantic and magnificent. We were at the end of our task (the first): We had created the city (the town plan). I noticed then that I had lost the box of the Modulor, of the only Modulor strip in existence, made by [Jerzy] Soltan in 1945, which had not left my pocket for six years.... A grubby box, splitting at the edges. During that last visit of the site before my return to Paris, the Modulor had fallen from the jeep on to the soil of the fields that were to disappear to make way for the capital. It is there now, in the very heart of the place, integrated in the soil. Soon it will flower in all the measurements of the first city of the world to be organized all of a piece in accordance with that harmonious scale.[12]

10. http://www.quarkindia.com/careers/chandigarh/.

11. Quark Press Release, "Big Bang Theory," http://www.quarkindia.com/presscenter/india_news/ie20031911.html.

12. Le Corbusier, *Le Modulor 2 1955 (Let the User Speak Next): Continuation of "The Modulor" 1948* (Cambridge, MA: MIT Press, 1968), 33-34.

Despite Le Corbusier's faith in his own virility, and in the fertility of his modular seed inadvertently sown in Chandigarh's virgin soil during a moment of uncontrolled ecstasy, there was a problem. The proportions shown on that first Modulor tape were wrong. There was a microscopic error in the architectural genome which, if left unattended, would lead to unimaginable mutations.

The error was first brought to Le Corbusier's attention sometime in 1950 by one R.-F. Duffau. It concerned, as Duffau put it, "the graphic demonstration out of which the first terms of the Modulor series are derived."[13] The geometrical relationships drawn on Le Corbusier's tape—the one with which he fertilized Chandigarh's soil—did not correspond to the mathematics. The error amounted to 1/6000, or .017%. But it was enough to send Le Corbusier's diagrammatic Modular figure (at Chandigarh, a universal "Indian"?) into inhuman contortions. It had to be corrected. And so it was, in 1955—after the designs for Chandigarh had been all but completed.

If we are to take Le Corbusier at his word, then—that the original tape, containing such an error, still somehow spawned Chandigarh's monumental "harmonies"—are we to believe that Chandigarh actually harbors a genetic mutation, a deviation from the Modular ideal? And that, far from originating in some indigenous trait to be regarded with neocolonial disdain—faulty craftsmanship, inadequately comprehending local assistants, etc.—this error in the code was lodged in the very mind's eye of the master himself?

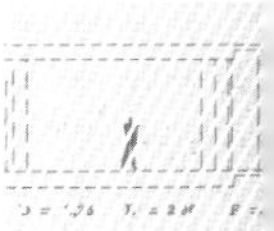

3.27

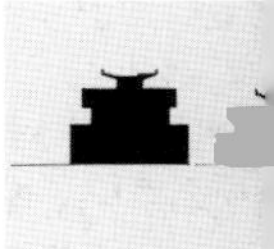

3.28

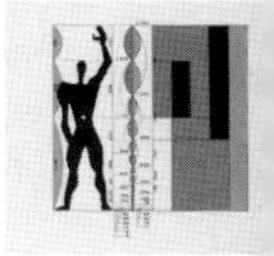

In other words, is it possible that, far from representing the realization of Le Corbusier's urban visions, Chandigarh represents something of a productive aberration? In fact, Le Corbusier's reflections on the use of the Modulor are full of such aberrations. At Chandigarh, for example, there is the discrepancy between the conceptual, "arithmetic" dimensioning of the High Court (12 x 12 x 18 meters) and the "texturique" (or visible) proportions of the Modulor, as applied to the *brise-soleil*. Of this discrepancy Le Corbusier admits: "It will be seen that, between arithmetic and texturique, there appeared some 'residues,' to be re-absorbed in the normal way."[14]

Once such discrepancies were overcome in "the normal way," design-by-Modulor had its practical advantages, as demonstrated by the small, medium, and large versions of the unbuilt Governor's house. The product of a "free imagination," the original design came in over budget. "We had built to the scale of

13. Ibid., 45.
14. Ibid., 217.

giants." So Le Corbusier and his team simply took out the Modulor scale, halved the generating cube, and adjusted everything accordingly, making a second round of adjustments to "put the Governor back into a House of Man."[15]

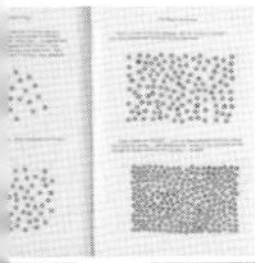
3.29

3.30

3.31

"THIRD WORLD PARADIGM" (DOTS)

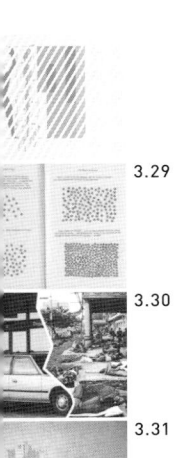

Who was this figure drawn on Le Corbusier's Modulor tape? There had been some variations proposed by others, as dutifully recorded by the master. These included a monkey (by students at London's Architectural Association), and a woman (by Le Corbusier's associate, Justin Serralta). But despite these overdetermined graphic challenges, the Modular survived as Man himself. And it was not until the 1970s that this universal Man would mutate into another figure—more Gandhi than Nehru—lodged in Chandigarh's unconscious: the "Indian."

In 1962, prior to designing the IIM campus, and just after returning from his stint in Le Corbusier's office applying the Modulor to Chandigarh's monuments, Balkrishna V. Doshi helped found the Centre for Environmental Planning and Technology (CEPT). He also served as the first director of its School of Architecture, then as director of the School of Planning, and finally as Dean of all of CEPT. He even designed the architecture school, with its open brick-and-concrete studios, from which have issued generations of architects hung over from drunken bouts with the auras of Kahn and Le Corbusier and later, with the aura of Doshi, along with that of his friendly rival Charles Correa.

Correa, a graduate of the University of Michigan and MIT, started big. Since the mid-1960s he had been a lead figure in the preparation of a master plan for New Bombay (Navi Mumbai), an enormous city-from-scratch across the river from Bombay/Mumbai. He incorporated many of the issues confronted in preparing the master plan for New Bombay into *The New Landscape* (1985), a manifesto for urbanism in a modernizing "Third World," with a title borrowed (without acknowledgement) from a work by one of his MIT teachers, Gyorgy Kepes. There, Correa reiterated an ambiguous lesson on density as taught by another of his MIT teachers, Constantinos Doxiadis, that replaced Le Corbusier's Modulor figure with a colored dot. Diagram the population of a village with two hundred fifty red dots, one blue (someone "different from the rest"); next a town of one thousand, with four or five floating blue dots; then a town of twenty-five thousand. Two blue dots finally meet, by chance. And now a city of a hundred thousand, where "we have several colonies where blue people reside...

15. Ibid., 222.

and furthermore, some of the red dots on the fringes of these colonies are turning... purple!"[16]

Celebrating India's dense cities as cauldrons of social transformation (Gandhi's "Quit India" movement, and the Calcutta resistance of the 1920s), Correa also notes an outsourcing in reverse, where "Today in the Gulf, a surprisingly large proportion of development is in the hands of Third World [urban] technocrats."[17] Still: "[t]here is a syndrome common to almost all Third World urban centres. They each seem to consist of two different cities: one is for the poor; the other (interlocked with it) is for the rich." Correa calls this juxtaposition (also of red and blue dots) the "Third World paradigm."[18] In conclusion, he doubles up it up with another ambiguous story of his own:

> In the 60s, when European hippies first started coming to Bombay, a lot of rich Indians complained bitterly about them. At dinner parties they would refer to those "terrible, dirty people with lice in their hair, begging." In response one would say, "It doesn't bother you when you see Indians under those conditions. Why do you get so upset when you see a European?" Finally, a friend gave me the answer: "Naturally a rich Indian goes berserk when he drives his Mercedes and sees a hippie. The hippie is signaling him a message: I'm coming from where you're going—and it's not worth going there. That upsets him terribly." But come to think of it, surely it is a message that should work the other way around as well! The hippie should realize that the Indian in his Mercedes, gross as he may be, is also sending a message, in fact, the very same one: I'M COMING FROM WHERE YOU'RE GOING.[19]

To this elliptical allegory of modernization, Correa appends an image of Bombay's new luxury hi-rise housing looming over a squatter settlement in the foreground, captioned "The Metropolis as mirage."

SANDSTONE (RED)

Simultaneously, Correa nurtured a professional practice oriented toward a maturing nation-state and to multinational capital. A snapshot of this is visible in his own contribution to the Bangalore skyline—the twenty one-story Visvesvaraya Centre, developed by the state-owned Life Insurance Corporation of India (LIC) and completed in 1980. Like Doshi's early work, Correa's office complex extended Le Corbusier's "voyage to the East" beyond the master's lifetime, into a set of raw concrete towers topped with periscopic heads that poeticized a hulking proto-industrial mass inhabited by

16. Charles Correa, *The New Landscape* (Bombay: The Book Society of India, 1985), 84-85.
17. Ibid., 87.
18. Ibid., 103.
19. Ibid., 132-133.

3.32

3.33

3.34

3.35

3.36

3.37

bureaucrats. But concrete was an inadequate carrier for the meaning that Correa sought, and along with such innovations as the folded concrete pavilion designed for Hindustan Lever in 1961—Correa's own Lever House—the Visvesvaraya Centre was relegated to the margins of subsequent monographs. Instead, Correa reasserted the promise of meaning in far more literal terms in his contribution to the Delhi skyline in 1986—the main offices of his Bangalore client, the LIC. Here Le Corbusier and Kahn were replaced by Kevin Roche and I. M. Pei as apparent sources. Except that Pei's signature triangular massing was now clad in the red sandstone typically quarried in the Delhi area or in neighboring Rajasthan, offset against expanses of Roche's signature mirrored glass and topped off by a functionless space frame spanning the empty plinth below.[20]

Yet this was no mere repetition of western models. On the contrary, like the man in the Mercedes, both Correa's writings and his architecture are rife with the tensions of "Indianness" written into that red stone. These tensions were already there in the sandstone monuments of the earlier, Mughal imperium. They were also prominently on display in the politically motivated sandstone detailing of Sirs Baker and Lutyens in New Delhi, only to be sublimated into the concrete and brick abstractions of Le Corbusier and Kahn. Thus did the red sandstone specter of "Indianness" resurface—literally—in the Delhi LIC (or Jeevan Bharati) and other Correa projects. Shortly thereafter red sandstone was again applied to British skin in Delhi, in the form of the screen wall fronting Correa's British Council, a center devoted to "cultural exchange" which opened in 1992. That same year also saw the opening of India's Permanent Mission to the United Nations in a recently postmodernized New York, again designed by Correa. There, on Forty-Third Street in midtown Manhattan, a red granite base, inlaid with an entrance door "made in India of wood and brass by traditional Rajasthani craftsmen," transmogrified into metal panels coated in reddish enamel as it wrapped the narrow tower above.[21] But even as Correa continued to use it superficially as he went on to explore the iconography of nine-square mandalas in other projects, red sandstone was, together with modular patterns modeled on indigenous settlements, being refined as a blunt instrument for smashing concrete modernism by the doyen of the Delhi scene, Raj Rewal.

20. Vikram Bhatt and Peter Scriver, *After the Masters* (Ahmedabad: Mapin Publishers, 1990), 144.
21. Charles Correa, *Charles Correa* (London: Thames & Hudson, 1996), 110.

MINI-MEGA

Two other Delhi monuments testify to the durability of red sandstone (with beige trim) in evoking the local in the interest of the global. The first of these is Rewal's 1976 State Trading Corporation (STC) headquarters in central Delhi near the neo-Roman circus of Connaught Place, on which Correa's LIC building stands. A mini-megastructure frozen in stone, the STC complex consists of three towers, the tallest of which is fourteen stories, with stacks of Virendeel trusses spanning between them. The towers were designed to accommodate the offices of a semi-governmental agency overseeing the export of Indian products. At the base was the government-run Cottage Industries shopping emporium, in which tourists, NRIs, and middle-to-upper class residents could purchase a wide variety of craft products. As representations of a traditional "India" from which a new modernity rises, these crafts provided a cultural foundation for the futuristic exertions of Rewal's architecture, grounded in red stone.

3.38

3.39

The second, equally demonstrative project by Rewal to exhibit megastructural tendencies—this time at a more genuinely mega-scale—was the Standing Conference of Public Enterprise (SCOPE) office complex, completed in 1989. Here interlocking mid-rise polygons housed a bewildering, seemingly infinite variety of government offices in seventy-five thousand square meters of sandstone-clad space punctured at regular, geometrically-controlled intervals by vertical cores. Again, the building intimates a specifically "Indian" architecture, whose link to its geographical region is supposedly secured by the very earth of which it is made—the global phenomenon known as "local stone."

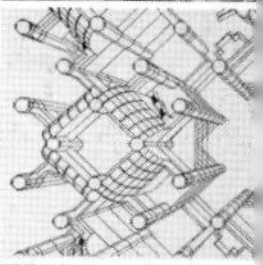
3.40

3.41

3.42

But the concluding chapter in the saga of red stone was written by another mega-project of the 1980s that went unrealized amid New Delhi's lush greenery until the 1990s: Ralph Lerner's Indira Gandhi National Centre for the Arts (IGNCA). A postmodern return to the symbolisms of Lutyens and Baker, the IGNCA was also evidence of a new stage in India's modernity, in which the raw materials of imperial imagery—Mughal motifs, taken up by the British—were recycled once again. This time, the recycling was passed through the lens of a rigorous, academic historicism by an American architect who had successfully tapped into the Indian geopolitical imaginary at a moment when this leader of the historically "non-aligned" nations was beginning to represent itself as having confidently emerged from the shadow of colonialism with solid historical foundations of its own. And, as in the equally postmodern efforts of Correa and Rewal, at the IGNCA these metaphorical foundations were built—again—of red sandstone.

Owing largely to shifts in the political fortunes of its namesake's Congress Party sponsors, the IGNCA was only partially realized. Still, throughout its lengthy construction period, visitors to the site could hear the continuous, background sound of masons chipping slowly at the recalcitrant stone which was expected to sing eventually of India's new global status. Alas, as the Indian economy was systematically "opened up" during the same period, government receded as the architectural custodian of Indian "culture," even as the far-right Hindu nationalist Bharatiya Janata Party (BJP) began their ascent to power fueled by a deadly culture war that began with the demolition of a mosque. Emerging in its wake, and singing the song of "Indianness" all the while (what the BJP called "India Shining"), was a new cult of lifestyle that began at home rather than in public. The earlier "housing colonies" built and presided over by the Delhi Development Authority (DDA) were gradually replaced by private, corporate enclaves, now called "housing estates." Alongside these sat subdivisions filled with new houses executed in populist, post-Chandigarh styles, including the aspirational style that one observer has called "Punjabi Baroque."[22]

3.43

IMPORT-EXPORT

But as with the STPI initiative, government-led efforts to (re)define "India" with the help of architecture did bear some fruit. For example, during his pre-sandstone "concrete" phase, Rewal designed a pair of permanent exhibition pavilions for the grounds of the International Trade Fair (Asia '72) in New Delhi. The project was the result of a competition whose brief was as much symbolic as it was pragmatic: to represent India's progressive industrialization to the world, for export. The resulting pavilions, the Hall of Nations and the Hall of Industries, each spanned large open exhibition spaces with truncated, pyramidal concrete space frames designed in collaboration with the engineer Mahendra Raj. Seen against the imported steel image of Correa's (later) LIC space frame, these were monuments to the lopsided ratio of (high) material cost versus (low) labor cost in India, which meant that Rewal and Raj had to perform the alchemical feat of transforming high-priced steel—the traditional material of the space frame—into labor-intensive concrete.

22. Gautham Bhatia, *Punjabi Baroque* (New York: Penguin Books, 1994).

GLOBAL VILLAGE

By 1990, Rewal's pavilions had been joined on their site by the National Crafts Museum, designed by Charles Correa. The museum incorporated into its precincts an earlier collection of rural huts constructed by the All India Handicrafts Board for Asia '72. Correa thus laid it out as a kind of abstracted village with the occasional, figural motif, such as the red tile awnings that surround interlocking courtyards. The museum's collection brought together for the first time representative crafts from the farthest reaches of the cultural amalgam called "India," with its twenty-eight states and three hundred-twenty-five languages, so that tourists, residents, and visiting craftspersons alike could compare various traditions and techniques and draw their own conclusions as to national identity. As its first director, Smita J. Baxi, described it, the museum was thus conceived as a prototypical component for a "university of crafts" that as yet had no campus—a center of knowledge about the diverse crafts practices and their histories that formed yet another fragile foundation on which India's modernity could be built.[23]

3.44

But more than merely making available a pan-Indian heteroglossia of crafts traditions for the first time to a general public, the museum literally enacted it, with actual, rural craftspeople performing (and selling) their crafts in the courtyards. This live performance reproduced the interpenetration of the rural and the urban—indeed their necessary coexistence, often on the same piece of land—which is all too apparent in the vast squatter settlements and "unauthorized" housing sectors that cover Delhi and other major cities. Earlier, such settlements had been inhabited by Salman Rushdie's "midnight's children" displaced by partition, and were later inventoried by Correa in *The New Landscape*. Today they are home to a new generation of rural migrants who are busy redefining cities around the world. It is often said (with middle-class annoyance) that Delhi's sometimes daily power outages are due in part to the electricity pirated by these settlements from the city's overtaxed, ancient infrastructure. Yet from those settlements emerges on a daily basis a vast corps of domestic workers to service the fast growing middle-class households of a fast growing service economy, closing the circle each day.

23. Smita J. Baxi, "The Crafts Museum at New Delhi," *Museum* 31, no. 2 (1979): 99.

3.45

NATIONAL SCIENCE

The other side of the coin that joined the production of culture with the new economy was also revealed in 1990, when Rewal's pavilions and the National Crafts Museum were joined on their site by the National Science Museum, designed by Achyut Kanvinde. In a move that complemented the project of the Crafts Museum, the National Science Museum and its companion, the Nehru Science Center in Mumbai (also designed by Kanvinde), were intended to introduce a broad Indian public to national and international advances in the sciences, and thus to encourage the developing nation's youth to pursue careers in science and technology. Such careers were further nurtured in the state-run Indian Institutes of Technology (IITs) located in each province, one of which was the fruit of Kanvinde's first major professional commission. Together, these institutions and others materialized Nehru's commitment to modernization as an engine of nation building, a project that explicitly included modern architecture, again with Kanvinde's assistance.

Having been sent by his (still British) government in 1945 to Harvard University's Graduate School of Design to study under Walter Gropius, Kanvinde returned to a liberated India in September 1947. At the time, an orientalist hangover still held sway on the architectural front, in the form of calls for an anti-modern "national style" made by the still-British head of Bombay's Sir J.J. College of Architecture, Claude Batley, among others. Equipped with a modernism which matched that of Nehru as well as Gropius, Kanvinde managed to meet with the prime minister to make known his distress at this state of affairs. Subsequently, in a March 1959 address to architects made at Kanvinde's invitation, Nehru officially endorsed modern architecture as an appropriate vehicle for India's national aspirations.[24] Three decades later, in the National Science Museum in New Delhi, Kanvinde synthesized these still-vivid aspirations in a cascade of program captured in a modular concrete frame. Orchestrated around the imagery of infrastructure, Kanvinde's cascade spoke—with Gropius but also with megastructuralists such as Kenzo Tange, as well as with Nehru—of the foundational power of science, technology, and industry.

24. Kazi Khaleed Ashraf and James Belluardo, eds., *An Architecture of Independence: The Making of Modern South Asia* (New York: Architectural League of New York, 1998), 14.

3.46

ALL THAT IS SOLID...

Thus was the landscape of late-twentieth century Delhi built on two types of foundations, concrete and sandstone, on which the nation's emerging role in the global economy could be seen to rest. One offered the presumably solid footing of techno-scientific calculation, while the other offered the more ephemeral but no less real footing of imagined cultural identity, more often than not rendered in dusky reds, trimmed with beige.

Other, hardly incidental contributions to this landscape were made by other, hardly incidental architects. At one end of the spectrum, for example, there was Kuldip Singh's solid monument to the public sector, the Delhi Town Hall, sculpted out of concrete in a manner that recalls Correa in Bangalore, as well as any number of other late-Corbusian modernisms worldwide, but with deeper recesses that register the blazing heat of the Delhi climate, or perhaps the deep thoughts of the bureaucrats inside. While at the other end of the spectrum, also in central New Delhi, is a monument to the private sector: the golden, shiny headquarters of the Delhi Land Finance Group (DLF). An essay in branding that exchanges "Indianness" for international glitz, the DLF headquarters presents a façade that, unlike the ponderous recesses of Singh's Town Hall, drowns its central, pseudo-classical "portico" in the brash liquidity of multi-national capital momentarily frozen in mirrored glass.

3.47

3.48

3.49

HAFEEZ

The Delhi Land and Finance (DLF) construction company was founded in 1946 and immediately rose to prominence as a builder of speculative housing to accommodate the massive influx of "midnight's children" moving to Delhi as a result of the 1947 partition. Later renamed the DLF Group, this private company—which is actually older than its more visible government counterpart, the Delhi Development Authority (or DDA, founded in 1957)—would eventually build twenty-one urban "townships" housing nearly a million people in and around the city.

The architect for the DLF headquarters (DLF Centre) in New Delhi is arguably India's most prolific—and most famous—practitioner: the inimitable Hafeez Contractor. By mid-2004, Contractor (or Hafeez, as he is affectionately known), had designed four million square feet of residential space, 2.5 million square feet of commercial space, and half a million square feet of shopping for the DLF Group. Most of this was in Gurgaon, a burgeoning "cyber-city" that had sprung up over the past decade near the airport, on the semi-rural outskirts of New Delhi, which was itself once on the semi-rural outskirts of Delhi proper, having now been encircled in dense sprawl by subsequent waves of urbanization.

By some accounts, Gurgaon harbors the largest privately owned conurbation in Asia, mostly in the form of the very large, irregular enclaves that together make up DLF City. As a set of non-contiguous spatial islands held together only by their brand name, DLF City is the Multi-National City (MNC) in microcosm. It is an entirely private city financed by speculative capital. There is virtually no public transportation.

3.50

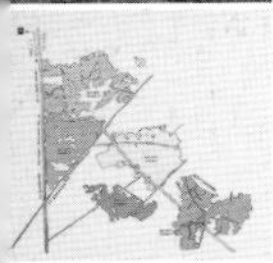
3.51

3.52

3.53

Not afraid of theorizing, its developers celebrated what they called the city's "walk to work concept: making global corporates feel at home," a concept, they continued, often heard but "rarely possible in today's congested metropolis." Not only does this supposedly reduce transportation costs (even as many workers endure two-hour commutes in company vans), according to the DLF Group it "reduces executive stress" and thus increases productivity. While on the home front, "it makes for much fuller family life," since "time available with the family is a lot more than would otherwise be possible."[25] Hidden in these proclamations is a tension, in which the bonds of the traditional, extended Indian family are threatened by the demands of commuting to the new utopia of the office park, and by the multiple allegiances of corporate life. This occurs both at the level of the so-called executive (the implied patriarch) and of the offspring, whose new job at the call center down the road (or two hours away) may require her to work evenings. In the Multi-National City, not only is your past their present, but your day is their night—the waking hours, that is, of potential credit card customers on the other side of the globe.[26]

And in more than one way, Hafeez can be called a multinational architect. His firm's public relations materials identify him as holding a Master of Science in Architecture and Urban Design (MSAUD) from the United States. In fact the degree is from the Graduate School of Architecture, Planning and Preservation (GSAPP) at Columbia University, which probably makes Hafeez that school's most prolific alumnus. But in terms of the cultural capital out of which the Multi-National City is built, it remains more important in the Indian context to identify oneself as having studied "abroad" (in the US, in Hafeez's case) than to name the specific institution. And like many of the founders of India's burgeoning IT industry to which DLF City caters, Hafeez returned to India after his studies, foregoing the temptations (or hardships) of life as an NRI in New York and

25. Text formerly on http://www.dlf-group.com/. Accessed June 2002.

founding his own practice in Bombay/Mumbai in 1982. Among his other works are any number of office buildings, including large projects for large multi-nationals like Citibank, Colgate Palmolive, and Proctor and Gamble; and any number of residential complexes with names like Broadway Avenue (Mumbai), City of Joy (Mumbai, projected), Dreams-AT (Mumbai, projected), Seawoods Estate (Navi Mumbai/New Bombay), Place Orchard (Pune), Vastu (Mumbai), and Lake Castle (Mumbai); as well as any number of institutions, including IIT Mumbai, and a projected twenty-acre campus for Infosys in the Chandigarh Technology Park (CTP).

"VERY, VERY AMERICAN!"

3.54

But just to the east of Delhi, DLF City faces stiff competition from an official high technology sector developed under the STPI scheme, the township of Noida. Among the new buildings on the Noida skyline is the headquarters of Adobe India, rendered in bright colors that, according to the company, reflect "the vibrant and fun filled work environment" inside.[27] The building, which opened in 2003, was designed by the New Delhi-based firm Spazzio. It contains an indoor gym, recreation room, library, and medical room, with a cafeteria that serves from 8 a.m. to 10 p.m., as well as outdoor volleyball and tennis courts. Work hours are flexible and are set by each employee "according to their lifestyle." What is more, work is supplemented by an institutionalized regime of "fun" presided over by a self-organized, employee-run Sports and Cultural Council that, like its counterparts in Silicon Valley, dedicates itself to reproducing the carefree abandon of college life.

All of this (post)modernity led the *Times of India* to declare the building "Very, Very American!" Here, in direct contrast to the deployment of red sandstone elsewhere for its "Indianness," cultural identity is imported. And among those architectural characteristics that (in addition to its overseas corporate parent) earned the building the designation "American," was the fact that the window glazing was from Glaverbel Belgium, the exterior aluminum panels were from Alucobond Germany, and the modular furniture was from the Canadian manufacturer Teknion. Everything imported. "Definitely American."[28]

26. Arjun Appadurai, *Modernity at Large: Cultural Dimensions of Globalization* (Minneapolis, MN: University of Minnesota Press, 1996), 31.

27. http://www.adobeindia.com/templates/ui/contentpage.asp?pageid=18.

28. Nita Trikha, "Very, Very American!" *Times of India*, 4 June 2003, Cities: Delhi, 1.

PRINCETON, GURGAON

Both Noida and DLF City/Gurgaon emerged from the latest phase of modernization serviced so adeptly by Hafeez Contractor. They did so by accommodating a middle-class flight from the city, and from the newly urbanized rural masses. In that sense, the MNC is paradoxical: a city that abandons the city, as the city, in turn, absorbs the village in the form of miles of urban poverty. This is a turning inward that is accomplished by moving outward, beyond the airport, which in the case of DLF City yielded five phased residential enclaves and a series of corporate offices, with requisite post-urban amenities. These gated enclaves go by such names as DLF Windsor Court, DLF Hamilton Court, DLF Regency Park, DLF Richmond Park, DLF Belvedere Towers, DLF Belvedere Place, DLF Silver Oaks, DLF Wellington Estate, DLF Oakwood Estate, DLF Ridgewood Estate, DLF Beverly Park, DLF Carlton Estate, and DLF Princeton Estate.

3.55

3.56

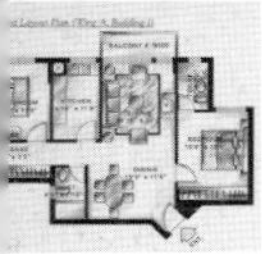
3.57

Their televisual names connect these objects to other objects in places like suburban New Jersey, where new condominium developments in the greater Princeton area offer an independent, homeowning lifestyle to the expanding NRI class of international, English-speaking technical workers trained in India's IITs and IIMs. Conversely, the "opening up" of the Indian economy during the 1990s brought tax breaks for NRI investors. And so, together with the upwardly mobile middle class who imagine themselves as "walk-to-work" executives, among the main clientele of DLF City is the NRI, for whom apartment units in Princeton Estate may represent both a potential investment in a rising real estate market, and a kind of displaced homecoming—a base from which to visit the family while still maintaining a safe distance.

INSIDE OUTSOURCING

Other such avatars of the outsourcing of identity in Gurgaon include DLF Square Tower, DLF Gateway Tower, and DLF Plaza Tower. There are also assorted shopping malls, as well as that all important lifestyle amenity for walk-to-work executives unable to tolerate their own family for very long: a golf course. Adjacent to DLF City Phase V, the golf course and country club comes complete with five lakes, "greens that play true," floodlighting (for night golf), and a downloadable application form that—like the city itself—helped construct the very golfers it serves, offering varying rates to "overseas corporate members," NRIs, individual residents, individual expatriates, and corporations, although it remains unclear whether these categories are in fact mutually exclusive.

Also adjacent to DLF City Phase V on Vishwakarma Road is the General Electric call center. Dedicated mainly to the back-office marketing and service operations of GE Capital, the call center is representative of the strange topologies of outsourcing. Anguished debates during the 2004 US presidential campaign about sending so-called American jobs overseas missed the point entirely, since a key job description for many call center operators has been the ability to produce a simulacrum of the "American," overseas. Here is an account from India's version of *Time* magazine, *India Today*: Meghna is a 23-year old call center operator somewhere in Gurgaon. When her phone rings, she becomes "Michelle." The caller is in Philadelphia, asking for a credit extension.

> Meghna is unruffled. Months of training, which included watching Hollywood blockbusters to pick up a wide variety of American accents and reading John Grisham thrillers to clear any linguistic obstacles, have paid off. Her computer screen even flashes the weather at Philadelphia as she tells a caller what a perfect day it is. Meghna signs off saying, "Have a good day." Outside her window it is pitch dark.[29]

3.58

3.59

Inside outsourcing, then, "Hari will become Harry, he will work this Diwali, and he will have a holiday on July 4."[30] So observed Ajit Isaac, CEO of Bangalore-based PeopleOne Consulting, a "full spectrum human capital services company" financed by JP Morgan Ventures. This is outsourcing: the displacement of national and cultural identity on the *inside* of an *exterior* space—inside the call center, out in Gurgaon, at night. In that sense, in mirrored symmetry with the NRI and the Resident Alien, the call center operator is a prototypical subject of the Multi-National City, a cyborg who switches identities by plugging into technological networks that scramble time and space into a topological knot.

3.60

3.61

3.62

And whether in Gurgaon or in Bangalore, outsourcing's strange topologies would not be possible without the technical infrastructure that provides the uplink—in the case of Bangalore's ITPL, the prominently placed satellite dish that, like the building's smooth surfaces, fulfills both a functional and symbolic role simultaneously.[31] This is a role prefigured, perhaps, by the cryptic symbolism of Le Corbusier's sculptural dome atop the Assembly building at Chandigarh, city of Nehru's technological dreams. There is also a large satellite dish poised prominently atop the GE Capital call center in Gurgaon, signaling the

3.63

3.64

29. Raj Chengappa and Malini Goyal, "Housekeepers to the World," *India Today* 1, no. 46 (12-18 November 2002), 10.

30. Samar Halakarnar, "Bangalore: The Buzz Is Back!" *Indian Express*, 8 November 2002, 15.

31. On the "broadcast urbanism" of satellite and telecommunications networks woven into the IT imaginary in India, see Keller Easterling, *Enduring Innocence: Global Architecture and Its Political Masquerades* (Cambridge, MA: MIT Press, 2005), 135-159.

building's status as a machine for producing multi-nationals of all kinds. On the inside, the cubicle space is divided into territories corresponding to regions serviced: North America, Europe, Africa and so on. The globe, internalized.

3.65

3.66

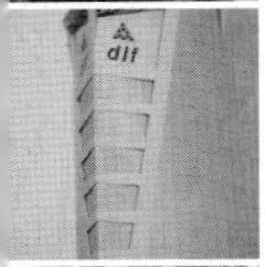

3.67

3.68

3.69

3.70

3.71

The interiors of GE Capital were designed by the Delhi-based firm of Framework Interiors, whose production was singled out in 2002 by the Indian periodical *Architecture + Design* as exemplifying "Multinational Design for the Multinational Mind." The mindset of Framework Interiors is no different than that of their American counterparts. They apply such Silicon Valley-style office planning methods as the relaxed, "open" office with designated social areas; or "hotelling," in which workers "plug and play" into different workstations on a daily basis, as well as "internal branding," or packaging the corporation from the inside-out to encourage brand-loyalty in the employees more than the customers. And naturally, the architect of the GE Capital call center in which Framework Interiors exercised their craft was Hafeez Contractor.

Again: despite the inclination of many Euro-American architects and critics to regard such developments as Gurgaon as emerging spontaneously out of the exotic, ahistorical jungles of globalization—Shanghai as "primitive hut," to name another—these cities are nothing if not historical. Not only is Hafeez's unapologetic postmodernism a remixed echo of earlier postmodernisms that Euro-American architects used to call historicist. In addition, looming large over private, postmodern cities such as Gurgaon is the hulking mass of Chandigarh: the modernist promise of a new future emanating from the recently decolonized public sector. In that sense, Hafeez materializes a kind of Corbusian alter-ego who will build in any style whatever, thereby also refusing the reactions to international modernism that advocate a more "authentically" Indian architecture.
As a result, Hafeez's postmodernism and the televisual image of the west that it projects (a kind of architectural equivalent to the pan-Asian Star TV) are surely instruments of power. But they also represent an inadvertent challenge to the jargon of authenticity associated with the rigid postmodernisms of national identity carved in stone.

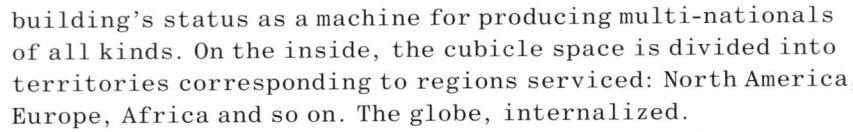

In addition to the GE Capital call center, among Hafeez's output in DLF City proper is DLF Square Tower, with an upside-down pyramid (the DLF logo) at its base—the figurative skyscraper top that once marked the skyline of "delirious New York," now inverted to become the ubiquitous emblem of the MNC: a glass atrium. But DLF City is not without a skyline. Not only does the bulk of DLF Square Tower hover over the still-vast fields formerly tended by villagers who are rendered increasingly invisible by its looming postmodernity. The entrance to DLF City, and to the new districts of Gurgaon into which it is embedded, is marked by Hafeez's DLF Gateway Tower, completed in 1999. The DLF Group duly celebrated this building's state-of-the-art technology, including "The 100% power back-up facility [that] makes sure that office efficiency is maximised at all times," a claim that reminds us that the politics of the MNC is often a politics of infrastructure.

GENERATORS (BACKUP)

In Delhi's residential neighborhoods, the use of individual backup generators in the event of a power outage is widespread, to the degree that the economic structure of a given neighborhood is starkly visible during a blackout by virtue of whose lights are on and whose are off. Industry has followed suit, offering not just backup generators in buildings like DLF Gateway Tower, but also the class prestige that goes along with them, which is analogous to the westernized names of the DLF housing estates.

3.72

3.73

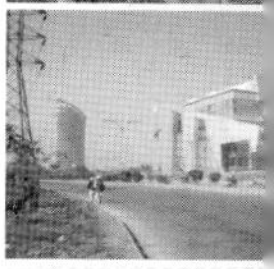

During blackouts in Gurgaon the efficacy of backup generators can in principle be measured by the glow of the glass atriums that feature prominently in other Hafeez buildings, such as DLF Atria and the Ericsson headquarters. While an equally potent architectural status symbol is the mirrored glass curtain wall that covers half of what the DLF Group calls Gateway Tower's "futuristic exterior." Again: your past is their future—or perhaps it is the other way around. One commentator writing in India's *Architecture + Design* describes—with tongue-in-cheek—a mirrored glass, spherical office building in Bangalore as "a globe building for a 'global' corporation," and therefore a Venturian "duck," albeit absent the usual irony.[32] Gurgaon has its own version, minus the spherical form: the Global Business Park. Are we to conclude, then, that this and other such buildings, including Bangalore's Digital Park, are decorated sheds—where the equation "glass = global" is applied as mere billboard to the otherwise unremarkable shell of an otherwise unremarkable office building?

32. Vijay Narnapatti, "Glass Box Slick: Dressing Up the Corporate Image, Bangalore Context," *Architecture + Design* 19, no. 6 (November-December 2002), 94.

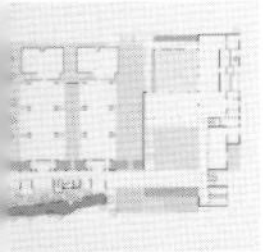
3.74

3.75

3.76

3.77

3.78

3.79

3.80

3.81

3.82

"NATURE"

In a kind of coda to this story, a more finely crafted architecture on the order of Correa's first LIC building downtown has finally made it to Bangalore's office parks, in the form of another campus for Hewlett Packard (HP). Not far from Digital Park, the home of Hewlett Packard GlobalSoft, this second HP campus was designed by Rahul Mehrotra Associates. Bunker-like, utilitarian office pods and an offset circulation spine surround its shaded landscaped court, which is bracketed off at one end by a food court and a gym. In the pods, the global curtain wall is replaced by subtly modeled and scored concrete, while the architecturally articulate spine mixes various materials and experiences in an effort to counter the actual monotony of office life. But most importantly, this campus is turned inside-out, thereby capturing in its crevices and its courtyards (distant relatives, it must be said, of Doshi's IIM) an internal "nature" made of trees, water, and shrubbery.

NORMAL?

Meanwhile, other clients in IT parks like those in Bangalore and Gurgaon have been known to request a specific percentage of curtain wall for their buildings. Still, the global curtain wall is more than merely a sign with structure behind. It is a surface with specific topological properties—a two-sided sign. Its enigmatic mirrors both reflect and fold the Multi-National City back onto itself, doubling up that city's strange exteriority into an equally strange intimacy. Such mirrors thereby defeat the logic of inside and outside, us and them, even as they reproduce it. This is not merely a matter of a false transparency, a false universality, where you can see out but you cannot see in, or vice versa. It is a matter of that mathematical property familiar to all digital architects, known as the "normal." Normal to one side of the mirror is its reflective opacity; normal to the other, its transparency. In this world, all mirrors are also windows. And their double valence is doubled many times over around the globe, mirroring doubled-up infrastructures like the backup generator and, like a revolving door, offering both entrances and exits, in and out of the MNC.

3

FROM **SILICON VALLEY** TO **NEW DELHI**

FEEDBACK

Delhi Land & Finance 2004

At the southern extremity of Gurgaon sits DLF City Phase V, the site of Carlton Estate and Princeton Estate, with the GE Capital call center adjacent and yet another new shopping mall on the horizon. Across the road there is the golf course. But by 2004, DLF Phase V remained incomplete. And so M/BA (Martin/Baxi Architects) decided to step in before Hafeez Contractor sealed the deal on the future of the MNC.

In M/BA's proposal, the irregular property outline of DLF Phase V is subdivided into thirty circular, secondary sectors, each its own closed world. Each of the circles is paved, while the interstitial landscape between them is left in its original state—presumably to be filled in with the huts and squalor reserved for those condemned to service India's new service economy. At the center of each circle is a sunken entry plaza for the building placed there. The remainder of the paved surface accommodates a zero-sum game of ecology and economy: a fixed area, which the occupants of each circle can choose to utilize in one of two ways, as parking or as solar energy source for backup power—but not both. Thus in each, a different pattern of solar panels and parking spaces develops, reflecting the differing priorities and politics of each circle—individual independence (more cars) or collective independence (more panels). Either way, as with the circles themselves, there are gaps in the system in the form of interference and irregular patterns.

The size of each building varies proportionately with that of its circle. Each is a cube with no discernible orientation, with a cubic, voided atrium at its center. Each cube is punctured on each of its six sides with a vortex formed by a mirrored curtain wall turned inside-out and sucked into the deepest interior, reflecting inward rather than outward, ad infinitum. The void is open to the elements by virtue of the six large holes. Inside are non-indigenous palm trees under which relaxed IT workers comfortably sit. The array of spaces surrounding the void is composed of three layers. On the outside, a high-resolution screen wall of multicolored metallic pixels shades the corridor that runs continuously around the perimeter. Inside is another, medium-resolution colored screen and inside of that, a low-resolution array of colored volumes that serve as both service cores and structure, subdividing each floor into units of indeterminate function (housing, offices, etc.). The distribution of pixel-units in each screen uses the proportions of Le Corbusier's Modulor to initiate an algorithm that digitally amplifies—rather than masks—Le Corbusier's original error. The results are different each time the algorithm is run for each layer of each building. There are thus no universal standards, as Modulor Man becomes a pixellated blur in which "arithmetic" and "geometry" are finally reconciled. Everything is number, translated directly into form.

Each cube has a different location in the overall array, a different size, a different façade pattern, and a different solar array/parking lot due to differences in local politics. Site circulation occurs in circles. At each tangential intersection there is a spherical, digital sign displaying a color-coded gradient, indicating which sector you are about to leave, and which you are about to enter. So, in place of neocolonial nomenclature like Beverly Park or Princeton Estate there is only color, digitally generated from the numerical average of all those other colors distributed on the respective building's façade.

Here, at DLF City Phase V, as at M/BA's Silicon Valley CVRP, or in their late entry into the Ground Zero sweepstakes, there are ultimately no NRI's, Resident Aliens, or walk-to-work commuters wandering about. Not because the boundaries that each confronts have finally been overcome, but because their topologies have been rearranged. Above all, the MNC embodies the signal, spatial paradox of our times: the further inside you go, the further outside you get. So the NRI's return "home," from the alienation of the Resident Alien to the India of Gurgaon and of Punjabi Baroque, is actually a voyage back into the black hole of displaced identity. While the flight from the city that this new city embodies is actually a return, to all of the dilemmas the "city" has posed and the promises that it has made—from Bangalore to Chandigarh to New Delhi, and around again. Spinning in the untimely circles of globalization, this architecture, which some have called "utopian realism," imagines other cities for other times. Hardly perfect, it reflects—even, at times, accentuates—the brutalities of our age, not because it serves the status quo, but because it proposes to change it rather than simply to wish it away. Although it may therefore seem closed, the MNC actually harbors an outside—a utopian "elsewhere"—within those claustrophobic spaces that serve the new imperium, and within those all-too-human humans who meander through its mirrored halls.

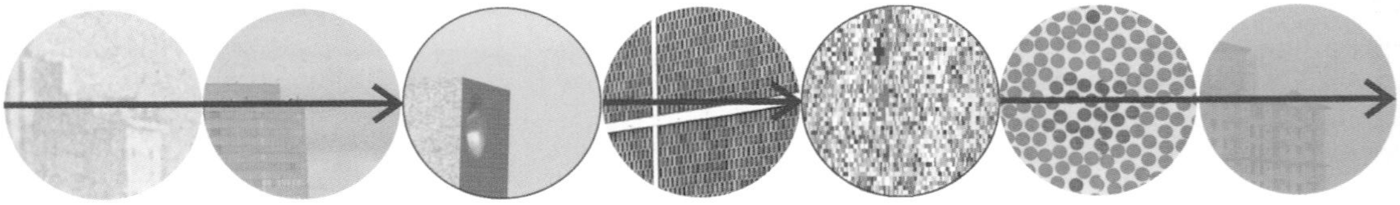

1

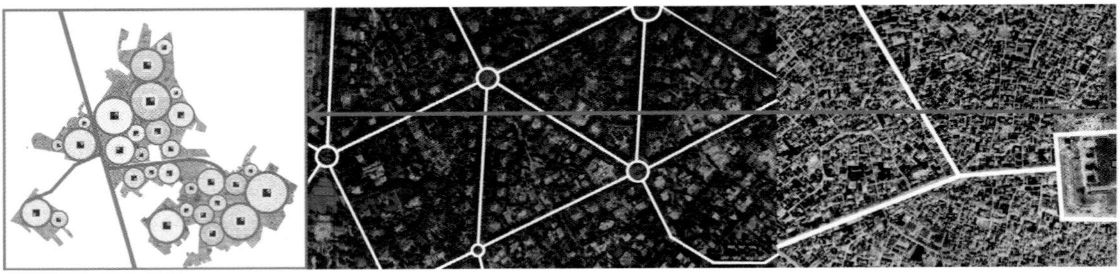

2

[1] Mirage of Circles. Fragments of Correa's *New Landscape*, DLF City/Gurgaon, and M/BA's screens.
[2] Lines and Circles, Old and New. L to r: New New Delhi (M/BA's DLF City Phase V), old New Delhi (Lutyens and Baker), and Old Delhi (Shahjahanabad).

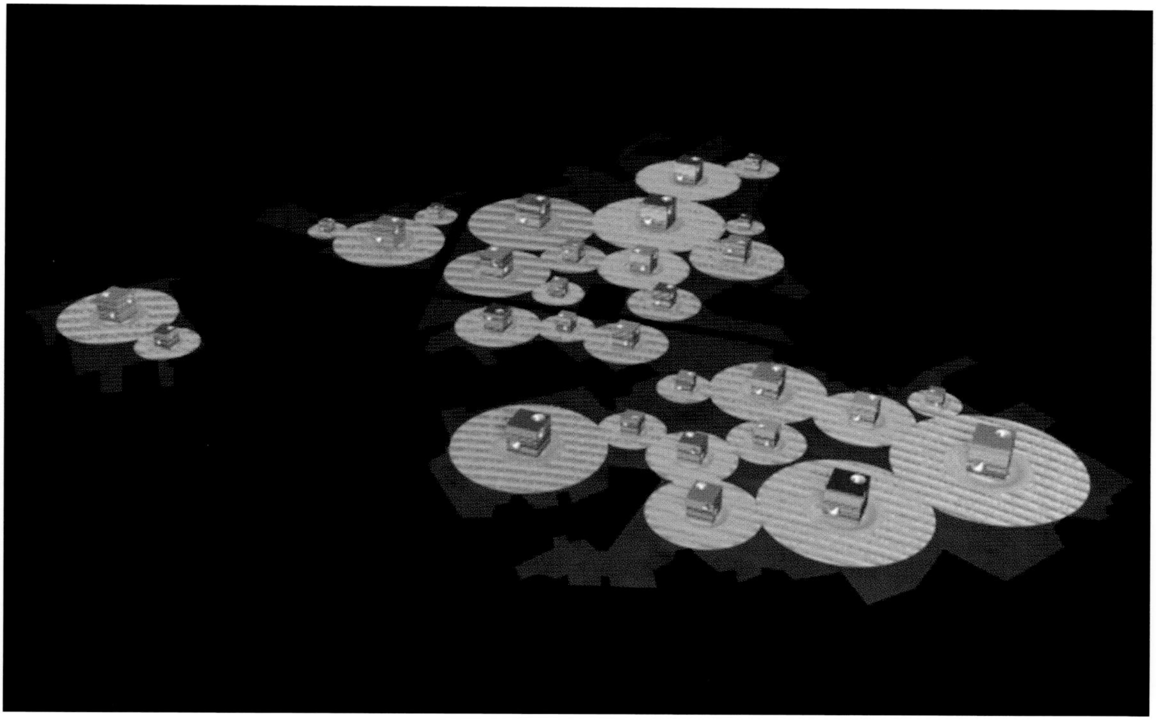

Delhi Land & Finance (DLF) City, Phase V, Gurgaon, 2004. Aerial perspective, night view. FAR =1.

1

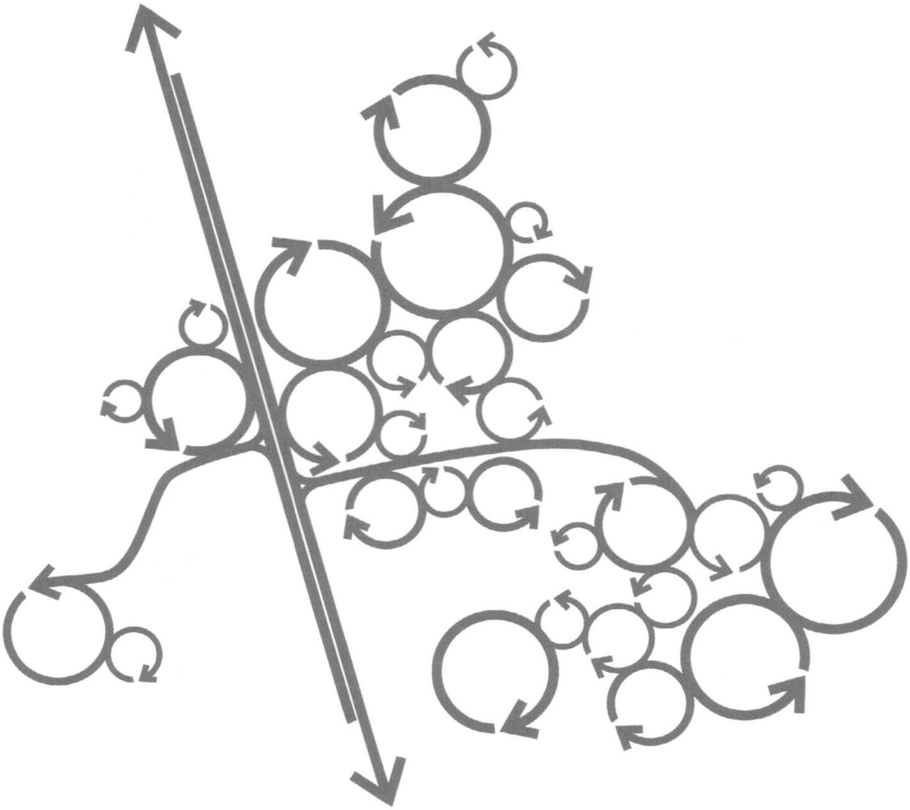

2

DLF2004

[1] Spherical traffic sign.
[2] Circulation, in circles

```
[Add Code:]
a=box length:.375 width:.5 height:.1
for j = 0 to 5 do
for i = 1 to 18 do
for t = 0.00 to 107 do (
x = (5.000^.5)/2.000
y = 1 + random 0.000 .2
box_instance = instance a
box_instance.pos = [(t/2) - 2 , (((y * x^i)-(y * x)) * 1.13) + (j*9) - 7 , 52.5]
)
for j = 0 to 5 do
for i = 1 to 18 do
for t = 0.00 to 107 do (
x = (5.000^.5)/2.000y = 1 + random 0.000 .2
box_instance = instance a
box_instance.pos = [(t/2) - 2 , 47 - ((((y * x^i)-(y * x)) * 1.13) + (j*9)), -1.5]
)
box_delete = delete a
```

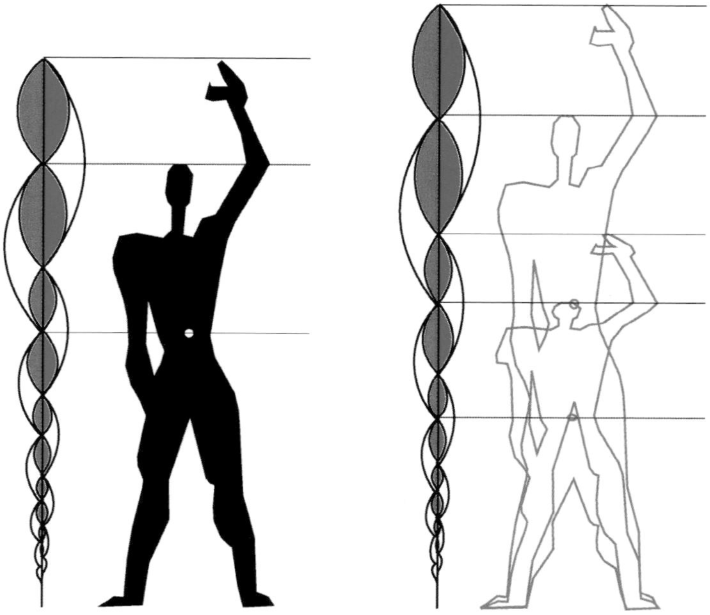

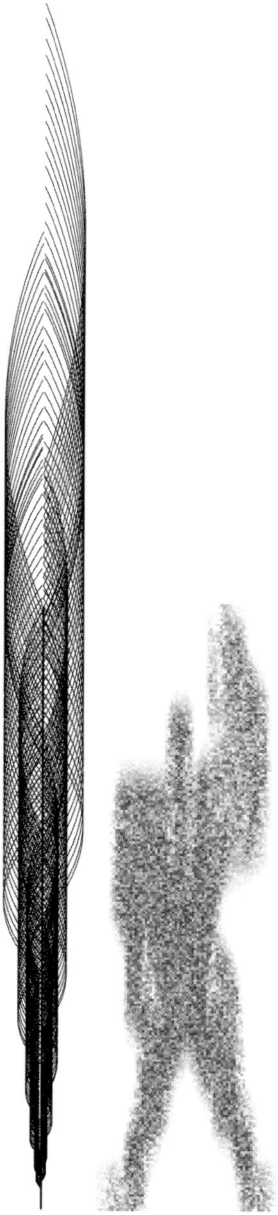

[Left to right]: Le Corbusier, Le Modulor, 1948; Le Corbusier, Le Modulor, 1955; M/BA, Le Modulor, 2004, with script used in M/BA DLF City Phase V.. Drawing by Urtzi Grau.

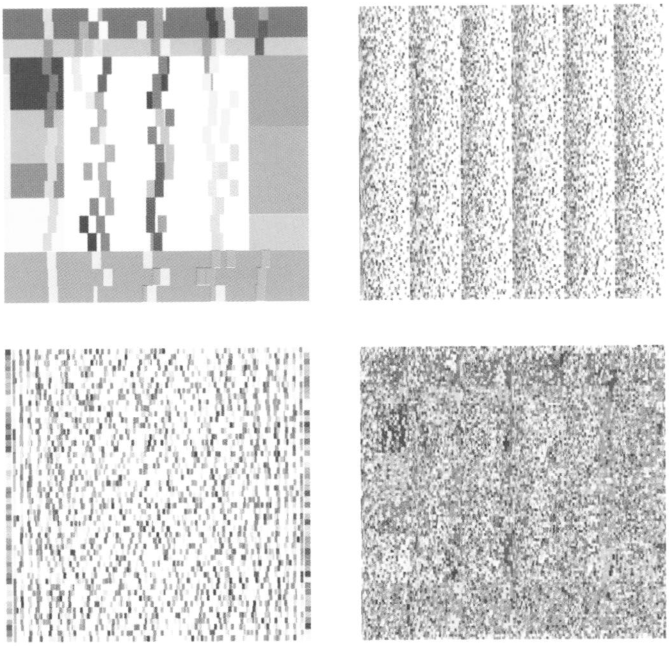

1

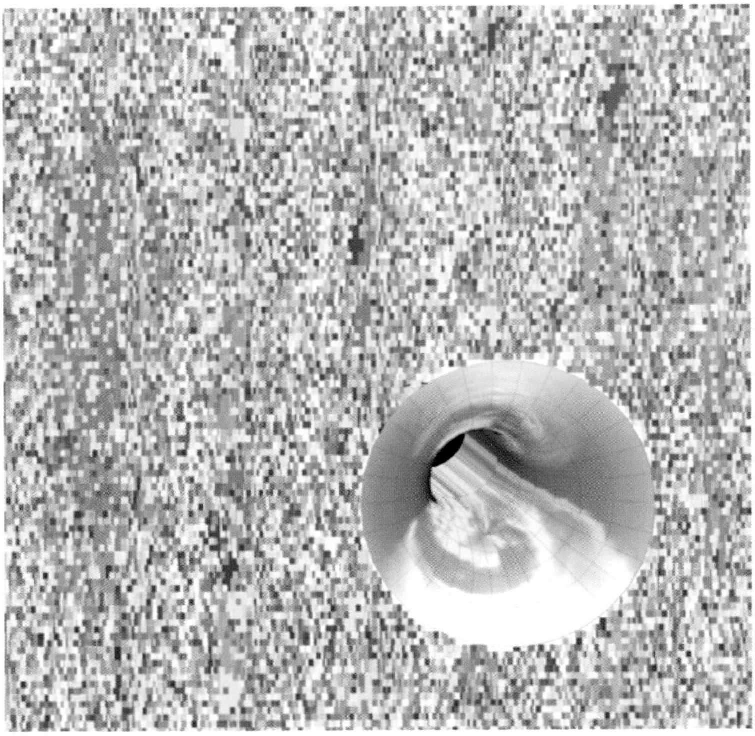

2

[1] Screen elevations.
[2] Typical building, elevation.

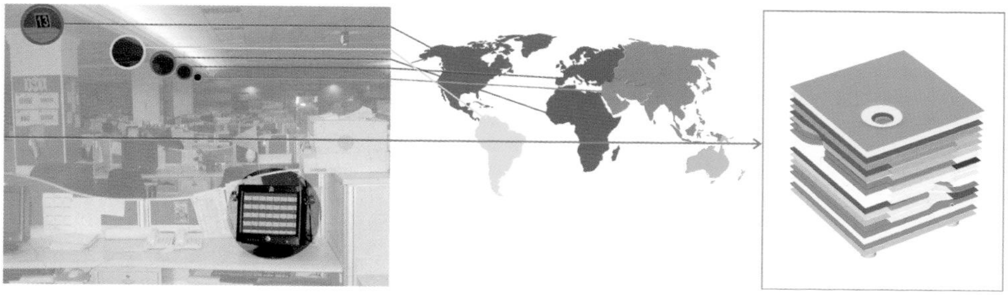
1

2-4

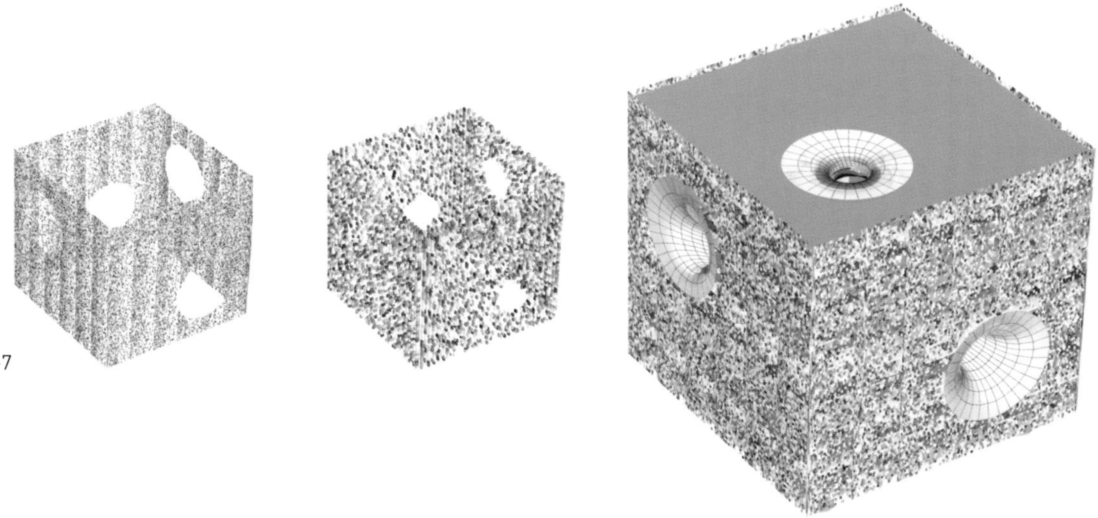
5-7

DLF2004

[1] Call Center as World. Call center numbered bays—where a number identifies the geographic region covered by a specific bay—mapped to color-coded world map, and transferred to color-coded floors in M/BA's DLF City Phase V. [2] Inner screens + (service cores/structure) + [3] Floors + [4] Open-air atrium + [5] Outer screens + [6] Middle screens = [7] Typical building.

1

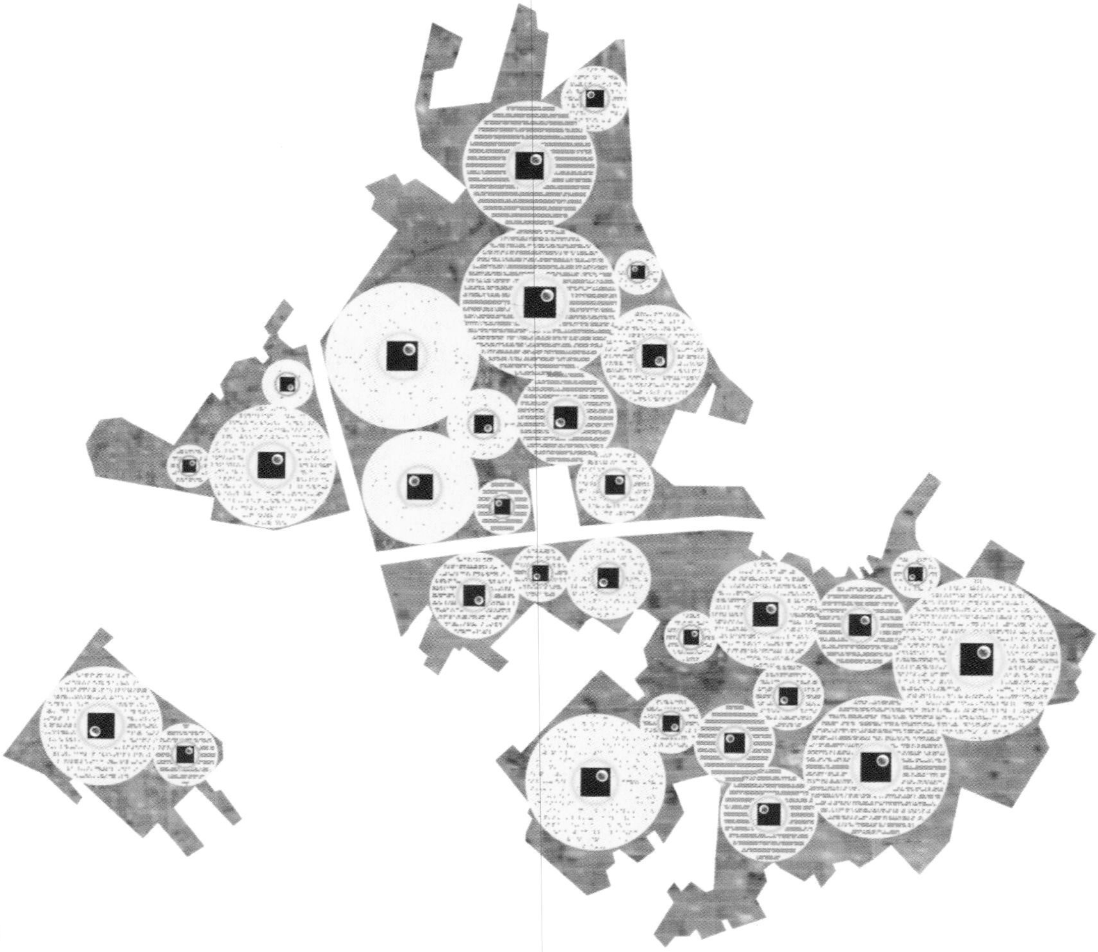

2

DLF2004

[1] Zero-Sum Game? Shopping malls, electrical infrastructure, and informal economies compete over possible futures in Gurgaon, and analogous scenarios (parking vs. solar panels) compete in M/BA's DLF City Phase V.
[2] Site plan.

1-3

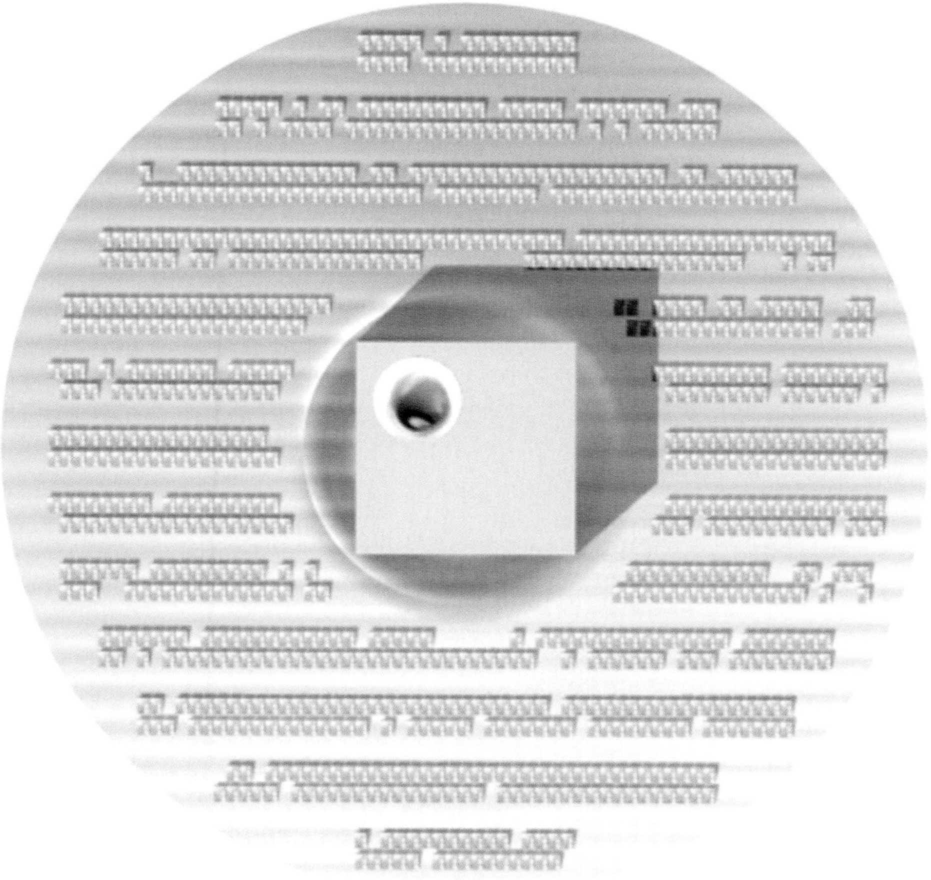

4

[1] Parking, [2] Parking + building, [3] Solar panels, and [4] Combination (typical plan)

DLF2004

Typical building, open-air atrium.

1

DLF Horizons: Buildings and open land scattered around DLF City, including M/BA's DLF City Phase V.

DLF2004

Roadscape.

Roadscape.

ACKNOWLEDGEMENTS

The research contained herein was made possible through collaborations of various kinds. Here are those who contributed directly:

SILICON VALLEY

Irene Cheng, Jennifer DeGaetano, Daniela Fabricius, Brian Loughlin, Waraluk Pansuwan

NEW YORK

Urtzi Grau, Michael Green, Corey Hoelcker

NEW DELHI

Urtzi Grau, Corey Hoelcker

Its public life began with an exhibition of work by Kadambari Baxi and Reinhold Martin (KB and RM), called Timeline: A Retroactive Master Plan for Silicon Valley held at Artists' Space gallery in New York in the spring of 2001. This exhibition was itself preceded by design studios on Silicon Valley taught by RM at the Graduate School of Architecture, Planning and Preservation (GSAPP) at Columbia University in 1998 and 1999. It was a time when, at Columbia and elsewhere, the promises of a "digital architecture" crossed paths with the irrationally exuberant bubble of the new economy, and the future of architecture was still thought by some to lie in machines sold by SGI (Silicon Graphics, Inc.). In these Silicon Valley design studios, Columbia architecture students traveled to northern California two years in a row to see for themselves. Both times they returned disappointed (it seemed) by the deadpan earnestness of SGI and company, though they were also encouraged by the strangeness encountered there and throughout the Valley.

These design studios were followed by another taught jointly (again at Columbia) by RM and KB in 2000. This time the subject was Atlanta-based CNN's virtual reality, in the wake of its parent company Time Warner's merger with America Online (AOL) earlier that year. That studio's particular site did not make it into the book, but its subject matter did, in the form of CNN's new home: the (formerly AOL) Time Warner Center in New York, which was proudly displayed to the studio group by a CNN executive, in a rendering signed by David Childs. While studying Atlanta, the home of John Portman's Peachtree Center and of CNN's former home in an enormous atrium, what we call here The Atrium Principle was developed.

Two years later, the research on Silicon Valley was presented to a bemused group of architects in Bangalore, at the very moment when the "winners" of architecture's Ground Zero sweepstakes were being announced. Shortly thereafter, RM conducted another design studio at Columbia—called a Think Tank, and designated a (Super)studio—that made a return trip to Silicon Valley, which was now in a state of metaphorical ruin (as befits any city aspiring to a spot on a new Grand Tour). This was followed by a design studio dedicated to replacing the newly completed, atrium-equipped Time Warner Center. Finally, as the book neared completion, RM conducted another Think Tank studio at Columbia that traveled to New Delhi and Gurgaon. This book would have been impossible without the contributions made by the many students who participated in these various studios and these various trips.

We are also immensely grateful to the team at Actar, including Ramon Prat, Albert Ferré, Michael Kubo, Reinhard Steger, David Lorente, and Anna Tetas for their support for the project, as well as for their collaboration in its realization. For feedback, conversation, and other assistance along the way, we would like particularly to thank Sonali Bhagwati, Michael Bell, Hafeez Contractor, Abhimanyu Dalal, Pradeep Dalal, Sohrab Dalal, Patrice Derrington, Keller Easterling, Jane Harrison, Laurie Hawkinson, Laura Kurgan, Brian Larkin, Timothy Lenoir, Duncan McCorquodale, Brian McGrath, Rahul Mehrotra, David Nieh, Janelle Porter, Felicity Scott, Rajmohan Shetty, David Turnbull, Bernard Tschumi, Henry Urbach, Kazys Varnelis, Anthony Vidler, Enrique Walker, Mark Wasiuta, Mark Wigley, and Mabel Wilson.

Finally, we remain grateful to all those others unnamed above—students, colleagues, and friends—whom we would like to think of as our fellow travelers.